# Exploring Rural
# ENGLAND
## & WALES

## OTHER BOOKS IN THE *EXPLORING RURAL* SERIES

**Series Editor: Andrew Sanger**

*France*: Andrew Sanger
*Greece*: Pamela Westland
*Ireland*: Andrew Sanger
*Italy*: Michael Leech
*Spain*: Jan S. McGirk

**Forthcoming:** *Austria, Germany, Portugal, Scotland*

*[handwritten annotations]*

Strip in new series book list — pick up repro from Exploring Rural Ireland

II
2

# Exploring Rural
# ENGLAND
## & WALES

## CHRISTOPHER PICK

**PASSPORT BOOKS**
a division of *NTC Publishing Group*
Lincolnwood, Illinois USA

½"

½"

IV9

# CONTENTS

*For the Try family of Beverley, and beyond*

# ACKNOWLEDGEMENTS

Many people have helped me to write this book. Thanks go to the Tourist Development Officers of County and District Councils throughout England and Wales; to staff of the various regional Tourist Boards; to the librarians of Upper Norwood Library, who obtained many books for me with their usual efficiency; to Andrew Sanger, the series editor, for patience and much advice; to many friends and relatives for their ideas and information; and to Jenny and Alison, for encouragment while I was writing.

Christopher Pick
London SE27

*England and Wales — the regions and routes*

# INTRODUCTION

Is there another country anywhere in the world that packs such a constantly changing pattern of landscapes into so small a space? I hardly think so. As J.B. Priestley, that great recorder of the English character, has remarked of England — but the same can be said of Wales too — there is always something new, something different, to be discovered 'round the corner'. A sudden glimpse, maybe, of a wooded valley guarded by a fiercely battlemented castle; the elegantly landscaped park surrounding a grand aristocratic mansion; the ruins of a medieval monastery abandoned now for 400 years; a prospect of distant mountains or of a sea shore stretching into a misty distance with seabirds wheeling high above. The interest and excitement derive not only from the form of the land itself — the moors and dales, the rock-strewn coastlines and remote marshlands, the gentle pastures and inhospitable peaks — but also from the varied imprints left on it by several thousand years of human activity. For in this time the land has been intensively cultivated, grazed, forested and mined, flooded to provide reservoirs or drained to create fertile farmland, fortified against internal or external threat, and reshaped by the architects of houses and landscapes and churches.

The 23 explorations in this book go round as many as possible of those corners Priestley describes. Some are through the less well-known backwaters of much-visited parts of the country. Others are in areas that deserve to be better known and more explored. Inevitably, for reasons of space, and to avoid making already quite complicatd routes even more tortuous, I have often had to omit many delightful places and landscapes. Some favourite places of mine (and, no doubt, of readers) have had to be left out. So please don't consider these routes sacrosanct. Use them as a guide to previously unknown parts of the country or as a fresh view of an already familiar area, but do seek out personal variations and diversions.

The tours are all circular (so you can join in wherever best suits you), and last from one to four days; their length varies from 55 to 240 miles. The start- and end-points are all towns where it's worth spending at least a night or two; some are well known (e.g. York, Bath), others (e.g. Stamford, Bedford) smaller and less visited. The routes deliberately avoid large towns and conurbations, motorways and, on the whole, major trunk roads. Most of the places of interest passed *en route* are described, though I've deliberately concentrated on those with some natural or historical link with the surrounding communities and countryside (e.g. rural life museums, country houses, heritage centres, nature reserves) rather than on theme parks and such like, which could be anywhere.

But visiting even the best of these attractions is no substitute for exploring on your own two feet, whether slowly wandering around country towns and villages or striding out across the countryside. A recent survey revealed that 43 per cent of visitors to Dartmoor stayed in their car or within 100 yards of it, and that another 32 per cent ventured no further than 1 mile! True, not everyone is mobile, but the 25 per cent who managed to escape the clutter of car parks and cars will have seen and heard immeasurably more of this unique part of Devon. Whenever possible, I've mentioned convenient walks, some which bring you back to your car, others that provide a pedestrian alternative to part of the route. There are of course many, many other walks: ask for advice at Tourist Information Centres and National Park Information Centres (see below) or simply follow the rights of way marked on Ordnance Survey maps.

## When to Travel

May and June, when spring's fresh greens remain vivid and there's a sense of new life in the air, are delightful touring months. So too are September and October, tinged with an agreeable melancholy at the prospect of the approaching winter. The busiest times are Easter week, the last week of May and the school summer holidays (roughly mid-July to early September).

Winter is not generally thought of as a time to go exploring, but what can beat the fresh air of a crisp sunny winter's day, especially with the prospect of a roaring log fire and a good dinner when you return to your hotel?

Several of these routes use difficult roads in mountainous areas. Take special care in poor weather, and in winter always check the weather forecast before you set out. The local Tourist Information Centre (TIC) should be able to advise, or consult the local office of the AA or RAC, or check the local telephone weather forecast.

## Touring from London

I'm firmly of the opinion that most of the best bits of rural England are a good distance from the capital. It's well worth trying to escape from London and the south-east for a few days to see a different and less hurried part of the country. However, for those with little time to spare, here is a list of routes that can be reached in a hour or two's drive from London.

**Around Bedford** M1 to junction 13, A421 north-east to Bedford or unclassified road to Husborne Crawley and then A418 to Woburn.

**Around the Cotswolds** M40 then A40 to Oxford.

**West Sussex and East Hampshire** A3 to Guildford then A31 to Alton.

**Weald, Marsh and Down** A21 to outside Tunbridge Wells or to Lamberhurst.

**East Suffolk** A12 to Woodbridge.
**Wool and Wheat** M11 to Cambridge or M11, then A11 to Newmarket.

## The Road Network

Main roads in Britain are classified A or B. (Motorways carry the prefix M.) Broadly speaking, A roads cover long distances, B roads are more local. Again broadly speaking, the lower the road number, the more heavily used and important the road. Thus A1 is the main road from London to Edinburgh, A1033 a minor road running east from Hull into Holderness (see page 41). But changes in traffic patterns since the system was established mean that it isn't always consistent — you may well find that a four-figure A road carries more traffic, and has been improved to a higher standard, than its two-figure neighbour. There are many, but sporadic, stretches of dual carriageway, largely on the low-figure A roads; these are indicated on motoring maps, which also show some A roads as 'primary', i.e. long-distance, routes.

A and B numberings are not immutable. Changes take place as new roads, by-passes etc. are opened and as road usage alters.

As well as A and B roads, there is a dense network of unnumbered country roads and lanes, which I generally refer to as 'minor' or 'unclassified' roads. These cross-country routes are much the most enjoyable to drive along, but don't expect to travel fast, and watch and listen for oncoming traffic — visibility is often poor, and you may well have to pull in to the side, or even reverse, to let an oncoming car pass. Unclassified roads are generally — but not always — signposted with the names of the villages they serve.

## Driving and Parking

Consult the *Highway Code*, available at bookshops and newsagents, for a detailed account of the rules of the road. Here are some brief points:
**Safety belts** must be worn at all times.
**Speed limits:** 30 miles per hour in built-up areas, unless signs are posted showing a higher limit (40 or 50mph); 60mph outside built-up-areas, but 70mph on dual carriageways and motorways.
**Priority:** unless there are signs to the contrary, traffic already on a roundabout has priority. At junctions and roundabouts, give way to traffic coming from the right.
**Parking:** look for local signs showing where roadside parking is permitted, and also for directions to off-street car parks. In general, parking is prohibited on roads marked with yellow lines. A single yellow line usually means 'no parking during working hours', a double line indicates a longer period.

## Maps

For long-distance route-planning, there are any number of motoring maps and atlases available. Choose whichever best suits your needs. I find the 3 miles to 1 inch atlases most helpful — several major British publishers (e.g. Bartholomew, Collins, Hamlyn) produce similar editions. For local explorations, Ordnance Survey's 1:50,000 Landranger series (mauve covers) is essential. This covers all Great Britain in 204 maps. *I list the OS Landranger maps required at the head of each route.*

## Information Sources

Much the best source of information about a particular place or area is the local TIC, which should be able to advise on a wide range of things such as opening times of attractions, local events, walks, accommodation (see below). Don't hesitate to ask. Most are friendly and efficiently run, and carry a wide range of leaflets, brochures, magazines and books (some free, some for sale). There are TICs in most major towns and cities, and in many smaller places as well; as you would expect, they are thicker on the ground in the more popular holiday areas. TICs generally open during standard shop hours. Many stay open in the evenings and at weekends as well, especially in summer, but a few have restricted opening times.

National Park Information Centres provide much the same service as TICs (but not accommodation-finding). Many of the Centres double as attractive and informative exhibitions/museums on topics such as the natural history and ecology of the park, and the social history of the area. They are also the base for a wonderful range of indoor and outdoor activities: lectures and films, walks, practical events of all kinds, organized by people who really know their subject. If you're exploring a National Park, don't fail to call in at one of the Information Centres.

The various regional Tourist Boards (addresses on page 173) provide more general information about the areas for which they are responsible. Some publish useful and reasonably priced booklets listing major attractions.

## Eating Out

Nowadays, eating out is generally a pleasurable experience in England and Wales, if often also a rather costly one. It's almost impossible to offer generalisations about where to eat, since prices and standards vary enormously. As a rule of thumb, look for establishments where, whatever the price, the owner does much of the cooking her/himself and takes a pride in the appearance of the dining-room. Pubs are often a source of good traditional English cooking (though sometimes the fare they offer can be quite dire), either at the bar or in a small separate dining-room. Indian and Chinese restaurants are usually good value too. Wholefood/health food/vegetarian restaurants have been springing up in recent years, and these are usually good value for money in pleasant surroundings. Light lunches and afternoon teas available at National Trust properties are often excellent.

*For each route I have named a limited number of eating places.*

Lunch is generally available from 12 to 2pm, afternoon tea from about 3pm to 5pm, high tea from 5pm onwards and dinner from 7pm. Don't count on being able to buy full-blown meals at other times, although, in summer especially, you will be unlucky not to find some sort of a snack somewhere.

A number of pub and restaurant guides are available, and these give good advice. The somewhat idiosyncratic *Good Food Guide* tends to recommend places in the upper price bracket. Egon Ronay's *Just a Bite* and *Good Food in Pubs and Bars* are tremendously useful.

Picnics are fun to eat, and fun to shop for as well. Village shops, especially in remoter areas, may have a limited amount of fresh food, but in many towns and villages you can buy delicious local cheese and fruit, pies and pastries, either at shops or in the market. A good crowd of local people queuing is a sure sign of quality.

## Accommodation

There's an enormous variety, from luxury hotels to modest guest houses and bed-and-breakfast establishments. As with restaurants, much depends on the standards and character set by the proprietor, and her/his determination to ensure a warm welcome for the guests. A wide variety of hotels and guest houses is mentioned in this book, with the accent on old coaching inns that have sometimes been serving travellers for centuries; but the examples don't pretend to be exhaustive.

Bed and breakfast is an excellent way of combining pleasant and resaonably priced overnight accommodation with meeting local people. You occupy your own room, which is almost always very comfortably furnished in a private home. Breakfast is often the traditional calorie- and cholesterol-packed meal of bacon and egg, toast and marmalade: with that inside, you may not want to bother about lunch. People who offer bed and breakfast generally put up a notice outside their house.

Another good way of finding a room for the night is through the local TIC. Most TICs operate a 'Local Bed Booking Service' for personal callers; the TIC staff carry details of local 'b & b' establishments and guest houses, and will make a booking on your behalf for the same or the next night. Some TICs also participate in another useful scheme, known as BABA: Book A Bed Ahead. BABA is a booking service for personal callers for accommodation for the same or next night in any other town with a TIC that also participates in the service. So, if you're staying in Bath tonight and want to spend tomorrow night in Wells, simply go to the TIC and see what's available.

For accommodation at the cheaper end of the market it's generally not necessary to book a long way ahead, except perhaps in the most popular holiday areas at peak times (e.g. Easter week, the week of the Late Spring Bank Holiday, and the school summer holidays). The situation varies a great deal with more expensive hotels depending on local factors and the fame of the hotel itself. If you call to make a reservation and find the hotel you've chosen is full, don't hesitate to ask the hotelier to recommend an alternative.

Many hotels offer bargain break weekends in autumn, winter and spring in order to keep their rooms full. These are generally excellent value — most regional Tourist Boards publish booklets with full details.

There's no comprehensive system of hotel classification in England and Wales. However, the Crown Classification Scheme (operated by the English, Scottish and Welsh Tourist Boards) is beginning to catch on. Inspectors visit the property and allot it one of six classifications (from 'listed' to five stars) according to the level of facilities and services offered. A low classification doesn't imply low standards — simply that the establishment concerned provides a simpler level of service. Hotels, motels, guesthouses, farmhouses and bed-and-breakfast places belong to the scheme, and display Crown Classification signs outside their premises and in publicity material.

## Opening Times

In the text I have shown the times of year and days of the week that museums, galleries, monuments etc. are open to the public. Information given is inclusive (i.e. April–Sept means 1 April to 30 Sept) and accurate as we go to press — and most places are finally realising the importance of keeping opening times consistent from one year to the next. More or less everywhere is closed on Christmas Day, and most places on Boxing Day. The nearest TIC should be able to provide more detailed information.

Standard opening times for EH (English Heritage) and CADW (Welsh Historic Monuments) are as follows:

*Summer* (15 March to 15 October): Mon–Sat 9.30am to 6.30pm, Sundays 2pm to 6.30pm.

*Winter* (16 October to 14 March): Mon–Sat 9.30am to 4pm. Sundays 2pm to 4pm.

## Public Holidays

The following days are public holidays, when banks, offices and most shops will be closed, and public transport may be restricted or non-existent:

1 January — New Year's Day
Good Friday and Easter Monday
1st Monday in May — May Day Holiday
last Monday in May — Late Spring Bank Holiday
last Monday in Aug. — Late Summer Bank Holiday
25 December — Christmas Day
26 December — Boxing Day

There's no predictable pattern as to whether museums, country houses etc are open or closed on public holidays, though those run by local authorities are more likely to be closed. Expect almost everywhere to be closed on Christmas and Boxing Day; some places may also close for 10 days to two weeks between around Christmas and the New Year.

# Abbreviations

The following abbreviations are used in this book:

| | |
|---|---|
| CADW | Welsh Historic Monuments |
| EH | English Heritage |
| NT | National Trust |
| OS | Ordnance Survey |
| RSPB | Royal Society for the Protection of Birds |

# Metric Conversion Tables

All measurements are given in imperial units. For readers more familiar with the metric system, the accompanying tables are designed to facilitate quick conversion to metric units. Bold figures in the central columns can be read as either imperial or metric, e.g.: 1lb = 0.45kg or 1kg = 2.20lb.

| in | | mm | in | | cm | yds | | m |
|---|---|---|---|---|---|---|---|---|
| .039 | 1 | 25.4 | 0.39 | 1 | 2.54 | 1.09 | 1 | 0.91 |
| .079 | 2 | 50.8 | 0.79 | 2 | 5.08 | 2.19 | 2 | 1.83 |
| .118 | 3 | 76.2 | 1.18 | 3 | 7.62 | 3.28 | 3 | 2.74 |
| .157 | 4 | 101.6 | 1.57 | 4 | 10.16 | 4.37 | 4 | 3.66 |
| .197 | 5 | 127.0 | 1.97 | 5 | 12.70 | 5.47 | 5 | 4.57 |
| .236 | 6 | 152.4 | 2.36 | 6 | 15.24 | 6.56 | 6 | 5.49 |
| .276 | 7 | 177.8 | 2.76 | 7 | 17.78 | 7.66 | 7 | 6.40 |
| .315 | 8 | 203.2 | 3.15 | 8 | 20.32 | 8.75 | 8 | 7.32 |
| .354 | 9 | 228.6 | 3.54 | 9 | 22.86 | 9.84 | 9 | 8.23 |

| oz | | g | lb | | kg | miles | | km |
|---|---|---|---|---|---|---|---|---|
| .04 | 1 | 28.35 | 2.20 | 1 | 0.45 | 0.62 | 1 | 1.61 |
| .07 | 2 | 56.70 | 4.41 | 2 | 0.91 | 1.24 | 2 | 3.22 |
| .11 | 3 | 85.05 | 6.61 | 3 | 1.36 | 1.86 | 3 | 4.83 |
| .14 | 4 | 113.40 | 8.82 | 4 | 1.81 | 2.48 | 4 | 6.44 |
| .18 | 5 | 141.75 | 11.02 | 5 | 2.27 | 3.11 | 5 | 8.05 |
| .21 | 6 | 170.10 | 13.23 | 6 | 2.72 | 3.73 | 6 | 9.65 |
| .25 | 7 | 198.45 | 15.43 | 7 | 3.18 | 4.35 | 7 | 11.26 |
| .28 | 8 | 226.80 | 17.64 | 8 | 3.63 | 4.97 | 8 | 12.87 |
| .32 | 9 | 225.15 | 19.84 | 9 | 4.08 | 5.59 | 9 | 14.48 |

| acres | | ha |
|---|---|---|
| 2.47 | 1 | 0.40 |
| 4.94 | 2 | 0.81 |
| 7.41 | 3 | 1.21 |
| 9.88 | 4 | 1.62 |
| 12.36 | 5 | 2.02 |
| 14.83 | 6 | 2.43 |
| 17.30 | 7 | 2.83 |
| 19.77 | 8 | 3.24 |
| 22.24 | 9 | 3.64 |

*Imperial to metric conversion formulae*

| | multiply by |
|---|---|
| inches to centimetres | 2.54 |
| feet to metres | 0.31 |
| yards to metres | 1.91 |
| miles to kilometres | 1.61 |
| square miles to km$^2$ | 2.59 |
| acres to hectares | 0.40 |
| ounces to grams | 28.35 |
| pounds to kilograms | 0.45 |

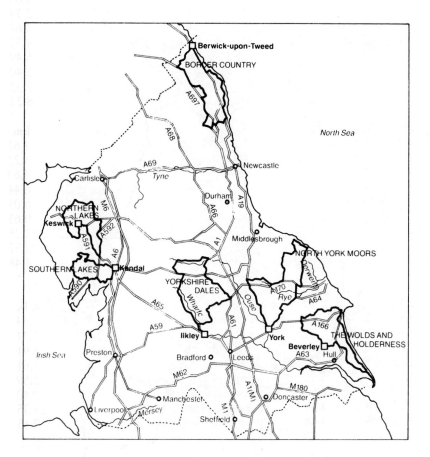

There's a special sharpness and clarity about the rural landscapes of the north of England. For the most part this is high, lonely country, with great stretches of moorland and some majestic mountain peaks, including, in the Lake District, England's highest summits. But it is not all challenge. Sparkling streams rush down from the weather-beaten tops to run through gentler valleys, past quiet stone-built villages. The Lake District offers a unique visual feast of water and mountain. In the north-east especially, castles and fortifications remind the traveller of the ever-present threat, throughout the medieval centuries, of raids and invasion by the hostile Scots from north of the border. And also on the eastern side lies a magnificent and relatively unexplored coastline, with miles of sandy beaches punctuated by tall cliffs and remote headlands, the habitat of countless seabirds.

## The Northern Lakes

*1–2 days/about 95 miles/from Keswick/OS maps 89, 90*

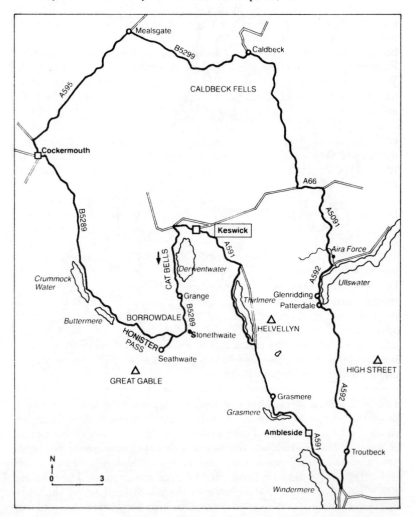

The Lake District packs a lot of contrasts into its 900 square miles. Water and mountains are the main ingredients of this magical combination. The water comes in many forms: the celebrated lakes strung out along the valley bottoms; lonely tarns hidden in folds in the hills; tumbling, crystal-clear becks; and, of coure, familiar to all but the luckiest visitor, the rain that, sweeping in from the Atlantic, waters the luxuriant vegetation. The hills offer equal variety. There are many grand peaks (including Scafell Pike, at 3,210ft England's highest), where you can enjoy invigorating walks or tackle Alpine-standard climbs. But the more accessible lower slopes offer as many pleasures: gentle strolls, by the water's edge or through woodland, and easy, well-signposted hikes — well worth tackling, for an immense sense of achievement is to be gained from leaving the mass of visitors behind and getting out into empty countryside.

As if the landscape were not enough, the Lake District is full of fascinating associations with the writers it has inspired over the centuries. The most famous is William Wordsworth. Others include the poets Robert Southey and Samuel Taylor Coleridge, the critic John Ruskin, Arthur Ransome, creator of the *Swallows and Amazons* stories, and one Mrs William Heelis, better known as Beatrix Potter, who set her tales of the adventures of Squirrel Nutkin, Mrs Tiggywinkle and her other inimitable, unforgettable characters in recognisable local settings.

Not surprisingly, the Lake District draws many thousands of visitors each year, and at high season, especially, the famous beauty spots can be unbearably crowded. Make the effort to seek out the less well-known spots, whether on four wheels or, better still, on two feet, and you will easily shake off the crowds.

This drive and the next provide a taste of the varying Lakeland landscapes. The first sticks broadly speaking to the brisker northern half of the area, while the second explores some of the gentler, more wooded southern hills and valleys.

Three practical points before setting out. First, in high season you will inevitably encounter patches of quite heavy traffic. Be patient — Lake District roads simply aren't made for fast driving. Secondly, in winter and spring, many high roads may be difficult to drive, if not totally impassable, in poor weather. Listen to weather forecasts and, above all, take local advice before you set out. Last of all, on the positive side, do take advantage of the excellent advice provided by the National Park's Tourist Information Centres; they have numerous ideas for walks (of all lengths and difficulties) and other activities.

**KESWICK** must be England's nearest approximation to an Alpine resort, delightfully situated at the head of Derwent Water and directly underneath the peaks of Skiddaw and Blencathra. There is an excellent range of shops, including **Fisher's**, which sells every imaginable item of walking and mountaineering equipment; you can even hire walking boots, which is useful if you're suddenly inspired to take off into the hills. The National Park Tourist Information Centre is in the **Moot Hall** (07687–72645), built in 1813, in the Market Square. The **Fitz Park Museum and Art**

**Gallery** (*open daily except Sun*), contains manuscripts by Wordsworth, Robert Southey (who preceded Wordsworth as Poet Laureate and lived at Keswick) and the novelist Hugh Walpole, whose *Herries Chronicles* are set in Borrowdale (see below), and also a good mineral collection. Pencils are the subject of another museum, the **Cumberland Pencil Museum** (*open daily*); Keswick was the first place in the world to make pencils, using graphite mined in Borrowdale from the 16th century onwards. Local trout and Cumberland ham and sausage (far, far tastier than pallid mass-production sausages) are all available in Keswick's good selection of eating places: try **Bryson's Tea Room** and **The Wild Strawberry** (both in Main Street), and the **Dog and Gun** and **Four in Hand** pubs (both in Lake Road). For accommodation, try **The Grange Country House Hotel** (07687–72500) or, simpler but still pleasant, guest houses such as **Foye House** (07687–73288) or the **Dorchester** (07687–73256).

We start by following the western shore of Derwent Water. Take B5289 west from the town centre, turn left on to the main A66, and almost immediately left again on to the unclassified road signposted Portinscale. This road runs the length of the lake — Lake District lakes are generally known as either 'mere' or 'water', as in Windermere and Derwent Water. — a little way in from the shore. At **Brandelhow**, the first Lake District property acquired by the National Trust, there are peaceful walks along the shore — in fact, you can walk right the way round to Grange (see below).

This may sound dictatorial, but really no visit to the Lakes is complete without taking a boat trip and climbing a mountain. The boat trip is easy: instead of driving take the regular launch service that runs round Derwent Water from Keswick, and get off at one of the three landing stages on the west side of the lake. The climb is almost as simple too. Though it's only 1,481ft high, a minnow compared with all the surrounding grand peaks, the delightfully named **Catbells** (where that 'excellent clear-starcher' Mrs Tiggywinkle lived) is a proper summit. It is also one of the best-loved walks of all the Lake District. Park near **Hawes End** and follow the path up and along the ridge; so long as you're reasonably fit and have sensible footwear, this shouldn't present any difficulties. After about 2½ miles, a path to the left will lead you down to the road again at the foot of the lake.

At **GRANGE**, just beyond the foot of Derwent Water, you can enjoy home cooking at **Grange Bridge Cottage** and buy examples of local craftsmanship at the **Lakeland Industries** shop. Turn right here on to B5289 and head south into **Borrowdale**, one of the most tranquil Lakeland valleys. Just off the road to the left stands the great **Bowder Stone**, a 2,000-ton boulder left behind by the glaciers that scoured the Lakeland valleys. Since you can ascend it on a ladder, it can't be as precariously balanced as it looks.

The mountains massed ahead are some of the main Lake District peaks: in the foreground Glaramara and Great Gable, behind them Scafell Pike. Past Rosthwaite, an unclassified road leads off to tiny

*View down Derwent Water*

**STONETHWAITE**, barely more than a dozen houses, where the **Langstrath Hotel** (059684–239) makes an excellent walking base. From Stonethwaite easy paths follow the beck into the hills: it's a real paradise for children, with the stream to play and swim in, stepping stones to clamber across and dams to build. The next unclassified road off B5289 runs from **SEATOLLER**, where there's a National Park Tourist Information Centre (059684–294), to **SEATHWAITE**, an important starting-point for many ascents. Seathwaite claims the highest annual rainfall in England: a dubious honour.

We continue on B5289, which now leaves Borrowdale and begins to ascend **Honister Pass**, gradient 1:4, 1,176ft high, through wild and lonely fells. At the summit, or hause, there are fine views all around. Mighty **Honister Crag**, whose slopes were once mined for slate, dominates the view to the left at the start of the slow descent, and then comes a spectacular view down to **Buttermere**, which, together with adjacent **Crummock Water**, is owned by the National Trust. The road runs along the edge of both lakes (there's a pleasant waterside path alongside Buttermere), which were once a single lake, divided by streams that eroded the hillsides after the last Ice Age. On the far side of Crummock Water is **Scale Force**, where the water tumbles 120ft between sheer rock walls; the walk to the waterfall is a relatively easy 4 miles, with views to a multitude of soaring peaks.

Beyond Crummock Water, the road runs north through the gentler, fertile landscape of Lorton Vale towards Cockermouth, joining B5292 a few miles outside the town.

William Wordsworth was born in **COCKERMOUTH** in 1770, and his sister Dorothy (herself an excellent writer, as her *Journals* show) the following year, in a handsome house built 25 years earlier on the town's main street. The rooms are furnished in period style, and some mementoes of the poet are on display; teas are served in the old kitchen. (*NT, open April–Oct daily except Thur.*) You can spend a pleasant hour or so exploring the rest of the town, which stands on the confluence of the rivers Derwent and Cocker and has been an important local commercial centre since the 17th century. The collections at the **Ethnic Doll and Toy Museum** consist of costumed dolls from all over the world and a large range of toys dating from 1900 to the present day (*open daily March–Oct*). TIC in the Riverside Car Park. Hotels here include the **Allerdale Court** (0900–822634), and the **Quince and Medlar** in Castlegate offers a much-praised vegetarian menu.

The next stretch runs round the back of the mountains to Caldbeck, through the great swathe of remote, unpopulated countryside that runs north to the Solway Firth. Follow the dead-straight A595 — the road follows the course of the Roman road connecting Cockermouth and Carlisle — north-east to Mealsgate, where turn right on to B5299, which eventually leads to **CALDBECK**. In the churchyard you will find the grave of the celebrated huntsman John Peel, decorated with hunting symbols, who died in 1854 as a result of a riding accident. The original version of *D'Ye Ken John Peel* was also written in Caldbeck in 1832; a plaque commemorates the house. At the end of the 18th century, when Caldeck's population numbered almost 2,000, there were no less than 13 water mills along the banks of Caldew beck. The waterwheel and pit machinery of one, the **Priests Mill** has now been restored (*open April–Oct daily except Mon, also weekends in Nov and Dec*). Here you can also enjoy home-cooked food in the wholefood cafe and buy crafts from the craftspeople working in the mill yard.

The Caldbeck Fells to the south are wild country, formerly the site of much mining activity. Follow unclassified roads south through **HESKET NEWMARKET**, where attractive 18th-century houses are grouped around the village green with a market cross, and then alongside Carrock Fell and through Mungrisdale. Turn left on to the busy A66 and right after about 1½ miles on to A5091, which eventually descends steeply to Ullswater.

Clearly signposted on the left shortly before you reach the shore is the path to **Aira Force**. There are good views of the 60 ft waterfall from bridges across the gorge.

Mountains drop down to the wooded shores of **Ullswater**, 7 miles long and the second largest Lake District lake. Its varying moods, one day basking serene in sunlight, another angry as the wind ruffles the water and the peaks are shrouded in rain clouds, never fail to entrance. There's an easy path along the far shore from Howtown around to Patterdale (see below), which is well worth walking; two 19th-century steamers, now oil-fired, will take you across the lake from Glenridding to Howtown. Dorothy and William Wordsworth were walking together on the banks of Ullswater somewhere below Aira Force when they saw that 'host of golden daffodils'. Dorothy recorded the scene in her notebook; her observations of Nature were an important source of her brother's poetical inspiration.

We turn right on to A592, which hugs the northern shore as far as **GLENRIDDING**, a busy tourist village and centre for walkers. Paths, including one via the dramatic ridge of rock called Striding Edge, lead up to **Helvellyn**, 3,116ft. National Park Tourist Information Centre in the main car park (08532–414). Hotels here are the **Ullswater** (08532–444) and the **Glenridding** (08532–228).

A592 runs through Patterdale and then slowly climbs up to Kirkstone Pass, passing Brothers Water on the right. **PATTERDALE** has a charming 19th-century church, dedicated to St Patrick, after whom the village is named, with notable embroideries done by a local lady, Ann Macbeth.

The views of the hills here are so fine that the temptation to abandon the car and set off on two legs is all but irresistible. So long as you are fairly fit, and have proper walking boots and rainwear, the ascent of Helvellyn is not hard; ask at the Information Centre for advice on routes (you don't have to go via Striding Edge) and weather conditions. If you want a long walk without any steep climbs, follow the path that runs west from Patterdale alongside Grisedale Beck and gradually ascends to Grisedale Tarn, underneath Dollywagon Pike at the end of the Helvellyn range, before descending quite sharply to A591 just south of Thirlmere, where you pick up this drive again. This 6-mile walk shouldn't take more than about three hours. More energetic possibilities lie in the lonely and lesser-known fells to the east of A592. Paths lead up from Hartsop village to High Street, a magnificent north–south ridge used by the Romans as a high-level road.

Back to four wheels! As you breast **Kirkstone Pass**, 1,450ft, a magnificent view opens up over Lake Windermere and the southern part of the Lake District. Think what it must have been like to struggle up here in a horse-drawn coach on an unmetalled road! Descending towards the lake, turn right just before Troutbeck on to an unclassified road. Keep straight on through the village, then descend alongside the Trout Beck and then right again on to A591 along the lake towards Ambleside.

On the left is the entrance to **Brockhole National Park Visitor Centre** (*open daily April–early Nov*). Here you can enjoy magnificent gardens, exhibitions on different aspects of Lakeland life, regular demonstrations of traditional crafts, launch trips, and a varied daily programme of slideshows, walks and talks. It all adds up to an excellent introduction to the Lake District.

**AMBLESIDE**, a major tourist centre with attractive historic buildings in the centre, including the 17th-century Bridge House, now the National Trust's oldest Information Centre and smallest shop. The National Park Tourist Information Centre is in the Old Courthouse in Church Street

*Dove Cottage*

(05394–32582); the mid-19th century St Mary's Church contains memorials to the Wordsworth family. There are many hotels here, including **Rothay Manor** (05394–33605), which also does a highly recommended afternoon tea, and **Smallwood House** (05394–32330). Restaurants include **Sheila's Cottage** (The Slack) and **Zefferelli's** (Compston Road).

Ambleside and Grasmere, a few miles north on A591, are very much Wordsworth country. William and his sister Dorothy settled at Dove Cottage in Grasmere in 1799, and the family — William had by now married his childhood friend Mary Hutchinson — moved to Rydal Mount, halfway to Ambleside, in 1813. **Rydal Mount** (*open daily, except Tues in winter*), the poet's home until he died in 1850, contains family furniture and portraits, first editions and personal mementoes; the four acres of garden are much as Wordsworth laid them out.

It was in his Dove Cottage years that Wordsworth wrote almost all the works by which he is now remembered during a period of intense creative activity that had virtually spent itself by the 1810s. Tiny **Dove Cottage** contains furniture and personal belongings, while the **Grasmere and Wordsworth Museum** (*both open daily*) is devoted to the works of Wordsworth and his fellow Lake Poets.

**GRASMERE** is a charming but often crowded village just to the north of the lake of the same name. The minute schoolroom where Wordsworth taught is now a gingerbread shop. The annual Grasmere Sports in mid-August include traditional local contests such as Cumberland wrestling, fell-racing and hound-trailing. A couple of weeks earlier, near the beginning of the month, sees the Rushbearing Festival, at which children parade traditional designs of rushes through the village streets and then lay them on the church floor; the festival commemorates the time when the church floor consisted of bare earth with a rush covering, changed annually. TIC in Red Bank Road (09665–245).

North of Grasmere, A591 runs through the fells once more, with the grand mass of Helvellyn to the right. (This is where the Patterdale–Grisedale Tarn walk described above finishes.) **Thirlmere** on the left was created out of two much smaller lakes at the end of the 19th century, as a reservoir to supply water to Manchester. If you're in a hurry, stick to A591. If not, turn left on to the quieter unclassified road that runs round the west side of the lake, which is surrounded by somewhat gloomy coniferous plantations. Nature trails lead off from car parks on each side of the reservoir. The water takes 26 hours to reach Manchester along a 96-mile downhill aqueduct.

At the northern end of Thirlmere, return to A591, which runs directly into Keswick.

# The Southern Lakes

*1–2 days/about 85 miles/from Kendal/OS maps 90, 96, 97*

The main streets of **KENDAL** (pop. 23,400) are lined with handsome grey limestone buildings; running off them are little alleyways terminating in old 'yards', where weavers and other craftsmen worked. From about the 13th century onwards the town was a major centre of the wool trade. The cloth produced was 'Linsey-Woolsey', a tough, hard-wearing combination of wool and linen. Kendal is still an important manufacturing centre (e.g. engineering, shoes), but the last cloth mill closed in the 1950s. See the large 13th-century parish church, the ruins of the Norman castle and three major museums. The **Museum of Lakeland Life and Industry** (*open daily*) in the Georgian Abbot Hall next to the church is a skilful recreation of the traditional, now almost completely vanished, Lakeland way of life, with period rooms, blacksmiths', wheelwrights' and weavers' equipment, costumes etc, and a section on Arthur Ransome. The **Abbot Hall Art Gallery** in the same complex contains works by John Ruskin and George Romney, the 18th-century Kendal painter, and furniture by Gillows of Lancaster, all set in elegant 18th-century rooms.

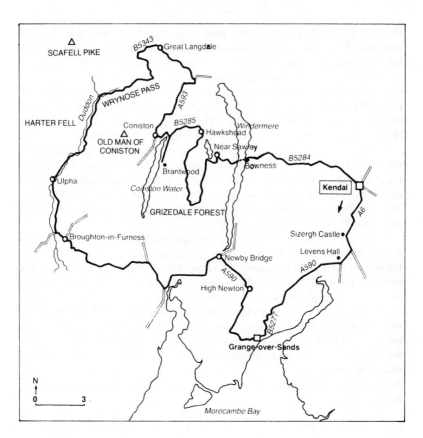

The **Kendal Museum of Natural History and Archaeology** (*open daily*) uses dioramas to explain local natural history and geology and also has displays on Lakeland people from prehistoric times onwards. Gourmets do well in Kendall. Among the many restaurants, try the **Brewery Arts Centre** (Highgate), which stages a lively all-year programme of theatre, concerts and exhibitions, **Farrers Tea and Coffee House** in Strickland-gate or **Eat Fit** (which changes its name to **Flavours** for evening meals) in Stramongate. The **County Hotel** (0539–22461) and **Lane Head Country House Hotel** (0539–31283/21023) are two of the local hotels. National Park Tourist Information Centre in the Town Hall, Highgate (0539–25758).

Follow signposts out of Kendal for the fast by-pass road and take this dual carriageway south to the next exit, where turn right on to A6. **Sizergh Castle** (*NT, open April–Oct Sun. Mon. Wed and Thur afternoons*) lies just to the north. Originally a 14th-century pele tower, a fortified bastion built for protection against Scottish raiders, it was transformed in later centuries into a substantial country mansion. There are no fewer than five exquisitely carved Elizabethan overmantels, plus fine furniture and paintings. The 18th-century gardens contain a rock garden with hardy ferns and dwarf conifers.

Roughly a mile to the south along A6, **Levens Hall** (*open Easter–mid Oct Sun–Thur*) is another extended pele tower with fine Elizabethan panelling and plasterwork. The beautiful gardens, designed in the 1690s, contain magnificent topiary — fantastical birds, animals, pyramids, castellated towers; there's also a collection of steam engines.

Follow A590 west across the broad Lyth Valley and then on south, turning off on to B5277 for Grange-over-Sands. This is a curious, relatively uncrowded finger of the Lakes that thrusts down into the expanse of Morecambe Bay. There are fells to the north, relatively low and wooded in the foreground, higher and starker behind, but to the south the scene is of mud-flats and marshes.

**GRANGE-OVER-SANDS** is a pleasant, sheltered 19th-century seaside and retirement resort, with gentle amenities such as bowling, tennis, swimming and gardens. **At Home** (Main Street) is a good place to eat; stay at **Netherwood Hotel** (04484–2552/4121), a late Victorian pile, or more cheaply at **Thornbank** (04484–2664).

Follow the unclassified road inland to **CARTMEL**, a pleasing village with medieval streets and an attractive market square. A priory was founded here at the end of the 12th century. Although the rest of the settlement was destroyed at the Reformation, the imposing church unusually survived intact; it was later restored in the 17th century. Admire the carved choir stalls and canopies, the stained glass and the Renaissance screens.

Return along unclassified roads to High Newton, and follow A590 west through Newby Bridge and Haverthwaite. **NEWBY BRIDGE** — the five-arched bridge dates from the 16th century — is about a mile from the foot of Lake Windermere. **Fell Foot Park** is a pleasant National Trust country park (*open daily*) on the edge of the lake; it's ideal for families. The entrance is a little way north on A592.

Newby Bridge is also the intermediate station on the steam-operated **Lakeside and Haverthwaite Railway** (*trains run at Easter and daily May–Sept*). You can see the locomotives and rolling stock at the station at **HAVERTHWAITE**.

Beyond Haverthwaite the road dips down to an inlet of Morecambe Bay. Bear right here on to A5092 and continue across the top of the Furness peninsula, joining A595, to **BROUGHTON-IN-FURNESS**, originally built as a stronghold strategically sited beneath the hills and overlooking the estuary of the river Duddon. The market square and town hall date from the mid-18th century.

It's time now to return to the hills. The next stage of the route involves some quite difficult driving through wild countryside. If this is not to your taste, or if the weather outlook is at all poor, drive north-east from Broughton on A593 (which itself has some quite steep sections) to Coniston, where you rejoin the main part of this exploration.

A short way beyond Broughton on A595, turn right on to the unclassified

*View into Great Langdale*

road that gradually climbs up the steep-sided Duddon valley, where the river tumbles past banks matted with wild flowers. A minute hamlet called **ULPHA**, where the church has some ancient wall paintings discovered during restoration work in 1934 and a pulpit carved from a fruit tree, is the only settlement along this lonely, romantic stretch of road. On the right are the Seathwaite Fells, and beyond them towers The Old Man of Coniston (2,621ft — known to readers of Arthur Ransome's stories as Kanchenjunga, the mountain scaled by the Swallows and Amazons); on the left is Harter Fell (2,129ft). Paths lead off all along this road, and there is a parking spot in Dunnerdale Forest.

From Wrynose Bottom the road climbs **Wrynose Pass** (1,270ft and 1:4 gradient in places). The Three Shires Stone near the top marks the junction of three former counties: Lancashire, Westmorland and Cumberland. The views are grand: the Coniston range to the south, symmetrical Pike O' Blisco to the north, Crinkle Crags and behind it Scafell Pike to the north-west.

The descent brings you to the Langdales, deep in the rugged central mass of mountains, and generally thick with walkers and climbers. Turn left just before Little Langdale Tarn and descend past Blea Tarn and the National Trust's **Old Dungeon Ghyll Hotel** (09667–272) and, now on B5343, along Great Langdale and past Elterwater to A593.

Turn right here and drive south to **CONISTON**, at the head of **Coniston Water**, scene of many record-setting powerboat runs by Malcolm Campbell and his son Donald. Malcolm set a new world water speed record here at 141mph in 1939, and Donald set a total of five records (the fastest 276mph) in the late 1950s, before dying in yet another attempt in 1967. You can cruise on the lake in the National Trust's restored steam yacht *Gondola*, built in 1859. (*Regular sailings late March–Oct.*) The **Yewdale Hotel** (05394–41280) is a good place to stay; eat at the **Bridge House Café**. National Park Tourist Information Centre in Yewdale Road (05394–41533).

There's no precise location for most of the places mentioned in Arthur Ransome's *Swallows and Amazons* stories. The lake is said to be a mixture of Coniston Water and Windermere, while Wildcat Island is generally identified as Peel Island on Coniston Water.

B5285 runs along the top of Coniston Water. Turn right down the eastern side to visit **Brantwood**, perfectly situated on the lakeside with some breath-taking views. John Ruskin, art critic, social reformer, essayist, poet and artist, lived here from 1872 to 1900; the house contains a collection of his lovely watercolours and drawings, and there are walks in the gardens, especially fine in spring when the daffodils, rhododendrons and azaleas make a glorious display. There's a bookshop, and a café serves lunches and teas. (*Open daily, but closed Mon and Tues mid-Nov to mid-March.*)

Return to B5285 and continue to **HAWKSHEAD**, whose pretty whitewashed buildings have made it a real tourist trap. Visit the **Old Grammar School** (*open daily April–Oct*), where Wordsworth went to school; among the exhibits is the desk on which he carved his name. You will find the newly opened **Beatrix Potter Gallery** (*NT, open Easter–Nov daily except Sat*) in the solicitor's offices once used by her husband, William Heelis. A must for all her fans, the gallery contains a selection of her original drawings and illustrations, together with displays not only on her writings but also on her life as a farmer and sheep-breeder and on her determined attempts, which included buying many farms to donate to the National Trust, to preserve her beloved Lake District. Half a mile north of the village centre is the 15th-century **courthouse** (*NT, open mid-April–Oct daily, key from NT shop in Hawkshead*), which contains a museum of local rural life. The bedrooms at the **Queen's Head** (09666–271) are pleasant and simple; downstairs you can sample excellent English cooking — pheasant, local sausage and hare for instance. TIC by the car park (09666–525).

Take the unclassified road south from Hawkshead through **Grizedale Forest**. An enormous range of activities is based at the Visitor Centre: sculptors and craftspeople at work, walks, orienteering trails, observation hides, unusual woodland sculptures. The **Theatre in the Forest** stages everything from lectures to plays and folk and classical concerts — take in a performance if you can; it's a magical place.

Follow the road south through Satterthwaite, and then turn north again through woodland and alongside Dale Park Beck to the southern tip of **Esthwaite Water**, where Beatrix Potter's Jeremy Fisher lived, and thence to **NEAR SAWREY**. In 1903 Beatrix Potter bought a little 17th-century farmhouse here called **Hill Top** (*NT, open April–Oct daily except Fri*), and moved north as soon as she was able to escape her London life overshadowed by her parents. Part of the house is now a museum — you can see the 'New Room', where she wrote many of her best-loved stories — the rest remains a working farm. The **Tower Bank Arms** next door, the inn illustrated in *Jemima Puddleduck*, serves bar meals.

Follow B5285 through wooded countryside to the shore of Lake Windermere, where the chain ferry will take you and your car across to Bowness; long queues are inevitable at high season. **Lake Windermere**, 11 miles long and 1¼ miles across at its widest point, is the largest and busiest of the lakes (it's also the largest in England) with a good deal of sailing and power-boating. The northern tip of the lake reaches the foot of the fells, but for the rest it is set amid softer, more wooded country. Steamers operate ferry services and cruises from Bowness.

BOWNESS is a busy lakeside resort chiefly devoted to supplying the needs of yachters and tourists. The **Windermere Steamboat Museum** north of the town on A592 (*open daily April–Oct*) has a large collection of vintage steam launches and other craft, many afloat in a large, covered wet-dock. **St. Martin's Church** (15th-century, restored in 19th) contains the grave of 47 people drowned in 1635 when the ferry capsized; they were on their way home from a wedding in Hawkshead. Eat in Bowness at the vegetarian **Hedgerow**, where tea-time specialities include Westmorland dream cake, or the **Nissi Taverna**, both in Lake Road. John Tovey's **Miller Howe Restaurant** provides an unforgettable theatrical cum culinary experience (your pocket book won't forget it for some time either); it's advisable to book well ahead (09662–2536). National Park Tourist Information Centre in The Glebe (09662–2895/5602 for accommodation).

Return to Kendal along B5284 through Crook.

## Border Country

*1–2 days/130 miles/from Berwick-upon-Tweed/OS maps 74, 80, 81, 75*

For centuries, the northernmost stretches of Northumbria were a no-man's-land, swinging between English and Scottish dominion: some historians claim that Berwick-upon-Tweed changed hands 14 times in just over 300 years before finally becoming part of England in 1482, others that it was a mere 13. Not for nothing were these nicknamed the 'Debatable Lands'. The physical evidence of these troubled times, first of border skirmishing and livestock-thieving, then from about 1300 onwards of military conflict on quite a large scale, is a series of impressive castles and fortifications. There is evidence too, on Lindisfarne, of Northumbria's early Christian heritage. The landscape provides impressive variety, from the conical granite peaks of the lonely Cheviot Hills in the west across heather-covered moorlands to the rich coastal plain and the golden sands, interspersed with rocky outcrops, of the North Sea coast.

Its Elizabethan fortifications are the most striking feature of **BERWICK-UPON-TWEED**, whose situation on the north bank of the Tweed betrays its Scottish origins. Unique in England — by the 1560s, when Berwick's fortifications were erected, most English towns felt free from attack and were abandoning their medieval walls and towers — these 1½ miles of gateways, ramparts and fortified arrowhead bastions were built to contemporary Italian designs, and were planned to make efficient use of artillery. Virtually nothing remains of the town's medieval walls, while the medieval castle was destroyed to form the railway station in 1844; much of the stonework was used by Robert Stephenson to build his handsome Royal Border Bridge, still crossed by main-line expresses. While there are no especially striking buildings, the 18th-century streets of the small town centre make a pleasing architectural whole. Berwick

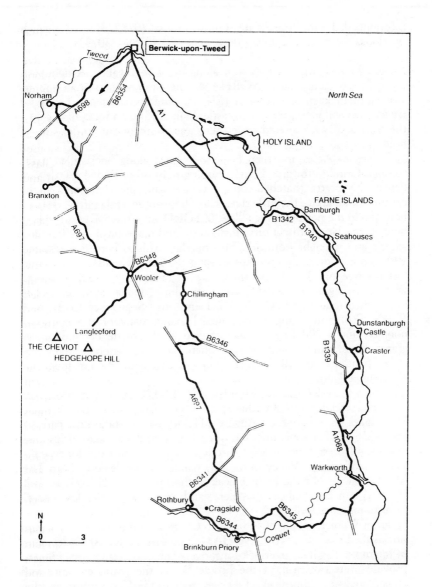

remained a garrison town until 1964. The **barracks**, built 1717–21, were one of the first purpose-built barracks in Britain. They now contain a local history museum (*open daily, except winter Sun and Mon*), a regimental museum (*open daily except winter Sun*) and an exhibition called 'By Beat of Drum', which recreates the life of the English soldier from 1660 to 1880 (*EH, standard opening times*). Eat at **Funnywayt' Mekalivin** in West Street or at the **Scotsgate Wine Bar** (Sidey Court off Marygate). Hotels include the **King's Arms** (0289–307454), whose restaurant is also recommended, and the **Walls Guest House** (0289–308320), which overlooks the river. TIC in Castlegate car park (0289–330733).

Leave by A698, which heads west along the Tweed valley. A right turn on to B6470 brings you to **NORHAM**, where the remains of an impressive Norman keep can be seen (*EH, standard opening times, but closed winter Tues and some Mon*). The castle, built *c.* 1160 on rocks high above the river and much altered since then, was an important border stronghold.

Return to A698 and then head south-west along unclassified roads through Grindon towards **ETAL**, turning right on to B6354 a little way before this pretty thatched-cottage village with the ruins of a 14th-century castle above the little river Till. There are several craft workshops here and in the neighbouring village of **FORD**, an attractive estate village built in the late 19th century, including hand-made furniture, spinning wheels and wrought ironwork. **Heatherslaw Mill** in Ford is a restored 19th-century corn mill (*open April–Sept daily, Oct weekends*).

Continue on B6354 and then take B6353 briefly into Crookham, where turn right on to A697 and then almost immediately left on to unclassified road to **BRANXTON**. Here, on 9 September 1513, some 10,000 Scots, including King James IV and many of the country's nobility, and 5,000 English soldiers died at the battle of Flodden. A granite cross, said to mark the spot where James fell, honours 'the brave of both nations' who died in this bloody engagement, the last fought in Northumberland.

Return to A697 and head south to **WOOLER**, an important market and commercial centre for this sparsely populated area; the Glendale Show takes place here each August. (TIC in the bus station car park — 0668–81602.) For some fine, but often boggy, walking, take unclassified roads south-west from Wooler through Earle and into the lonely hills along the Harthope Valley to the tiny hamlet of Langleeford. Both The Cheviot (at 2,674ft the highest peak of the range) and Hedgehope Hill (2,348ft) can be climbed from here, and there are gentler lower-level paths to follow as well.

From Wooler, follow B6348 east to Chatton, and turn south along an unclassified road to **CHILLINGHAM**. The **castle** (*open April–Sept daily in afternoons*), which overlooks the river Till, was fortified in 1344 to provide protection against the hostile Scots; the grand entrance was constructed when more peaceful times came in the 17th century and the grounds were landscaped in the early 19th century. In the wooded park (*open April–Oct daily except Tues*) lives a herd of wild white cattle, the only survivors of the beasts that roamed Northumberland in the Middle Ages. Coloured creamy-white with black-tipped crescent-shaped horns and black muzzles, they have on several occasions barely survived the hazards of winter weather and disease. Bring binoculars if possible, for these shy creatures like to conceal themselves in the remoter corners.

To rejoin A697, follow unclassified roads south along the river to Old Bewick, turn right on to B6346, and then left on to the main road. About

9 miles further south, turn right on to B6341 for Rothbury. Ahead there are lovely views to the heathery Simonside Hills, while the delightful river Coquet, famous for its salmon and trout, flows through the town. **ROTHBURY** would make an excellent holiday base; there are walking, fishing, pony-trekking and bird-watching in and around the town, which has a steep tree-lined main street and a shady green. Stay at **Orchard Guest House** (0669–20684) or, a little way outside town, at **Whitton Farmhouse Hotel** (0669–20811). Northumberland National Park Information Centre (0669–20887).

**Cragside** lies a mile or so away on B6344, a massive mansion built in Wagnerian Gothic style for Lord Armstrong, the Tyneside inventor and industrialist. Everything is larger than life here: the house took 30 years to build (initially designed as a hunting lodge, it was later extended by the Arts and Crafts architect Norman Shaw), and was the first in the world to be lit by hydro-electricity; in the grounds 40 miles of drives and footpaths were built, as many as 7 million trees and shrubs were planted, streams diverted and artificial lakes created. Thirty rooms can be visited, including some grand interiors, there is a Museum of Energy in the Visitor Centre, while on a 3-mile walk known as the 'Power Circuit' you can inspect the water-driven turbines and other machinery. (*NT, house open April–Sept daily except Mon; park, Power Circuit and Museum April– October daily, weekends rest of year.*) National Trust restaurant and shop.

With the coast our goal, we head east from Rothbury on B6344 along Coquetdale. The road passes **Brinkburn Priory** (*EH, standard times in summer only*) founded 1135 in a delightful situation amid riverside woods.

*Warkworth Castle*

All that remains is the church, sympathetically restored in the mid-19th century. Continue on B6344, turn left on to A697, and then right on to B6345. Follow this road across A1, through Felton and Acklington, and so to the sea at Amble, at the mouth of the Coquet.

Set in a loop of the river Coquet a mile to the north along A1068, **WARKWORTH** is dominated by its castle, originally Norman but largely rebuilt in the 14th and 15th centuries as a stronghold for the Percy family, who controlled Northumberland throughout the Middle Ages. In contrast with other castles further north, there hasn't been much later rebuilding here, and the ruins retain something of a medieval feel. (*EH, standard opening times.*) A narrow stone bridge with a fortified gatehouse arch crosses the river, and streets of grey stone 18th- and 19th-century houses cluster around the castle walls. St Laurence Church is largely Norman, and half a mile upstream (access by boat only) is the **Hermitage**, a tiny 14th-century chapel built in the rock (*EH, open summer weekends*).

The rest of this route keeps close to the coast, where there is a succession of fine, empty sandy beaches. Drive north on A1068, and bear right on to B1339 at Lesbury. Leave this road to visit **CRASTER**, a tiny fishing port famous for its undyed oak-smoked kippers, which you can sample in the restaurant next to the smoking sheds. South of the village is **Howick Hall**, home of the Grey family since the early 14th century, where the gardens (*open April–Sept afternoons*) have splendid displays: daffodils, rhododendrons and azaleas, shrubs, a silver wood (planted to commemorate a 25th wedding anniversary).

The ruins of **Dunstanburgh Castle** (*EH, standard opening times*) stand on a rocky promontory in a romantic, lonely spot high above the shore. Originally built in the early 14th century on the site of earlier strongholds, it belonged to John of Gaunt during the Wars of the Roses, when it changed hands five times. There's no access by road — but a fine walk instead along the coast north from Craster (1 mile) or south from Embleton (1½ miles).

Joining B1340 beyond Embleton, drive north past a series of fine beaches with facilities for sailing, wind-surfing and water-skiing, to **SEAHOUSES**. The harbour was built relatively recently, in the late 19th century, for fishing and the lime trade, but now the village is largely a mini-resort, although fishing continues and there's generally something of interest happening in the harbour. The **Marine Life Centre and Fishing Museum** (*open daily April–Nov*) consists of a seawater aquarium and a recreated fisherman's cottage. Stay in the **Olde Ship Hotel** (0665–720200) by the harbour (accommodation closed in winter).

From Seahouses, take a boat trip (weather permitting) to the **FARNE ISLANDS**, a group of 28 uninhabited islands — some so small they are barely more than outcrops of rock — 2–5 miles out to sea. In early summer over 17 species of seabird — puffin, kittiwake, eider duck, guillemot, razor bill, tern, fulmar among them — breed here in huge numbers. So crowded are the rock faces you can hardly believe there is room for another bird! The islands are also a breeding-ground for grey seals — the only one on the entire east coast of Britain — and if you're

*Farne Islands Seal*

lucky you will see dozens of these gentle creatures, basking lazily on sun-drenched rocks, or lumbering clumsily towards the water and then, in pointed contrast, racing sleek and swift through the waves. (These words were written before disease decimated the seal population of the east coast in 1988.)

Landing is permitted on only two islands, Inner Farne and Staple, between April and September; the most interesting time to come is during the breeding season, mid-May to mid-July, but then landing times are severely restricted for obvious reasons. Two 7th-century saints, Aidan and Cuthbert, lived as hermits on the Farnes; Cuthbert died on Inner Farne in 687, and a chapel was built to his memory in 1370. Note that while some boat trips land on Inner Farne and Staple, others go round the islands, including the Outer Farnes; details from the TIC (0665–720884) or from local boatsmen.

The imposing red sandstone walls of **Bamburgh Castle** (*open Easter–Oct afternoons*) tower 150ft high above the sea a couple of miles north along the coast. The last of a long line of fortifications dating back to the Iron Age, the present castle has Norman origins and was badly damaged during the Wars of the Roses. It was extensively rebuilt in the mid-18th century and again at the end of the 19th by Lord Armstrong (see Cragside above), who, among other improvements, installed in the banqueting hall a replica of the hammerbeam roof of Westminster Hall, London. Inside are collections of porcelain, furniture, paintings, arms and armour and a museum devoted to Lord Armstrong.

**BAMBURGH** village, one of the prettiest along this coast, huddles beneath the castle walls. The **Grace Darling Museum** (*open daily mid-April–Sept*) tells the story of the stormy night in September 1838 when Grace Darling and her father, the lighthouse keeper on the Farnes, rescued nine people from the wreck of the luxury steamer *Forfarshire*. Grace is buried in the village churchyard. Eat in Bamburgh at the **Copper Kettle**, where the baking is especially recommended; places to stay include the **Lord Crewe Arms** (06684–243) and the **Mizen Head Hotel** (06684–254).

B1342 runs inland to A1, where turn right and head towards Berwick (about 12 miles).

After 5 miles a right turn off the main road near Beal takes you over the causeway to **HOLY ISLAND**, or Lindisfarne; note that it is safe to cross only during the 2 hours before low tide, and the 3½ hours after it. Christianity spread across the north of England from the monastery established on Lindisfarne by St Aidan in 635. Another early Christian connected with Lindisfarne was St Cuthbert, who became bishop in 664. During his period in office the monks of Holy Island produced the richly illluminated Lindisfarne Gospels, now one of the treasures of the British Museum. The monks left the island during the 9th century in the face of increasing Danish raids, and the present **priory** (*EH, standard times*), now roofless and ruined, dates from the 11th century. The **castle** (*NT, open April–Sept daily except Fri*) high on a pyramid of rock at the south point of the island, was built in 1550 and converted into a private residence by the architect Edwin Lutyens in 1903; the small walled garden below the castle walls was designed by Gertrude Jekyll. Mead, the honey and herbs drink traditionally brewed by the monks of Lindisfarne, continues to be made on the island in a modern winery open to the public. Try to come to Holy Island at a quiet time of year: sometimes the rather touristy atmosphere makes it hard to sense the history and spirituality of the island.

# The North York Moors
*2–3 days/about 135 miles/from York/OS maps 94, 100, 105*

The moors are the central feature of this route: a brooding heathery mass of flat-topped hills, cut through by tiny deep-set valleys and interrupted by slab-like stretches of conifer plantations and by the remains of iron workings. Small fishing villages perched along the North Sea coast and the gently rolling Howardian Hills, a picturesque setting for some of Yorkshire's grandest historic mansions and for delightful limestone hamlets, provide contrasting landscapes.

**YORK** (pop. 120,700) is an almost perfect medieval city, with evidence from more than a thousand years of history. See above all the **Minster**, built 1220–1470 and now magnificently restored after the disastrous fire in 1984, a wondrous example of the skill of medieval craftsmen and masons; admire especially the stained glass, the choir screen, on which appear portraits of every medieval monarch, and the exquisite 14th-century chapter house. The **Castle Museum** (*open daily*) in a former 18th-century prison contains a series of authentic historical reconstruc-

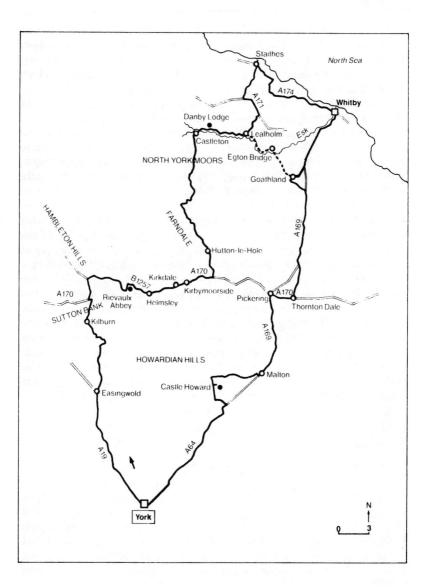

tions, including a full-scale Victorian street complete with shops. At the **Jorvik Viking Centre** (*open daily*) you travel in electric time-cars back to the sights, sounds and smells of Viking York, while the **National Railway Museum** (*open daily*) contains locomotives and rolling stock from the earliest days of rail travel. Much of the pleasure of York comes from walking the walls and the narrow medieval streets such as the Shambles and Stonegate, whose overhanging buildings are so close that you can almost reach from one to the other. During such wanderings you'll come across interesting shops — the city is especially strong on books and antiques — and a wealth of lesser-known churches and secular buildings: for instance, **St. Mary's** in Castlegate, now converted into a Heritage Centre, the **Merchant Adventurer's Hall** and the **Merchant Taylor's Hall**, both fine examples of medieval guild halls, and the 18th-century **Judges' Lodgings**. There are numerous places to eat in the city — try **Taylors** in Stonegate, a good old-fashioned coffee house, and the restaurant in the Tudor **St William's College** at the east end of the Minster. Stay, among many others, at **Jorvik Hotel** (0904–53511) or, at the upper end of the price range, at **Ladbroke Abbey Park Hotel** (0904–658301). TICs in De Grey Rooms, Exhibition Square (0904–21756/7), and at the railway station (0904–643700).

Despite York's unique atmosphere, best appreciated out of high season, it is worth tearing yourself away. Head north on the busy A19 across the Vale of York, the plain that divides the Dales and the Moors, to Easingwold. Turn off here on to the unclassified road to **COXWOLD**, a lovely limestone village at the western end of the Howardian Hills. Just south of the village is **Newburgh Priory** (*open mid-May–Aug Weds, also Suns in Aug*), a 12th-century priory converted into a house from the 16th century onwards; the grounds include a wild water garden. Coxwold's vicar during the 1760s was the witty and eccentric novelist Laurence Sterne. His house, called **Shandy Hall**, is at the other end of the village; here he wrote *A Sentimental Journey* and much of *Tristram Shandy* too. Still looking much as it was in Sterne's day, it now houses a collection of books and manuscripts. (*Open June–Sept Weds and Suns.*)

On now to **KILBURN**, tucked at the foot of Roulston Scar on the steep scarp slope of the Hambleton Hills. **Kilburn White Horse**, 105yds long, 75 high, was cut out of the grassy hillside by the local headmaster and his pupils in 1857; originally it was painted with whitewash, but now chalk chippings from the Yorkshire Wolds are used. Stacks of sawn oak indicate the workshop of **Robert Thompson Craftsmen** (*open Mon–Sat*). Robert Thompson, who died in 1955, was a local wood-carver whose furniture and ecclesiastical carvings, inspired by the medieval master-carvers, became famous world-wide for his signature, a little mouse hidden somewhere on each piece. Thompson's grandsons maintain the business, employing a team of about 30 craftsmen, each of whom interprets the mouse trademark in their own fashion.

Continue straight on at the north end of the village, along the minor road that climbs through woodland to the top of Sutton Bank. The road is narrow and very steep (1:4); be prepared to reverse should you meet oncoming traffic. Use the car parks along this road to walk to the White Horse, or else turn left on to A170 and park at the top of Sutton Bank, where the National Park Information Centre (0845 597426) is an excellent source of information about local walks and activities. The views from **Sutton Bank** are stupendous: west to the Pennines, north to the Cleveland Hills, east towards the North Sea, and south to York, where the Minster towers should be clearly visible. This is a grand spot for a

*Rievaulx Abbey*

walk. One path runs down to **Lake Gormire**, a natural lake with no visible source of water. Another possibility is to follow the Cleveland Way, which runs north from Sutton Bank along the scarp.

Follow the unclassified road north from Sutton Bank; this is an old drove road once used for driving cattle south to market. Take the second turning off to the right, and pursue this road through Old Byland and then on a steep and winding route downhill through woods above the river Rye to Rievaulx (pronounced 'Reevo').

**Rievaulx Abbey** (*EH, standard opening times*), was founded by Cistercian monks in 1131, the first Cistercian foundation in the north of England. It soon flourished; within 50 years, it owned 6,000 acres and 14,000 sheep, and some 500 lay brothers were employed to keep its estates in order — the 140 or so monks had little time for outside work, being required to attend church seven times a day. The nave, the first part of the church to be built, is plain and severe; the choir, constructed a century later, is a splendid example of English Gothic. There are also extensive remains of the monks' living quarters.

From the village, follow the unclassified road north through woodland to the junction with B1257. On the right is the entrance to **Rievaulx Terrace** (*NT, open daily April–Sept*), a long, curving grassy terrace overlooking the Abbey. If the Abbey is a triumphant proclamation of the medieval faith, the Terrace, with its two temples (Doric at one end. Ionic at the other) and its carefully contrived panoramas over the Abbey, equally represents the essence of 18th-century civilisation. It was laid out for Thomas Duncombe, a local landowner, in about 1758.

Now follow B1257 into **HELMSLEY**, a friendly market town on the southern edge of the Moors. It's a busy shopping and tourist centre (TIC in the Town Hall on the Market Place — 0439–70173) and a focus of the annual Ryedale and Helmsley Festival each summer. The **castle** (*EH, standard opening times*) dates from the 12th century and has complex defensive earthworks. Several hotels and inns border the spacious market square (market day Friday), including the **Black Swan** (0439–70466) and the **Crown** (0439–70297), where you can get an excellent, substantial high tea.

Take A170 east out of town. After about 3 miles, beyond Beadlam village, the main road turns sharp right. Carry straight on to the unclassified road, following signs to **St Gregory's Minster** in **KIRKDALE**. An Anglo-Saxon inscription on the sundial above the doorway of this tiny, isolated church tells how it was rebuilt by 'Orm, Gamal's son', in about 1060 after being destroyed in a Danish attack. The original minster was built in about 654 and dedicated to Pope Gregory, who sent Augustine to establish Christianity in England.

Follow the unclassified road across the ford, and rejoin A170, turning left in just over 1 mile for Hutton-le-Hole. The main road by-passes **KIRKBYMOORSIDE**, whose main claim to fame is that George Villiers, 2nd Duke of Buckingham, the rich, witty, drunken favourite of Charles II, died here in 1687. **Hatters Castle Coffee Shop** on the cobbled market square serves curd tart, a Yorkshire speciality that every visitor should sample.

Moorland sheep graze the grassy banks of Hutton Beck as it tumbles down from the moors and flows through the middle of **HUTTON-LE-HOLE**. The village is self-consciously pretty in a chocolate-box sort of way — little white bridges run across the stream, the gardens burst with colour — and hence is packed with visitors. But the **Ryedale Folk Museum** (*open daily Easter–Oct*), housed in 18th-century farm buildings, makes it well worth stopping here. The museum contains reconstructed buildings from the moors villages, including two yeomen's cottages, one 500 years old, the other 200, an iron foundry, a blacksmith's shop, a dairy and a 16th-century glass furnace, all with original furniture and equipment. It adds up to a vivid portrait of life on the moors, and demonstrates how hard that was until well into the present century. (TIC in the museum — 07515–367.)

Take the road running north from the village, which soon climbs on to the moorland tops. In poor weather, when the rain lashes down and the wind races in from the north, this is bleak and unforgiving terrain. At good times, with the sun beating down, it is gloriously exhilarating: crisp, clean air, a purple mass of heather, birds wheeling in the sky.

The main road, which this route rejoins later, continues right over the moors along Blakey Ridge. We take the second turning to the left and gently descend into **Farndale**, one of the loneliest and loveliest of the moorland valleys. Farndale is best known for its daffodils: not the cultivated variety found in millions of urban back gardens, but the small wild flowers native to this country. The walk along the banks of the river Dove from the hamlet of **LOW MILL** to the even tinier settlement at **CHURCH HOUSES**, where the **Feversham Arms** serves pub meals, is delightful at any time of the year, and especially lovely around Easter, when the daffodils appear in thick profusion. For a longer hike, climb up to the moors on the west side of the valley and follow Rudland Rigg, a broad ancient trackway running north. If you've time, you can make an entire circuit above Farndale on the Rigg and then on the bed of the old railway that transported the iron ore mined high in the moors — but this major walk will occupy a good part of the day.

From Church Houses take the steep unclassified road that climbs up to the tops, and turn left on to the main road along Blakey Ridge past the isolated **Lion Inn**. The road reaches 1,300 ft at **Rosedale Head**, where two crosses, called the Ralph Crosses, stand out against the skyline.

Young Ralph is close to the road, Old Ralph a little way off half-hidden in the heather. Bear right at Rosedale Head (NB: do *not* take the sharp right turn that eventually runs down into Rosedale) north across Danby High Moor and along Castleton Rigg, eventually descending to the Esk valley at Castleton.

Attractive stone villages and farmhouses and winding flower-banked lanes make **Eskdale** a delight to explore. There's a feeling of intimacy in the valley, which contrasts with the wide views and sense of space gained from the moors on each side.

Drive east from Castleton to **DANBY**. On the far side of the village, the National Park's **Moors Centre** (*open daily Easter–Oct — 0287–60654*), housed in a 19th-century shooting lodge, has excellent displays on the history and wildlife of the Moors, a brass-rubbing area and a country bookshop; the 13 acres of grounds are ideal for picnics and walks, and several trails are laid out. There is also a tea room.

From the Centre, follow the unclassified road that runs north of the river and roughly parallel with the railway to **LEALHOLM**, a popular tourist spot set in a narrow, steep-sided part of the dale. Stepping-stones cross the river.

Our route now divides. The shorter alternative runs along winding

*Staithes*

roads with many steep ups and downs through Glaisdale and on to
**EGTON BRIDGE**, home of the annual Gooseberry Show, and
Grosmont. Look out for the tiny stone Beggar's Bridge over the river near
Glaisdale. **GROSMONT**, where iron ore was mined during the 19th
century, is the terminus of the North York Moors Railway (see page 35);
the loco sheds can be visited. From Grosmont take the unclassified road
running south-east up on to Sleights Moor, where you rejoin the main
route on A169.

The coast is the target of the longer route. Climb steeply out of
Lealholm up on to the moors, bear right towards Stonegate and then left.
Turn left again on to A171 and follow this road for about 2½ miles,
turning right for Staithes just before the parking spot at Scaling Reservoir.
This road crosses Borrowby Moor and then descends steeply into
Dalehouse, crossing A174 to reach old Staithes. Cars are prohibited from
much of the village; car parks are clearly indicated.

**STAITHES**, a traditional fishing community and still an important
lobster port, is protected by two great cliffs, Cowbar Nab and Old Nab.
Cottages and narrow cobbled alleyways tumble down to the harbour. The
boats used here are traditional cobles, with a sharp bow, a square stern
and broad amidships; you may also see the frilly Staithes bonnets being
worn. Captain Cook, who was born a few miles away in Marton, was
apprentice to a draper in Staithes and lived in a cottage by the harbour.
Try the **Cod and Lobster Inn** for fresh crab sandwiches.

**RUNSWICK BAY**, the next harbour down the coast, is another
charming fishing village with red-roofed cottages clustering around the
harbour and a sandy beach. The **Royal Inn** serves good pub food.

A174 runs south into **WHITBY**. There is much to see in this bustling
fishing port: the inner and outer harbours, the 12th-century parish
church (Bram Stoker used its gloomy graveyard as the setting for the first
scene of his novel *Dracula*), and the ruins of the **Abbey** (*EH, standard
opening times*), standing majestic on the cliff top. The first monastery was
built here in 657; seven years later the Synod of Whitby committed the
English church to the Roman rite rather than the Celtic, which had
predominated in the north of England, and also laid down the method of
fixing the date of Easter. The Danes destroyed the first abbey in the 9th
century, and it was not refounded until 1708. Captain Cook set sail for
the South Seas from Whitby in ships built in the town; the **Captain Cook
Memorial Museum**, which occupies the merchant's house in Grape
Lane where Cook lodged as an apprentice, has period furniture, maps
models, etc. (*Open May–Oct daily except Tues.*) Apart from a patch of
amusement arcades, Whitby remains a place of great character, with
many narrow passageways and steep-stepped paths to explore. Local fish
and chips are *the* food to eat here; there are many establishments around
the harbour — the **Magpie Café** in Pier Road is especially recommended.
Hotels include the **Royal** (0947–602234) and the **White House** (0947–
602098) and many guest houses. TIC in New Quay Road (0947–602674).

Head west from Whitby along A171 (i.e. towards Middlesbrough, *not* Scarborough), and then fork left on to A169 a couple of miles out of the town. A169 climps up on to the roof of the moors past turnings for Grosmont (where our shorter alternative route feeds in).

Turn right off the main road and descend to **GOATHLAND**, a straggly village with attractive stone houses that makes a good base for exploring the eastern part of the Moors. There are lots of excellent walks: the path to **Mallyan Spout**, a 70ft waterfall, descends through steep woods; another route leads up to **Wheeldale Moor** and to **Wade's Causeway**, a well-preserved stretch of Roman road; a third runs to Grosmont (3½ miles) along the bed of the horse-drawn railway built in 1836. This last path takes you through the minute hamlet of **Beck Hole**, where there is an even minuter pub, the **Birch Hall Inn**, and an excellent tea room. Goathland also has a station on the **North York Moors Railway**, which runs across the Moors from Grosmont to Pickering. Opened in 1845, the line was closed in 1965 and re-opened as an enthusiast-operated steam service in 1973. A regular timetable is operated between Easter and October. The train runs through lovely countryside, especially around **Newtondale**, which is inaccessible by car; get off at the station there and explore on foot. The evening Pullman service, on which a luxury five-course meal is served at your seat, is a must for nostalgia addicts; the food's good too. Stay in Goathland at the **Mallyan Spout Hotel** (0947–86206), the **Whitfield House Hotel** (0947–86215) or at the **Heatherdene Hotel** (0947–86334).

Return now to A169 and head south, past the 154ft high, 100-ton radomes of the **Fylingdales Ballistic Missile Early Warning Station**, built in the early 1960s and now said to be technically obsolete; four-minute warnings start here. After 6 miles, where the main road swings right, carry straight on to **THORNTON DALE**, another picture-book village at the foot of the Moors. Stocks stand on the village green, there is an ancient market cross, and stone cottages are surrounded by beautifully tended gardens.

**PICKERING**, west along A170, is a busy market town (market day Monday). The **castle** (*EH, standard opening times*) started as a motte-and-bailey construction around 1200; later a circular shell keep and two curtain walls were added. **Beck Isle Museum** in a Regency house has collections on local history and rural life (*open April–Oct daily*). The parish church contains 15th-century wall paintings. TIC in the station (0751–73791), which is the southern terminus of the North York Moors Railway (see above).

From Pickering travel along A169 to Malton. Look back to the mass of the Moors climbing up behind Pickering. At Malton, pick up A64, which crosses the eastern edge of the gentle Howardian Hills.

To get to **Castle Howard** — the hills are named after the Howard family, not the reverse — follow signposts right off A64. Familiar to every television viewer as the setting for the adaptation of Evelyn Waugh's novel *Brideshead Revisited*, the house — or should one rather call it a palace? — was built between 1700 and 1760 by two most distinguished architects, Vanbrugh and Hawksmoor. The magnificent exterior is matched only by the treasures inside: furniture, china, paintings, costume. There are renowned rose gardens, and the 1,000-acre landscaped park contains two lakes, Hawksmoor's Mausoleum and Vanbrugh's Temple of the Four Winds. (*Open Easter–Oct daily.*)

Continue on A64 to return into York.

## The Yorkshire Wolds and Holderness

*1–2 days/about 150 miles/from Beverley/OS maps 100, 101, 106, 107, 113*

This is a Yorkshire quite different from the brusque tops of the Moors and the swift rivers characteristic of the Dales. The Wolds are a band of windswept chalk domes, rising to 800ft in places and scattered with a few isolated villages. Sheep were the mainstay of the Wolds' prosperity until about the 18th century; nowadays, where they once grazed, vast hedgeless fields of cereals stretch out towards the horizon. To the east, the hills descend to the boulder clay of Holderness, a stretch of remote reclaimed marshland ending in the sand dunes and crumbling cliffs that face the ever encroaching North Sea. There is evidence of Dutch settlement here, with drainage channels dividing the fields and handsome houses with Dutch gables.

Start at **BEVERLEY**, county town of the former East Riding and also of Humberside, its much-disliked successor. (A decade and a half on from the officious abolition of Yorkshire's traditional Ridings, local people still consider themselves of Yorkshire stock: a boy born in Humberside can aspire to play cricket for Yorkshire.) To Beverley, which owes its original affluence to the medieval wool trade, belong two of the finest medieval churches in the country, the twin-towered Minster and, at the other end of town, the parish church of St Mary's. Both have a wealth of intricate carving in stone and wood; look

*The Beverley 'imp', St. Mary's Church, Beverley*

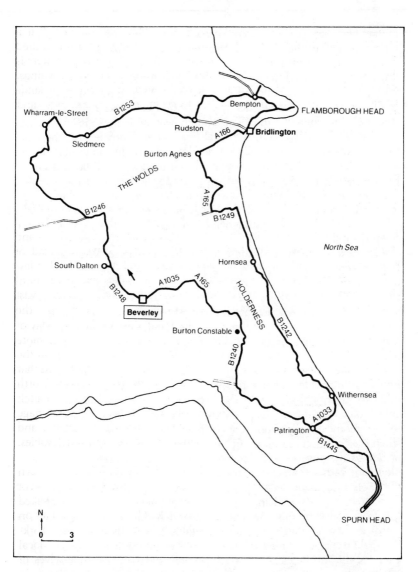

for the misericords and canopied Percy Shrine in the Minster, more misericords, the minstrels' pillar and ceiling bosses in St Mary's. Between the two churches are rows of red-brick Queen Anne and Georgian houses, some now occupied by chic boutiques and gift shops, and the cobbled Saturday Market, which lives up to its name with a bustling weekly fruit and veg and general market. The open octagonal market cross dates from 1714. On the west side of the town, the Westwood is a large stretch of common land leading up to the racecourse. Stay at the **Beverley Arms** (0482–869241) or in simpler style at the **Eastgate Guest House** (0482–868464). **Butterdings** in the market place serves not too expensive salads and hot dishes as well as afternoon tea. TIC in the Guildhall, Register Square (0482–867430).

Leave the town through the North Bar, the only survivor of the five gates that surrounded the town in the Middle Ages, and head north along A164, turning off after about 1 mile on to the Malton road, B1248. Soon you'll see the tall and slender spire of **SOUTH DALTON** church, a landmark for miles around. The church was built in 1858–61 by J.L. Pearson for Lord Hotham, the local landowner. Turn left off the main road to explore this estate village (the Hothams still live in the big house) with its duck pond and to enjoy good pub food at the **Pipe and Glass**. Return to B1248, then turn left on to B1246 just beyond Bainton and then right in North Dalton. Follow this unclassified road as it climbs up to the highest ridge of the Wolds through Huggate, across A166, and into **THIXENDALE**, a delightful hamlet snuggling at the foot of several steep-sided dales.

Our next destination, the deserted medieval village of Wharram Percy, lies no more than a couple of miles north of Thixendale — as the crow flies, that is. But cars not being crows, the journey is much more circuitous. Leave Thixendale by the road running roughly east, turn sharp left after 2 miles in Burdale, left again on to B1248 after another 2 miles, and almost immediately left once more in the hamlet of Wharram le Street. You will reach the entrance to Wharram Percy on the left after about ½ mile.

There are at least 3,000 deserted medieval villages scattered across the English countryside. What makes **WHARRAM PERCY** so special is that 40 years of annual archaeological excavations have produced a remarkably detailed picture of village life over 5,000 years, from Neolithic times to the present day. We know how many villagers there were — about 150 when the community was at its peak, in the early 14th century — the sort of houses they lived in, the animals they kept (they preferred horses for ploughing rather than the oxen generally used), the crops they grew and the tools they made — there was iron-smelting as well as leather- and wood-working in the vicinity — even what they ate (mutton and beef, fish from the fishpond plus dried cod and haddock, bread made from wheat and barley, but hardly any vegetables). It is these intimate details that help to bring Wharram Percy alive. If you come in July, you can join a guided tour of the excavations. But there's plenty to see at other times; information boards explain the layout of the village, a medieval house and the medieval fishpond have been reconstructed, while St Martins, the village church, still stands. (*EH, open all year.*)

Return now to Wharram le Street and drive straight on at the crossroads along the unclassified road to Duggleby, where a right turn onto B1253 will carry you down to **Sledmere House**, home of the Sykes family since the 18th century. The house (*open May–Sept afternoons except Mon and Fri*) is a remarkable mixture of the Georgian and Edwardian; it dates from 1751 but was extensively remodelled after a fire in 1911. There are fine paintings, tapestries and furniture, including Chippendale and Sheraton pieces, a 100ft-long vaulted library, a tiled Turkish room and a pipe organ, on which recitals are given on Sunday afternoons. The grounds were landscaped by the ubiquitous Capability Brown; there's also a pleasant tea room. In the village, look out for the monument to the Yorkshire Waggoners, a force of local farmworkers raised by Sir Mark Sykes in 1912; the carvings movingly portray them in peacetime and then in war. An earlier Sykes, the elder Sir Tatton, who died in 1863, is commemorated by another Wolds landmark, a 120ft tower that stands out against the skyline a couple of miles south of Sledmere along B1252. A man of much vigour, he hunted, raced and boxed, bred sheep and established the Sledmere stud, besides farming and endowing local schools. His monument was erected by 'those who loved him as a friend and honoured him as a landlord'.

From Sledmere, follow B1253 east to **RUDSTON**. A 25ft high prehistoric monolith stands in the churchyard, which is also the burial place of the novelist and journalist Winifred Holtby (1898–1935), who was born in the village. *South Riding*, her best-known novel, is set in the towns and villages of the East Riding. All along this stretch of road there are fine wide views south over Holderness and east to the coast; look out for the beacon of Flamborough Lighthouse.

Our next destination is the coast at Bempton, which is best reached by a back route that avoids the often crowded outskirts of Bridlington (known locally as Brid). Turn left off B1253 in Rudston towards Burton Fleming. Take the first unclassified road right and follow this round to a crossroads; turn right here, drive through Grindale and then take the first left, continuing across A165. A left turn by a level crossing will bring you into Buckton, where you turn right onto B1229. Bempton is reached almost immediately, and here you turn left through the village, following the road until it terminates in a car park next to an RSPB shop and information centre.

The chalk cliffs at **BEMPTON**, 300–400 ft high and continually beaten by wind and waves, are one of the finest spots to watch sea birds in England. Here lives the only mainland colony of gannets in Britain; you'll also spot puffins, razorbills, guillemots, kittiwakes and herring gulls, each species inhabiting its own particular level in the cliffs. During the breeding season especially, June and early July, the noise as the birds wheel and caw is deafening.

The walk along the clifftop path towards **FLAMBOROUGH HEAD**, where the Wolds drop into the sea, is not to be missed. The scenery is dramatic: stacks rising sheer out of the sea, majestic arches cut by the relentless action of the waves, minute, inaccessible coves. After this, the Head itself (which you can reach by car through Bempton and Flamborough villages), despite fine views south down the Holderness coast, seems scruffy and a bit unkempt, with some unattractive caravan developments.

From Flamborough take B1255 towards Bridlington. The 18th-century **Sewerby Hall**, on the outskirts of the town, contains the municipal art gallery and a collection devoted to Amy Johnson, the pioneer aviator; outside there are 50 acres of parkland, an 'Old England' walled garden, a small zoo, an aviary and other similar attractions. (*Park open all year, house Easter–Sept.*) **BRIDLINGTON** (pop. 27,800) has a genuine working harbour and fish market, plus lots of other traditional seaside entertainments, a brand-new leisure centre and even a rock factory (sticky rock, that is). TIC at 25 Prince Street (0262–673474/ 679626/606383.)

Five miles from Brid, the Driffield road, A166, runs past **Burton Agnes Hall** (*open April–Oct daily*), a grand Elizabethan mansion built at the very beginning of the 17th century of a mellow red brick. Inside is a succession of ornately furnished and decorated rooms; especially notable are the oak panelling in the drawing-room, the stone and alabaster chimney-piece in the great hall and the massive oak staircase, not to mention the present owner's somewhat incongruous collection of French Impressionist paintings. Like most great country houses, Burton Agnes was built to replace a more modest predecessor. Unusually, that earlier building, a rare 12th-century Norman upper-hall house, now known as **Burton Agnes Manor House**, is still standing; it has a superb vaulted stone undercroft. (*EH, standard opening times.*)

Now we leave the hills behind and enter the flat land of Holderness. Take the unclassified road that runs south from Burton Agnes over the railway, through Gransmoor and on into Lissett. Turn right here on to A165, and then left in Beeford, the next village, on to the coast road, B1249. This is a strange and little-known shore: virtually deserted even in high summer, wild in winter when forbidding waves crash on to the beach. You can stop to stroll, sunbathe or even swim (the water can be painfully chilly) more or less anywhere. Two good spots are Skipsea and Atwick, or you could drive north to Fraisthorpe, where part of the beach is given over to naturists. (East Riding naturists are a particularly hardy breed — one New Year's Day I spotted an enthusiast clad in nothing but green wellies!)

**HORNSEA** is an old-fashioned resort like they used to make them before the days of package tours. The award-winning **folk museum** (*open Easter–Oct daily*), which occupies a 300-year-old farmhouse on the main street, recreates village life as it was a century or so ago, with several rooms furnished in period style and displays on local history and crafts. A little way inland, Hornsea Mere is a large freshwater lake where herons, grebes, cormorants and many other species gather. **Ashburnham Guest House** (04012–5118) is a comfortable place to stay. TIC in Floral Hall, the Esplanade (04012–2919).

From Hornsea it's an easy 13-mile drive back to Beverley, along B1244, A165 and A1035. However, Spurn Point, 30 miles to the south, is not to be missed if your taste runs to wild and eerily remote country. Continue south on B1242 to Withernsea, and then take A1033 to **PATRINGTON**, where the soaring spire of St Patrick's Church, nick-named the 'Queen of Holderness', is visible from far off. Inside this cathedral-like church, largely built in the 14th century, is much elaborate stonework.

Driving along B1445 through Easington and Kilnsea and then out on to Spurn itself seems like travelling to the end of the world — and a pretty lonely and precarious world at that, with the endless expanse of the North Sea on one side, the murky, swirling waters of the vast Humber estuary on the other. **Spurn Point**, now owned by the Yorkshire Wildlife Trust which operates a small shop and exhibition, is a slender spit of dunes largely built up of debris swept down from the eroding cliffs around Flamborough and Bridlington further north. Vulnerable to changing tides and weathers, it has shifted its position several times during the last few centuries, drowning whole villages in the process; from time to time it also gets cut off from the mainland during stormy weather. This is a great place to spot seabirds, watch shipping — Goole, 50 miles upstream, is a major inland port — or simply to be alone with your thoughts.

There's only one way back from Spurn: the way you came. From Patrington, follow A1033 to Hedon, and then strike across country on B1240 to Sproatley. Here there's another splendid Elizabethan mansion, **Burton Constable Hall**, home of the Constables, who have owned land in the East Riding since the 11th century. The house (*open April–Sept Suns and Bank Holidays, also Thurs in July and Aug*) was built in 1570 but remodelled in the 18th century, the interiors by Wyatt and Robert Adam, the grounds by Capability Brown. The special collections include one of carriages and agricultural implements, another of 18th-century scientific instruments. There's also a country park and children's zoo here.

To return to Beverley, at first follow unclassified roads to South Skirlaugh, then A165 and A1035.

*Burton Constable Hall*

# The Yorkshire Dales

*2–3 days/about 140 miles/from Ilkley/OS maps 92, 98, 99, 104*

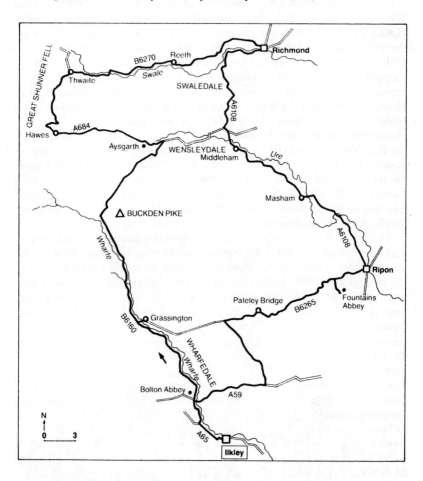

The Dales — the name is the Norse word for valley — are some of Yorkshire's most inviting and harmonious countryside. Beneath the rocky, windswept summits, many rising to 2,000ft and more, lie green and gentle valleys, patterned with stone walls and dotted with isolated farmsteads; stone villages cluster along river banks. Farming, for centuries the principal Dales livelihood, and still a precarious one, was formerly supplemented by lead-mining; the remains of old workings can be found on many hillsides. Today, on the harsher, western side of the Dales unsightly limestone quarries deface the landscape. This route explores the more pastoral eastern and northern valleys, where the darker gritstone predominates — a land and people already familiar to the countless readers and television viewers of James Herriot's tales of his life as a local vet.

We start in **Wharfedale**, one of the easier and more approachable dales. **ILKLEY** is a friendly, bustling town that first developed as a spa resort in the 18th century and then expanded with the coming of the railway in the 19th. There's a pleasant main street with canopied shops and a Victorian shopping arcade. See also All Saints' Church, which has three Saxon crosses, and the displays of local history and archaeology at the Manor House museum (*open daily except Mons*). **Betty's** is the place to sample traditional local fare such as spiced Yorkshire teacake or a Yorkshire cheese lunch with blue and white Wensleydale; much more expensive is the **Box Tree**, noted for superb French cuisine. Places to stay include the **Rombalds** (0943–603201) and **Craiglands** (0943–607676) **Hotels**, both on the edge of Ilkley Moor — made famous worldwide through the Victorian comic ballad *On Ilkla Moor Baht'at* — which descends virtually into the centre of town. The TIC in Station Road (0943–602319) has details of many excellent local walks on the Moor.

The first leg of this route follows the Wharfe back towards its source high in the fells. North on the busy A65, you're almost immediately out into the country. Turn right on to B6160 for **BOLTON ABBEY**, where the ruins of the 12th-century **priory** stands on a great bend in the river (*open daily*). The nave survived Henry VIII's dissolution in 1539 and is now the parish church. The monks who founded Yorkshire's great medieval abbeys and priories were highly efficient landowners. They cleared woods and marshland, introduced sheep-farming and established the present pattern of roads and tracks — many monastic fortunes were based on wool. There is a fine walk from the priory alongside the river. You can either go up as far as the footbridge or (more fun) the stepping stones and then return to the village on the opposite bank, or continue upstream through romantic woodland to the **Strid**, where the river, turbulent and deep, rushes through a narrow rocky chasm, and on to **Barden Tower** (3 miles), a ruined 15th-century tower-house.

B6160 continues up the valley, past Barden Tower and through **BURNSALL**, the first of a succession of picture-postcard riverside villages, whose church contains a 14th-century alabaster Adoration of the Magi, to **GRASSINGTON**. The museum in the main square is devoted to local life, an annual Arts Festival is held each June, and the National Park Information Centre (0756–752748) is a fruitful source of information about local walks (both guided and self-guided) and other activities. As in all these small Dales communities, it's well worth taking time to stroll round the streets and tiny passageways and the market square; generations from the 17th century onwards have all built in the local stone, and the result is most pleasing and harmonious.

The head of Wharfedale is the target now, as B6160 climbs into ever wilder country past **Kilnsey Crag**, a dramatic limestone outcrop, and through Kettlewell to Buckden; Great Whernside and Buckden Pike (2,310ft and 2,302ft) are the mountains looming on the right. There's a not too stiff walk along the Dales Way from Kettlewell to Buckden on the opposite side of the valley from the road. Beyond Buckden the road divides. Take the left fork to explore **HUBBERHOLME**, a remote hamlet with a beautiful riverside church. Then return to B6160, which climbs Kidstones Pass before descending into Wensleydale.

A left turn on to A684 brings you almost immediately to **AYSGARTH**. Aysgarth Force consists of three separate sets of falls, over 1 mile long in all; the Middle and Lower Falls are reached along a frequently muddy woodland path. The river here is the Ure; unlike other dales, Wensleydale derives its name not from its river, but from the village of Wensley, further downstream. There's a National Park Information Centre near the Falls (09693–424).

**ASKRIGG**, further west on the opposite side of the valley from the main road, is the location for the Darrowby scenes in the TV adaptation of *All Creatures Great and Small*. The real-life James Herriot practised in Thirsk, just beyond the eastern edge of the Dales, serving the farmers of Wensleydale and Swaledale.

Despite its small population, about 1,000, **HAWES** is a major centre for the northern part of the Dales, with a weekly livestock market, a creamery where Wensleydale cheese is made, good shops and a general market. You can watch rope being made in the **Ropeworks** and buy rope and other craft goods there as well. Visit also the **Museum of Upper Dales Life**, which portrays farming and mining in the Dales, and the **National Park Information Centre** (09697–450) (*both open April–Oct daily*), both housed in the old railway station. **Simonstone Hall** (09697–255) and **Stone House Hotel** (09697–571) are two hotels and guesthouses; have morning coffee or afternoon tea at **Cockett's Hotel** in the Market Square — recommended for its baking.

Continue north on A684 and turn right on to an unclassified road as soon as you've crossed the river. There's a magnificent view ahead to the rugged mass of Great Shunner Fell (2,340ft). **Hardraw Force**, 96ft of a shimmering curtain of water, is said to be England's highest above-ground waterfall — well worth a visit; the entrance is through the Green Dragon Inn.

Turn left a little beyond the pub, and prepare yourself now for one of the Dales' tougher drives, over Butter Tubs Pass into Swaledale. The Butter Tubs are a series of shallow limestone potholes just off the road; hart's tongue and other ferns thrive on the rocks, but take care, for the ground is often slippery.

**Swaledale**, the most northerly of the major dales, is also one of the more remote, narrow and sinuous where Wensleydale is lush and pastoral, its villages and farms built of the local grey-brown sandstone. A brief diversion to the left along B6270 when you reach the valley bottom brings you to **THWAITE**, where **Kearton Guest House** (0748–86277) dispenses warm Yorkshire hospitality and cooking. But our route follows the river eastwards on B6270, through **MUKER**, where an excellent shop sells wool goods and the pioneer naturalists and wildlife photographers Richard and Cherry Kearton (1862–1928 and 1871–1940) went to

*Thwaite*

school, and alongside the Swale to Reeth. There are numerous footpaths, including one along the riverbank all the way from Muker to **REETH**, which is becoming something of a tourist trap. The village was formerly a major lead-mining centre, and also had an important hand-knitting industry; both are recalled in the **Swaledale Folk Museum** (*open April–Oct daily*). Seven annual fairs and a weekly Friday market were once held here; now there's an annual Show each September and sheep sales in the autumn.

Rather than stick to the main road in the valley to reach Richmond, follow the old road (unclassified) through the hills via Marske. There are excellent views over Richmond and, if the day is clear, the towers of York Minster will stand out to the south.

The powerful Norman castle (*EH, standard opening times*) with its massive 12th-century keep (good views from the top) dominates **RICH-MOND**, the rest of which is largely Georgian and built of local stone. Take time to wander round — the Market Square (market day Saturday) and Newbiggin, broad and cobbled, are both fine architectural compositions. The tiny, exquisite **Georgian Theatre**, restored in the early 1960s, has scarcely changed since it was built in 1788; many of the original seats and boxes survive. Take in a performance if you're staying overnight — if not, at least make sure you visit the interior (*open May–Sept afternoons*). Hotels in Richmond include **Frenchgate** (0748–2087), **King's Head** (0748–2311) and **West End Guesthouse** (0748–4783). TIC in Friary Gardens (0748–3525/5994).

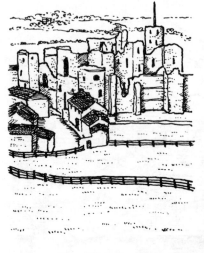

Leave Richmond west on A6108, at first along the Swale valley and then over into Wensleydale again, now broader and more wooded than further west. The massive 60ft tower of **Middleham Castle** (*EH, standard opening times*) dates from 1170, the rest from later centuries; Richard III lived here as a boy, and later again for 10 years after his marriage in 1472. Racehorses exercise on the moor beyond the castle.

Three miles further on the ruins of **Jervaulx Abbey**, founded in the mid-12th century, lie close to the road. The monks here are said to have introduced the art of cheese-making to Wensleydale. Wild flowers carpet the ruins.

*Middleham Castle*

**MASHAM** (pronounced Mass'm) has a spacious market square where in past centuries huge numbers of sheep and lambs were sold at the sheep fair each September. Outside the parish church (mixed Norman, 15th-century and Victorian) stands a 9th-century Anglo-Saxon cross carved with delightful human and animal figures. Theakston's beer has been brewed in Masham since 1827; don't leave before non-drivers have sampled a pint of their potent 'Old Peculier'. **Bank Villa** (0765–89605) is a pleasant Georgian guest house.

On the way to Ripon, the road passes **Lightwater Valley** (*open late May–early Sept daily, also weekends Easter–late May and Sept*), where you can enjoy all the thrills of an up-to-the-minute theme park. There's also a working farm and other more peaceful attractions.

**RIPON** grew up around the church built by St Wilfrid, one of the founders of the Christianity in the north of England, in the 7th century. Its crypt survives underneath the central tower of the present church, which dates from the 12th and 13th centuries and acquired cathedral status in the 1830s. Admire the magnificent west front and, inside, the 15th-century misericords, with a motley and delightful collection of carvings: among others appear pigs, an owl, fox and geese, and Samson and Jonah. The TIC (0765–4625) and a small museum are in the timber-framed, 13th-century **Wakeman's House**, in one corner of the market place. The wakeman was the town's night watchman and hornblower — a horn is still blown each evening at 9 in the market square. Poised on the edge of the Dales and the broad Vale of York, and within easy driving distance of the North York Moors (see pages 28–36), Ripon makes an excellent touring base. **Crescent Lodge** (0765–2331) is a praised bed-and-breakfast establishment, **Ripon Spa Hotel** (0765–2172) an up-market country house hotel.

The final leg of the tour turns back towards the Dales west along

B6265. After abut 2 miles turn off left to **Fountains Abbey**, the Cistercian foundation on the banks of the river Skell. This was untamed country when the monks settled here in 1132. They took to sheep-farming with great zeal and equally great success, and built themselves one of the country's most impressive and prosperous abbeys, a valuable prize for Henry VIII when he dissolved the monasteries in the late 1530s. The ruins are especially interesting to explore, since the plan of the monastery has been preserved virtually intact. Fountains stands now in a magical setting: the 18th-century landscape of **Studley Royal**, with classical temples and follies, a water garden and a deer park. You could spend hours here, looking at the abbey and walking in the landscape garden — it's an ideal place for a picnic, or alternatively you can have a light lunch or tea in the tearooms by the lakeside and next to the abbey. (*NT, open all year.*)

Now follow B6265 past **Brimham Rocks**, an area of fantastically shaped pillars and blocks of millstone grit (*NT*) through Pateley Bridge on the river Nidd. A few miles further on, turn left at Greenhow Hill on to an unclassified road which then runs through wild, high country alongside the river Washburn and Thruscross Reservoir to join A59 at Blubberhouses, near the head of Fewston Reservoir. Take A59 west to Bolton Abbey, and return to Ilkley.

# 2  MIDDLE ENGLAND

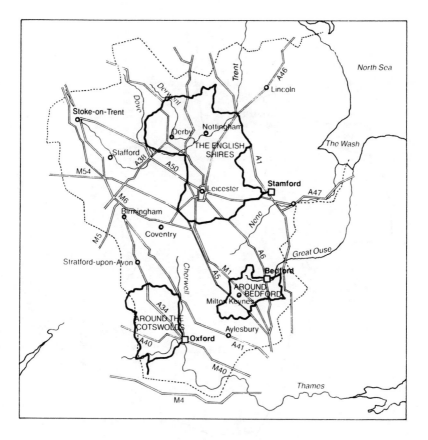

A few high spots aside, middle England tends to be neglected by tourists. This is a pity, but understandable, for it is all too easy to define the area by the features it lacks — spectacular mountains, fine beaches — rather than to identify its positive qualities. Here are rolling acres of productive agricultural land, punctuated by numerous small market towns built of local materials (limestone, sandstone, brick), and also by several industrial conurbations. The principal characteristic of the counties of middle

49

England is that they are not primarily tourist centres, loaded with events and 'attractions' calculated to appeal to travellers and holiday-makers, but modest, workaday places that get on with the jobs in hand.

## The English Shires

*2–3 days/about 190 miles/from Stamford/OS maps 141, 130, 120, 119, 128, 140*

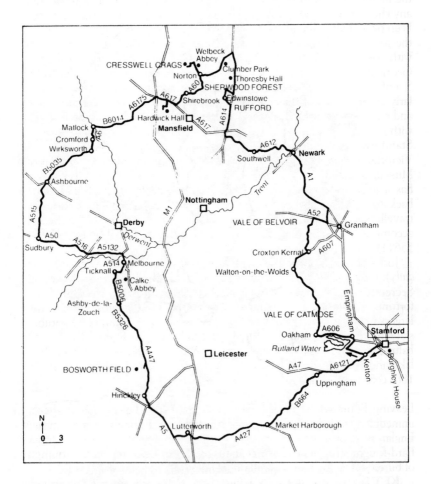

This exploration takes in a great swathe of the shire counties of the east Midlands: Leicestershire, Nottinghamshire and Derbyshire. The land here has been the main source of wealth for centuries. It is fertile farming country (arable predominates to the east, dairy to the west), rich also in minerals; coal, ironstone and gravel are still mined extensively. The main centres are in and near the three county towns, around which our route weaves through lightly populated and often surprisingly remote country.

Although just within Lincolnshire, **STAMFORD** has little in common with the bare Fenlands to the east. Standing on the edge of the long belt of limestone that curves up the country from the Cotswolds, the town is as handsome a memorial to the solid and enduring qualities of the local stone, and to the innate sense of style of 18th-century stonemasons and the merchants and professional men who employed them, as you will find anywhere in England. Nor, unlike many Cotswold towns, has Stamford been over-prettified and over-conserved — it makes its living, as it has for the past three centuries or so, as a market-town for the surrounding area with some small industries. The houses and civic buildings are largely Georgian; the churches are several centuries older, dating from Stamford's medieval prosperity as a cloth-making centre. Look particularly at St Mary's (13th-century tower, topped by a 14th-century spire, and nave rebuilt in 15th century) and at All Saints', where painted angels with golden wings decorate the chancel roof. In nearby All Saints' Street, **Stamford Steam Brewery Museum** (*open April–Sept Wed–Sun*) is a Victorian steam brewery complete with original equipment. **Stamford Museum** (*open May–Sept daily except Sun mornings, Oct–April Tues–Sat*) has a local history collection. Parts of the **George** (0780–55171) date back to 1597; it has given long service as a coaching inn welcoming travellers on the Great North Road — and good reports of both food and accommodation continue. TIC in the Museum in Broad Street (0780–55611).

Just south-east of the town is **Burghley House** (*open Easter–early Oct daily*), built 1540s–80s by William Cecil, Elizabeth I's Lord Treasurer and Secretary of State who later became Lord Burghley. As befitted his fortune and status, Cecil built on a grandiose scale, creating one of the largest mansions of Elizabethan England, with a succession of sumptuous state rooms inside and decorated externally with elaborate towers and balustrades, turrets and chimney-shafts. The fine park, with its serpentine lake and elegant stone bridge, was laid out by Capability Brown in the 18th century.

Leaving Stamford by A6121 west, you cross into Leicestershire almost immediately. Signs also announce that this is Rutland. For centuries England's smallest county, in 1974 Rutland was demoted, but only after a hard-fought struggle, to District status as part of Leicestershire: a triumph of bureaucratic logic over local independence.

**KETTON** is the first of a series of attractive villages built of mellow limestone; there is a fine 13th-century church with an attractive 14th-century spire. Turn right off the main road in Ketton and head towards **Rutland Water**, proclaimed as Europe's largest artificial lake. The flooding of 3,100 acres of good agricultural land in the 1970s to satisfy demand for water in nearby towns created another source of local resentment at outside intervention. The lake has become a major water sports centre — sailing, fishing, windsurfing — and is attractively landscaped with picnic areas, a perimeter path for walking and cycling, and a nature reserve at the western side. One of the picnic areas is at **Normanton**, once a village, of which all that remains is Normanton Church. The church, originally a plain 18th-century structure with a more elaborate tower and porch added in the 19th, stands somewhat incongruously on a spur of land jutting out into the water. It has now been converted to a **Water Museum** (*open April–Sept daily, also winter Suns*).

From Normanton follow the minor road — good views across the horseshoe-shaped lake — east past the dam, and turn left on to A606 shortly before **EMPINGHAM**, whose tall church tower (14th century) is a local landmark. There are attractive stone houses here plus a circular dovecote. A606 runs west towards Oakham past more picnic areas; from the one at Whitwell you can take a 45-minute pleasure cruise (*April–Sept daily except Mon*) around the lake.

**OAKHAM**, the county town of Rutland, has a lively twice-weekly market; an octagonal Buttercross stands in the market place, together with the town's stocks. The buildings of Oakham School, founded 1584, are scattered around the town. Visit the great hall of **Oakham Castle** (*open Tues–Sat and Sun afternoon*), a magnificent example of late 12th-century domestic architecture; several hundred horseshoes hang on the walls — by tradition a peer of the realm visiting Oakham for the first time presents a horseshoe. **Rutland County Museum** (*open daily except Mon also closed Sun Nov–March*) recalls the county's domestic and agricultural life. **Rutland Farm Park** (*open May–Sept daily except Mon*) has rare breeds of farm animals, Shetland and Exmoor ponies, and old farm equipment. The name of the **Whipper-in Hotel** (0572–56971) is a reminder that the land hereabouts is good hunting country: **Normanton Park Hotel** (0780–720315) is another comfortable establishment, within sight of Rutland Water. TIC in the Museum, Catmos Street (0572–2918).

There now follows a long stretch on backroads which climb gradually from the Vale of Catmose to the gentle heights of the Leicestershire Wolds. This is remote, windswept country, with views stretching in all directions. Leave Oakham on B668, but turn immediately on to the unclassified road heading for Ashwell, Wymondham and Waltham-on-the-Wolds. Turn right here on to A607, and then left again near Croxton Kerrial, following signposts to **Belvoir Castle** (*open mid-March to Sept daily except Mon and Fri, also Suns in Oct*), home of the Duke of Rutland. Commanding magnificent views over the Vale of Belvoir (pronounced Beevor), the castle has been built and rebuilt many times since the 11th century, the last time in the early 19th century, with many mock-medieval effects. Inside there are Gobelin tapestries and paintings by Van Dyck, Reynolds, Hogarth and Holbein (portrait of Henry VIII) among others; the gardens contain classical statuary and a mausoleum.

Descend into the Vale of Belvoir along minor roads through Woolsthorpe, turning right on to A52 at Sedgebrook. For speed's sake, the best route now to Newark is along main roads: east on A52 and then north on A1, taking A6065 into the town centre.

NEWARK's castle, strategically situated beside the river Trent, was built *c.* 1125; King John died here in 1216. Unlike the large majority of English castles (except those within reach of the raiding Scots), which for all their defensive features never saw much action, Newark suffered a long siege by Parliamentary forces during the Civil War. It never fell — the commander eventually surrendered with honour on the orders of Charles I, whereupon the castle was dismantled. The Norman gatehouse, the west wall and the south-west tower, whose undercroft contains an exhibition of castle history, survive (*open Easter–Sept daily except Mon and Thurs*). Handsome buildings surround the cobbled market place, including Clinton Arms (0636–72299), where Gladstone made his first public speech. The spire of the nearby parish church, St Mary Magdalene, is higher than the length of the ground plan. The museum (*open Mon–Sat except Thurs afternoon, also open Sun afternoon April–Sept*) in Appleton-gate has material on local archaeology and history; visit also Millgate Museum of Social and Folk Life (*open Mon–Fri, also on Sat and Sun April–Sept*). Gannets in Castlegate is recommended for wholefood meals. The town's TIC might win a contest for the most intriguing address: The Ossington, Beast Market Hill (0636–78962).

Leave Newark on A617 west, and after crossing the Trent branch left on to A612 along the Trent valley to SOUTHWELL (pronounced Suth'll), hardly more than a large village clustering around the glorious Norman Minster, recognisable from far off by its three towers, one square, two pyramidal. Inside, look especially at the lovely choir screen and at the riot of delicately carved foliage in the chapter house: countless varieties, perhaps inspired by nearby Sherwood Forest. The ruins of the 14th-century Bishops' Palace stand outside the church, and there are attractive 18th-century houses in the village. In the timber-framed Saracen's Head (0636–812701) Charles I spent his last few hours of freedom in 1646.

*Southwell Minster*

Follow the minor road through Edingley and Farnsfield, and turn right on to the main A614, which runs north towards the remnants of Sherwood Forest and on to the Dukeries. In the Middle Ages, the Forest — a huge stretch of mixed pastureland, wood and heath used as a royal hunting ground — covered much of northern Nottinghamshire, offering a hiding-place for outlaws. One such was Robin Hood, whose exploits in robbing the rich and powerful to help the poor have been the stuff of romantic legend since medieval times. The three great estates a few miles north of the present-day Forest give their name to the Dukeries: Thoresby (Earl of Manvers), Clumber (Dukes of Newcastle) and Welbeck (Dukes of Portland).

First of all A614 passes **Rufford**, a Country Park and Craft Centre based in the grounds of a Cistercian abbey dissolved by Henry VIII. (*Open daily, but Craft Centre weekends only Jan and Feb.*) It is a most attractive place, with formal gardens, woodland and parkland walks, and a lovely lake, while the craft centre stages regular exhibitions of work by top-class potters, jewellers, textile-, glass- and metal-workers. The shop is well stocked with high-quality pieces. Picnic in the park, or else enjoy a light lunch or tea in the restaurant.

Follow B6034 north-west from Rufford to **EDWINSTOWE**, a small village on the edge of the most beautiful parts of the forest. Robin Hood is said to have wed his Maid Marian in St Mary's Church. Just beyond the village, **Sherwood Forest Visitor Centre** (*open daily*) is a good place to start exploring the forest. There is an exhibition — entitled 'The legend of Robyn Hode and Mery Scherewode' — talks, a shop, waymarked walks, and regular special events; the Centre also serves as a TIC (0623–822490/823202). The surrounding **country park** includes Major Oak, said to be over 1,000 years old and one of the largest in England, and another nicknamed Robin Hood's Larder, where the outlaw is said to have hung his venison.

To reach **Thoresby Hall** (*open Easter Sun and Mon, the May–Aug Suns and Bank Holiday Mons*) continue north on B6034, turn right on to A616, and then left on to A614 travelling north. The house, rebuilt in the flamboyant 'manorial' style of the 1860s, is the only one of the three great houses still occupied by its original owners. It is a monumental pile, 180ft square, with a huge great hall, 29 rooms on the principal floor, and 78 bedrooms. Deer graze in the park, which contains a lake and extensive woodland.

Perhaps even more magnificent is **Clumber Park** (*NT, open daily*), a couple of miles further north along A614. The house (built 1770 but twice rebuilt in the 19th century) was demolished in 1938, in order to meet a tax bill, but the newly repaired Victorian Gothic chapel (fine stained glass and wood carvings) still stands, delightfully situated beside the lake. The 3,800-acre park contains classical temples, fine walks and vistas, and a magnificent double lime avenue. National Trust shop, restaurant and café.

Follow the unclassified road that crosses Clumber Park and B6005 and then runs alongside the Great Lake in the grounds of Welbeck Abbey, now an army college and not open to the public. Beyond Norton, you have a choice. Turn right on to A60 and then left on to B6042 after about 2 miles to visit **Creswell Crags**, a spectacular limestone ravine and site of some of the earliest man-made artefacts found in Britain. Many of the finds are displayed in the **Visitor Centre** (*open Feb–Oct daily, Suns only in winter*), and there are woodland and lakeside walks to enjoy.

If the Crags don't appeal, turn left on to A60 and continue south for about 2 miles, turning right on to B6031. Follow the road past spoil heaps — this area is the heart of the productive North Notts/Derbyshire coalfield — turning left onto B6407 beyond Shirebrook and then right on to A617. In the village of **Glapwell** turn left, following signs to **Hardwick Hall** (*NT, house open April–Oct Wed, Thur, Sat, Sun and Bank Holiday Mon afternoons, garden April–Oct daily, country park daily throughout year*).

Hardwick is an imposing Elizabethan mansion, built for the redoubtable Bess of Hardwick in the 1590s, and scarcely altered since. Much of the furniture, tapestries and needlework listed in the inventory Bess compiled in 1601 remains. The second-floor state rooms are especially fine, notably Bess' Great Chamber, decorated with a sumptuous plaster frieze. Outside there are formal walled courtyards and herb gardens, with parkland beyond. One word of caution: Hardwick is very popular, and admission may be limited to avoid congestion. National Trust restaurant.

We head now for Matlock, on the edge of the Peak District, with increasingly clear views towards the high, hard summits. Drive west from Glapwell on A617, take A6175 west at the roundabout by junction 29 of M1 to Clay Cross, turn left on to A61, and soon right on to B6014.

Running across the head of Ogton Reservoir, this road descends to **MATLOCK**, a series of small settlements, developed as a spa in the 19th century, strung out along the wooded Derwent valley. You may think Matlock is too touristified, but it does make a good base for exploring the wild countryside of the National Park, which begins on the far side of the river valley. Dominating the town are the **Heights of Abraham** (*open Easter–Oct daily*), a 1,100ft wooded crag reached by taking the cable car across the gorge; here you can visit two show caves, enjoy woodland walks and experience a 'multivision programme' which explains the geology and history of the Heights. Other attractions include the **Aquarium and Hologram Gallery** (*open April–Oct daily, also winter weekends*) a wildlife park at **Riber Castle** (*open daily*) built in the 1860s high above Matlock town, **Gulliver's Kingdom** (*open Easter–mid-Sept daily*), a theme park for families with young children, and the **Peak District Mining Museum** (*open daily*), which tells the story of lead-mining, the Peak District's main industry for some 2,000 years. But perhaps the most pleasant thing to do in Matlock is simply to stroll through the lovely parks and gardens, to hire a rowing boat on the river, or enjoy the late-summer riverside illuminations. There are places to eat and stay to suit all tastes and pockets: try **Strand Restaurant**, where meals are sometimes served to the accompaniment of a jazz trio, **New Bath Hotel** (0629–583275), where the pools are fed by thermal water, or **Winstaff Guest House** (0629–582593). TIC in the Pavilion, Matlock Bath (0629–55082).

There's a greater sense of history in **CROMFORD**, some 3 miles south along A6 and then right on to B5036. Here in 1771 Sir Richard Arkwright set up the first water-powered cotton spinning mill in the world. This important relic of the early industrial revolution is now being restored, together with the model village Arkwright built nearby, and there is also an interpretative exhibition (*open daily, but closed Nov–Easter Mon and Tues*). The towpath of the Cromford Canal, built to carry Arkwright's products to the growing towns of the East Midlands, provides pleasant walks.

Continue south on B5036 towards Wirksworth, past **Black Rocks**, a massive outcrop of gritstone where there is a picnic site and good walks. The **High Peak Trail**, a 17½-mile footpath along the track of the former Cromford and High Peak Railway, passes nearby.

**WIRKSWORTH**, a handsome stone-built hillside market town, was formerly a major lead-mining centre; George Eliot used the town as a model for Snowfield in *Adam Bede*. Inside the imposing church is a late 7th-century coffin lid with carvings depicting the life of Christ, and elsewhere there are attractive houses from the 16th to 18th centuries.

B5035 runs south-west across the hills to **ASHBOURNE**. This pretty little town, whose buildings mix Pennine stone with the red brick of the Midlands, would make a good exploring base for the southern part of the Peak District. There is a fine 13th-century church, 'the cathedral of the Peak', and along Church Street, the long 'double' main street, there are 18th-century houses and the 16th-century Grammar School. Look for the gallows on the signboard of the **Green Man and Black's Head Royal Hotel** (0335–43861), which stretches across St John Street; the name commemorates the merging of two coaching inns in 1825. The **Gingerbread Shop** sells not only the town's traditional delicacy (plain or chocolate-coated) but also salads, sandwiches, quiches and so forth. TIC in the Market Place (0335–43666).

Follow A515 south across gradually lower country towards **SUDBURY**, turning left on to A50 and then almost immediately right to reach the village and **Sudbury Hall** (*NT, open Easter–Oct Wed–Sun and Bank Holiday afternoons*). This late 17th-century house, home of the Vernon family, is one of the pleasantest of Derbyshire's many country houses, not least because it receives fewer visitors than many others. There is lovely plasterwork and carvings and a handsome Long Gallery. The basement has been turned into a **Museum of Childhood** with displays about childhood life in the past, including chimney climbs — ideal for energetic kids bored with traditional stately homes! National Trust tea room and shop. Take time to stroll around the attractive brick-built village, which largely dates from the 17th century.

Follow A50 east, continue straight on along A516 and in Hilton bear right along A5132 through Willington and alongside the river Trent. Beyond Barrow upon Trent turn right on to A514. If it is a summer Wednesday or weekend, branch left on to B587 to visit **Melbourne Hall** (*house open June–Sept Wed afternoons, gardens April–Sept Wed, Sat, Sun,*

*Bank Holiday afternoons*). The 17th-century house contains fine paintings and furniture; one room commemorates Lord Melbourne, Queen Victoria's first, much-loved Prime Minister, who lived here. The renowned formal gardens, laid out in the 1690s, contain wide lawns, a lake, a yew tunnel, interspersed with little statues and monuments. The church is 12th-century, and there is an attractive mixture of 17th–19th-century buildings in the village.

Continue south on A514 as far as Ticknall, where signs will direct you to one of the National Trust's newest and most publicised acquisitions: **Calke Abbey** (*house open Easter–Oct Sat–Wed afternoon, admission by timed ticket; park daily throughout year*). When the Trust received the house, built in the first years of the 18th century, it was in the most perilous condition: urgent repairs and conservation, to both the fabric and the contents, were necessary, and will continue for some years after the rooms in the front of the house open to the public in 1989. The Harpur-Crewe family, Calke's former owners, had scarcely altered the inside of the house for many generations, and it is a jumbled treasure trove of furniture, pictures, cartoons, books and maps, textiles, cases of stuffed birds, minerals, shells and curiosities, trophy cattle heads, china, textiles and metalwork. Essential preservation, not 'smartening up' and renewal, has been the aim of the repair work, and so the decorations retain their rather shabby appearance. The extensive outbuildings include a handsome stable block and riding school. The late 18th-century walled kitchen and flower gardens are also being restored, together with the church, built in the 1820s and a good example of the early Gothic revival style. Beyond lies a 750-acre park.

Take B5006 south from Ticknall to **ASHBY-DE-LA-ZOUCH**, named after a Breton family called la Zouch who acquired land here eight centuries ago. The wide main street leads to spa buildings developed in the 19th century and to a 70ft memorial cross designed by Gilbert Scott in memory of Lady Loudoun, a local benefactress. The Norman manor

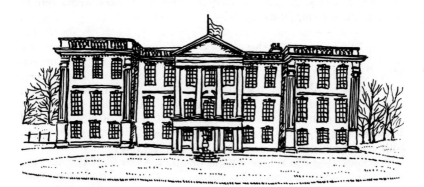

*Calke Abbey*

house was converted into a fortified castle (*EH, standard opening times, but closed Thurs and alternate Fris in winter*) in the 15th century and suffered a year-long siege during the Civil War. Stay at the **Royal Osprey Hotel** (0530–412833), built in the 1820s for visitors to the spa. TIC in the Museum, Lower Church Street (0530–415603).

Leave Ashby along B5326, turn right on to A447 in Ibstock, and then right near Cadeby, following signs to **Bosworth Battlefield**. On 22 August 1485 these quiet fields witnessed the concluding battle of the 30-year Wars of the Roses between the two great feuding houses of medieval England, York and Lancaster. Richard III, last of the medieval English monarchs, was killed, and was succeeded by the Lancastrian claimant, Henry Tudor. The exhibition in the **Visitor Centre** (*open April–Oct every afternoon, Battle Trails daily throughout year*) vividly sets the historical background and recreates the course of the battle, and Battle Trails guide you across the actual site of the fighting. There are regular special events, e.g. jousting and battle re-enactments.

For speed's sake, there follows a stretch of main road driving, south on A447 to Hinckley and then south on A5 (Roman Watling Street) for about 7 miles to the junction with A427. Follow this road through Lutterworth, over M1, and then east through the gentle landscapes of southern Leicestershire to **MARKET HARBOROUGH**. The largely 15th-century parish church, dedicated to St Dionysius, has a fine limestone steeple. Nearby stands the timber-framed **Old Grammar School** (*early 17th century*) (*both open Mon–Sat*); wooden posts support the first-floor schoolroom, under which a market used to be held. Take time to explore the square and nearby streets: Market Harborough remains a classic English market town that has evolved quietly over the centuries. TIC in the Pen Lloyd Library, Adam and Eve Street (0858–62649).

The final leg takes us through fine hunting country back into Rutland, north-east along B664 to **UPPINGHAM**, dominated by its public school. Then take A47 east, turning left on to A6121 to Stamford. Russet-coloured ironstone is the predominant building material in southern Rutland, in contrast with the limestone encountered further north at the start of this drive.

# Around Bedford

*1–2 days/about 100 miles/from Bedford/OS maps 152, 153, 165*

Most people pass through the northern tips of Bedfordshire and Buckinghamshire on the way to somewhere else. This happens nowadays with rail and road travel, just as it did 200 years ago when the Grand Union Canal was opened and long before that, when Watling Street was one of the Romans' main routes north. What you will find, if you take time to discover it, is an appealing variety of countryside, with quiet villages built of local materials, stone in the north, brick further south. There are no dramas in the landscape here — but it does possess a modest

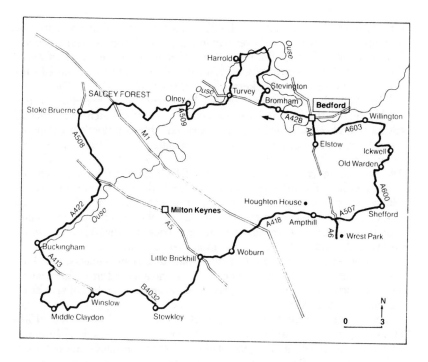

beauty that well repays exploration. Bedford's most celebrated son is John Bunyan (1628–88), tinker turned spiritual teacher and writer. Many of the places Bunyan portrayed in the spiritual journey he described in *The Pilgrim's Progress*, his best-known work, can still be identified in and around Bedford today.

The most pleasant part of **BEDFORD** (pop. 74,800), the country town of Bedfordshire and a local commercial centre, is alongside the river Great Ouse, where there are attractive Embankment Gardens and waterside walks. At one end of the early 18th-century stone bridge, **St Paul's Square** has some pleasing buildings — none individually outstanding, but together they make a harmonious whole; the spacious church is largely 14th and 15th century. Nearby, **Bedford Museum** contains displays of local history and natural history, and the **Cecil Higgins Art Gallery** (*both open Tues–Sat, also Sun and Bank Holiday Mon afternoons*) has nationally important collections of watercolours, prints, sculpture, glass and ceramics, as well as exquisite examples of Bedfordshire lace. The **Bunyan Museum** (*open April–Sept Tues–Sat afternoons*) contains a collection of editions of *The Pilgrim's Progress* and some of his personal possessions. The museum occupies part of the mid-19th-century **Bunyan Meeting House**, built on the site of the meeting place in Mill Street Bunyan founded in 1672; bronze doors at the church entrance depict scenes from *The Pilgrim's Progress*. The **Swan Hotel** (0234–46565) is a late 18th-century inn on the corner of St Paul's Square and The Embankment; its staircase, thought to have been designed by Christopher Wren, came from Houghton House (Bunyan's House Beautiful — see below). Other houses in the town include **De Parys** (0234–512121) in tree-lined De Parys Avenue and the **Shakespeare Hotel** (0234–213147). The **Park** pub in Kimbolton Road, just outside the centre, serves beer brewed by Charles Wells, the local independent brewery, and, at lunchtime, a good selection of cheeses, and the food at **Saracen's Head** in St Paul's Square is also spoken of highly. TIC in St Paul's Square (0234–215226).

A428 travelling west crosses the Ouse at **BROMHAM**. The river, whose gentle meadows form the constant backdrop of the first part of this drive, follows a tortuous course — and our route, through a succession of secluded, little-known riverside villages is almost as indirect. Old Bromham bridge, 26 arches and dating back to the 13th century, survives, despite a battering by motor traffic. In the 17th-century **Bromham Mill** (*open April–Oct Wed–Sun and Bank Holiday Mon*) a museum of milling has been created around the restored machinery, and there are also natural history displays and an arts and crafts gallery. You can picnic by the river.

Turn right in Bromham along an unclassified road to **STEVING-TON**, where the beautifully restored **post mill** (erected 1770 and retaining sails) is a landmark (*open daily — keys from Royal George in Silver Street*). In the Middle Ages the holy well in the churchyard, whose waters never freeze or dry up, was a place of pilgrimage. Both the well and the village cross appear in *The Pilgrim's Progress*; Christian loses his burden at the cross. The church has a Saxon tower. **Stevington Country Walk** is a 1¾-mile walk along the old Bedford–Northampton railway with fine views over the river valley.

Follow minor roads to Pavenham, then Felmersham, then **ODELL**, a quintessential English village, with a fine 15th-century church and pretty thatched stone cottages. A castle once commanded the bend in the river — the remains of the mound, now occupied by a private house, can be discerned. There are enjoyable walks in Odell Great Wood north of the village.

Between Odell and Harrold, a **country park** developed from old gravel working offers riverside walks and pleasantly landscaped scenery; there is a nature reserve, and wildfowl can be spotted on the lakes. (*Visitor Centre opens April–Oct afternoons except Mon, also Sat and Sun afternoons in winter.*)

Until the 18th century, **HARROLD** was an important centre of the local lace industry. Thread and patterns were distributed, and finished items collected and sold, in the elegant early 18th-century octagonal Market House on the village green. Nearby stands a lock-up, built 1824. The church, St Peter's, is largely 13th-century, and there are other old cottages scattered through the village.

Leave across the long narrow river bridge (11 arches) and then turn right in Carlton alongside the river to **TURVEY**, another attractive stone village. Most of the cottages are 19th-century, although the two big houses are several centuries older. Continue straight on in Turvey through two hamlets, Newton Blossomville and Clifton Reynes. In Emberton turn right on to A509.

The soaring four-tiered spire, 185ft tall, of **OLNEY** church, St Peter and St Paul, just across the river, dominates the view. The town is another former lace-making centre; if I wanted to show someone an unpretentious but good-looking small English town, Olney would be high on my list. There are buildings of all periods, none especially remarkable, but together they give the town a character of its own. The **Cowper and Newton Museum** (*open Easter–Oct Tues–Sat, and June–Sept Suns; also Tues–Sat afternoons in winter*) commemorates the poet William Cowper, who lived here 1768–86, and his friend John Newton, the local curate. Together they wrote such well-known hymns as 'Glorious things of thee are spoken' and 'How sweet the name of Jesus sounds'; Newton also wrote 'Amazing grace'. The poet's possessions are displayed, and there are exhibits on local history and the lace trade. Olney is also famous for the Pancake Race, run each Shrove Tuesday. **White House Guest House** (0234–711478) is a comfortable and friendly place to stay.

Take the unclassified road through Weston Underwood (the **Cowper's Oak** pub occupies a handsome stone house) to Stoke Goldington, turning right on to B526. After about 1½ miles, turn left on to a minor road running through **Salcey Forest**, where there are some pleasant walks and picnic spots, and then over M1 to Hartwell. Continue straight on here, crossing A508 to descend to Stoke Bruerne.

A pleasant canalside village, **STOKE BRUERNE** is also home of the **Waterways Museum** (*open daily, but closed Mon Oct–March*), which tells the story of the construction of the Grand Union Canal and of the way of life of the canal families who operated the brightly painted narrow boats until well into this century. There is also a mile-long walk along the towpath as far as the entrance to Blisworth Tunnel.

Take A508 south alongside the canal to Old Stratford, on the edge of Milton Keynes, where follow A422 west alongside the Ouse to **BUCKINGHAM**. Again, it is the ensemble that shapes the character of this largely Georgian hill-top town rather than any single outstanding building, although the red-brick town hall and the Old Gaol (both 18th century) and the 15th-century chantry chapel (*NT but only open by prior written request to the Buckingham Heritage Trust, The Old Gaol, Market Hill*), later used as a Latin or Grammar School, are exceptions. Film and home movie enthusiasts will not want to miss **Buckingham Movie Museum** (*open Wed–Sun*). There is good central European cooking at the **Austrian Coffee Room** in West Street, while in the Market Square the **White Hart** (0280–815151) has been receiving guests since the 15th century.

Strike south from Buckingham on A413 across a belt of gently undulating and surprisingly remote countryside, and follow signposted minor roads to **Claydon House** (*NT, open April–Oct Sat–Wed afternoons*) in **MIDDLE CLAYDON**, which has elaborately decorated rococo state

*Pavilion at Wrest Park*

rooms, a grand staircase and a Chinese room among other treasures. Florence Nightingale lived here for many years, and a museum with her personal possessions can be seen. Teas are available in the house.

From Middle Claydon, make your way through East Claydon to Winslow, where take B4032 east through Stewkley to Soulbury. Follow an unclassified road from here to Great Brickhill, then across A4 at Little Brickhill and so to Woburn. All these villages are on the wooded greensand hills that run east–west across central Bedfordshire; though quite narrow and low (the highest point is about 500ft), the ridge nevertheless produces distinctive scenery.

There are attractive brick cottages (brick-making is a substantial industry around here) in **WOBURN**, along with Market House, built in 1830. Antique shops have sprung up here, in the lee of the antiques centre at the Abbey. Stay here at the **Bedford Arms Hotel** (052525–441) or more cheaply at the **Bell Inn** (052525–280). TIC in Old St Mary's Church, Bedford Street (personal callers only).

**Woburn Abbey**, home of the Dukes of Bedford, could easily claim a good half day of your time. The house contains priceless paintings (including a score or so by Canaletto), furniture and other treasures. Outside, there is a 3,000-acre deer park, **Wild Animal Kingdom**, whose inhabitants include elephants, lions, tigers and white rhino, plus lots of other fun attractions, such as a railway, carousel and sea-lion shows. (*Abbey and Park open April–Oct daily, also Jan–March Sat and Sun only. Wild Animal Kingdom open mid-March to Oct daily.*)

Drive east from Woburn on A418 over the motorway and on to **AMPTHILL**, which has handsome Georgian buildings, including town houses, almshouses and the **White Hart Hotel** (0525–406118). The mainly 14th-century church stands at the head of an elegant small square. Henry VIII was fond of the town, and Catherine of Aragon stayed here while Henry was divorcing her. There are good walks in Ampthill Park on the edge of the town, which would make an unhurried exploring base for the surrounding area. TIC at 12 Dunstable Street (0525–402501; open Mon–Fri only).

The ruins of **Houghton House** — Bunyan's 'House Beautiful' — stand on top of the steep hill (the 'Hill of Difficulty') to the north of the town. The house was built in 1615 for the Countess of Pembroke, at least partly by Inigo Jones. (*EH, open any reasonable time.*) There are excellent views north towards Bedford and south to the line of the Chilterns, Bunyan's 'Delectable Mountains'.

Continue east along the greensand ridge to Clophill, where turn right on to A6 and then left shortly to **Wrest Park House and Gardens** (*EH, open mid-March–mid-Oct Sat, Sun and Bank Holiday Mondays*). Some rooms in the mid-19th century house can be seen, but it is the formal gardens, laid out between about 1700 and 1850, that are the principal attraction, with great lawns, classical statues and temples, an artificial lake and ruins. Teas are served in the Orangery.

Retrace your route briefly on A6 north, and turn right onto A507 to Shefford, where turn left on to A600 and then right on to a minor road to Old Warden, a village right on the edge of the greensand ridge. Just to the east the landscape alters quite suddenly, with flat clay fields of cabbages and brussels sprouts.

But **OLD WARDEN**, with its lanes of thatched cottages built of a mellow honey-coloured stone, village cricket pitch and late 12th-century church (much sinuous wood-carving inside), feels far removed from the bracing winds of the east. The recently restored **Swiss Garden** (*open April–Oct Wed, Thur, Sat, Sun and Bank Holiday Mon afternoons, but closed last Sun in month*) belongs to a late 19th-century house built for Joseph Shuttleworth and later converted into an agricultural college. Also based here is the **Shuttleworth Collection**, which contains historic aircraft and road vehicles. (*Open daily; flying displays usually on last Sunday of the month.*)

Drive north on unclassified roads through **ICKWELL**, where a maypole stands on the village green, to Northill and Mogerhanger. Turn

*Moot Hall, Elstow*

left here on to A603. In the next village, **WILLINGTON**, are Tudor stables and a dovecote with nesting boxes for 1,500 pigeons. (*NT, open by advance appointment only; tel. 02303–278.*)

A603 runs directly into Bedford, but first there is an important diversion to Elstow, a small village on Bedford's southern outskirts. Take B562 on the edge of town and then turn on to A6 south. John Bunyan was born in **ELSTOW**, and although his birthplace has not survived, there are Tudor cottages restored to their appearance in his time. The timbered **Moot Hall** (*open April–Oct Tues–Sat and Sun and Bank Holiday Mon afternoons*), built in about 1500, was originally used as a market-house, with small shops and storage space for market stalls; the large upstairs room was used for meetings and for hearing trading disputes. The building is now a museum of 17th-century life, with a reconstruction of a working room and a collection of early editions of Bunyan's books. Nearby is **Elstow Abbey** (13th-century but restored in the 19th), where Bunyan was baptised and whose bells he used to ring, until he abandoned this 'vain' practice. The church's door and wicket gate described in *The Pilgrim's Progress* survive, and the belfry appears as the castle from which Beelzebub shoots arrows at those approaching the wicket gate.

# Around the Cotswolds

*2–3 days/about 135 miles/from Oxford/OS maps 164, 174, 163, 150, 151*

Wool made the fortune of the Cotswolds. Often processed and woven locally, the long, thick fleeces of the sturdy Cotswold sheep, the Cotswold Lion, fetched high prices both in England and on the Continent. With the profits of their business, which at times supplied more than half of England's cloth, wool merchants used the local soft, mellow limestone and the skills of indigenous craftsmen to build and embellish handsome houses, churches, halls, almshouses. The result is a succession of gentle villages and small towns that grow naturally and harmoniously out of a peaceful landscape by-passed by the Industrial Revolution. The Cotswolds' present-day wealth comes from agriculture (largely arable since the wool trade moved north in the 18th century), and increasingly from tourism. The area is also becoming a haven for prosperous long-distance commuters (mostly to London and the West Midlands) and for weekenders and retired people.

The eastern Cotswolds form the core of this route. We also explore less well-known neighbouring areas: the Thames Valley west of Oxford towards the river's source and the gentle Vale of White Horse, which takes its name from the great creature carved on the chalk downs; the Vale of Red Horse, as the quiet Warwickshire ironstone landscape beyond the Cotswolds is known; and the pastoral countryside of north Oxfordshire, around the river Cherwell.

Though there is much industry on the city's periphery, a bird's-eye view

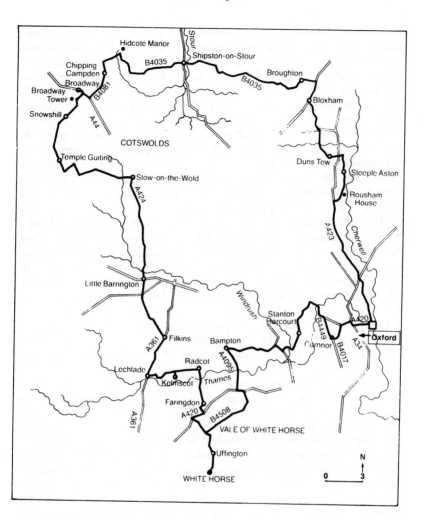

of the centre of **OXFORD** (pop. 110,000) reveals an intricate pattern of domes, spires, quadrangles and ancient college buildings, all linked by narrow streets and alleys. The best, in fact the only practical, way to explore is on foot. The university is England's oldest; the first colleges (there are now 35 in all) were founded in the 13th century. Most college chapels and quadrangles are open to visitors in the afternoons, though access may be restricted in early summer, when exams are imminent. The oldest quadrangle is **Merton College**'s Mob Quad. The largest and, in many people's view also the most handsome, is **Christ Church**'s Tom Quad; the hall here has a magnificent timbered roof and a fine collection of portraits, the chapel (*open daily*), which serves as Oxford's cathedral, fine fan tracery and a superb chapter house; there is also a **picture gallery** (*open daily*) with works by Rubens and Leonardo among many others.

**Magdalene College** has 15th-century cloisters, a group of fine 18th-century buildings, and a lovely deer park running down to the river Cherwell. There is striking modern architecture too, notably at **St Catherine's College**. Scattered amidst the individual colleges are many historic university buildings. Degree ceremonies are held at the semicircular **Sheldonian Theatre** (*open Mon–Sat*), designed by Sir Christopher Wren; there is a magnificent painted ceiling inside, while outside the busts of Roman emperors stand astride the walls. In nearby Broad Street is the **Bodleian Library and Divinity School** (*open Mon–Fri and Sat morning*). The library, one of the world's oldest and largest, contains many rare manuscripts, while in the collection of the 15th-century Divinity School (note the fine fan vaulting) is the only known copy of Shakespeare's first published work.

The city has many museums. One of the newest, and not at all a traditional museum, is the **Oxford Story** (*open daily*), near the Sheldonian in Broad Street. This uses the latest audio-visual techniques and well-researched reconstructions to take you back to the Oxford of the Middle Ages. The **Ashmolean Museum** (*open Tues–Sat and Sun afternoons*) has practically everything: Egyptian, Greek and Roman antiquities, Chinese ceramics, Persian and Indian paintings, a fine collection of drawings by Michelangelo, Pre-Raphaelite and French Impressionist paintings. See also the **Museum of Modern Art** (*open Tues–Sat and Sun afternoon*) and the natural history collections at the **University Museum** (*open Mon–Sat*).

**Brown's** in Woodstock Road is an all-day café serving sandwiches, salads, hot dishes and afternoon tea. A couple of miles outside the city centre, the riverside **Trout Inn** at Godstow is a delightful place to enjoy a drink and good pub food. Oxford has numerous places to stay: **Eastgate Hotel** (0865–248244) in The High is at the top end of the price range, the **Old Parsonage Hotel** (0865–54843/513144) at the beginning of Banbury Road a cheaper establishment. TIC in St Aldates (0865–726871/3).

Oxford lies in the middle of a clay plain, between the Chilterns to the south-east and the Cotswolds, whose dip slope rises gradually, almost imperceptibly, in the north-west. But we make for the hills by an indirect route along the Thames Valley towards the river's source.

Leave the city centre on A420 west, which turns into a dual carriageway after crossing the watermeadows on the edge of the city. At the roundabout junction with A34 (the Oxford by-pass), continue straight on along A420, but then take the first exit, to Cumnor. As soon as you have left the dual carriageway, turn right on to B4017, and then left again alongside Farnmoor Reservoir on to B4044. At the junction just south of Eynsham, follow B4449 to **STANTON HARCOURT**.

This is an attractive village lying amid water meadows near the confluence of the Thames and the river Windrush, which rises high up in the Cotswolds. **Stanton Harcourt Manor** (*open irregularly April–Sept; tel. 0865–881928 for details*) contains some remarkable buildings, including the Great Kitchen, one of the best-preserved medieval kitchens in the country with a pyramidal roof surmounted by a griffin weathercock, and the 15th-century Pope's Tower, so called because the 18th-century poet Alexander Pope lived at the Manor while translating Homer's *Iliad*. The Manor was the home of the Harcourt family from the 12th to the 18th centuries; there are elaborate statues and effigies to various Harcourts in the Norman church.

B4449 runs past gravel pits and across the Windrush, briefly joins A415 (turn right), and then veers left to **BAMPTON**, where, every Whit Monday, teams of Morris dancers perform. There is a fine church, its tall buttressed spire a well-known local landmark, and some pleasing Georgian houses around the little market square.

Take the unclassified road that heads south towards the Thames, which it crosses on the delightfully named **Tadpole Bridge**. The river bank path that runs west makes a good walk through quite lonely countryside; you could walk past Radcot Lock to Radcot (see below) and meet your driver there.

The hills ahead are the **Berkshire Downs**, which retain their traditional name, despite having been moved into Oxfordshire. This great sweep of chalk hills is scattered with prehistoric fortresses and burial chambers; the ancient Ridgeway, now a long-distance path, runs along the summit. The lush valley at the foot of the Downs is the lovely **Vale of White Horse**, made famous as the boyhood home of Tom Brown of the 19th-century novel *Tom Brown's Schooldays*.

Turn left in Buckland on to A420, then right almost immediately on to a minor road, then right again on to B4508. A left turn in Fernham brings you across the little river Ock to **UFFINGTON**, birthplace of Thomas Hughes, Tom Brown's creator. See the **Tom Brown School Museum** in Broad Street (*open Easter–Sept weekends and Bank Holiday Mon afternoons only, but closed late Aug Bank Holiday*). **White Horse Hill** (856ft) rises up above the village. The angular, sparsely delineated white horse, some 360ft long, 130ft high, dates from about 100BC. The best view is from the Vale, but it's fun to climb up to examine it close-to as well. Drive south from the village, across B4507 and uphill. Paths lead from the car park to the horse and to **Uffington Castle**, a prehistoric fortification on the summit, with spectacular views.

Return to Fernham, and cross B4508. Bear left in Little Coxwell across A420 to **GREAT COXWELL**, where the **Great Barn** (*NT, open daily at reasonable hours*) is a 13th-century stone monastic barn; the interior roof construction is a complex pattern of timber supports and beams.

Beyond the barn, turn right on to B4019, which brings you to **FARINGDON**, a pleasant small market town with a pillared 17th-century Market Hall and a 13th-century church. **Bell Hotel** (0367–20534) is a 16th-century inn with a popular restaurant. TIC in the Pump House also on Market Place (0367–22191).

A4095 runs north out of town, past Faringdon Hill. The stone tower on top is a folly, erected in 1936 by Lord Berners, and said to be one of the last follies built in this country. Soon after crossing the Thames at

*Kelmscot Manor*

**RADCOT**, where the bridge saw an important engagement in the Civil War, turn left on to an unclassified road that runs across water meadows towards Lechlade.

A left turn off this road brings you to **KELMSCOT**. William Morris, artist, painter, writer, social reformer, lived at **Kelmscot Manor** (*open April–Sept first Wed in month only*) from 1871 until his death in 1896. The Elizabethan house contains Morris wallpapers and textile designs, as well as family portraits.

**LECHLADE** is the highest navigable point of the Thames, and in years past was an important port. Cloth, Single Gloucester cheese (a less rich version of Double Gloucester), even stone for St Paul's cathedral was loaded on to Thames barges here. Nowadays a flotilla of sailing boats, motor cruisers and rowing boats occupies the water. The fine 15th-century wool church with its magnificent spire, recognisable from miles off, contains fine carvings.

And now, at long last, the Cotswolds. A361 heads north, across the river Leach. Turn right in Broughton Poggs for **FILKINS**, where **Cotswold Woollen Weavers** (*open daily except Sun morning*) utilise the traditional skills of carding, spinning and weaving to produce a range of rugs, clothes and materials on expertly preserved machinery. Visitors can observe all the various stages of production; there's also an exhibition and a coffee shop. Encouraged by the success of the woollen weavers, other craftsmen have moved into the village.

Return to A361 and turn off left in the village. (NB: do not travel beyond the built-up area of the village on the A road.) This minor road runs through lonely country, with hardly more than a farm in sight, across A433 and A40 to the **BARRINGTONS**, Little Barrington on the south bank of the river Windrush, Great Barrington on the north side. Christopher Wren used stone from the quarries here for St Paul's cathedral and many of his City of London churches. One of the local quarry-owning families was the Strongs, and Thomas Strong was Wren's master mason at St Paul's; it was Thomas who laid the cathedral's foundation stone. **LITTLE BARRINGTON** is a characteristic Cotswold village: grey limestone cottages with steep-pitched roofs of local slate around the village green.

The road continues over the rolling wolds, eventually meeting A424, where turn left for **STOW-ON-THE-WOLD**, at almost 800ft the highest town in the Cotswolds. There are many handsome buildings and a plethora of antique shops, most pretty expensive. Two great sheep fairs were held each year in the large market place, at which some 20,000 beasts would change hands; the tradition continues today with the annual Horse Fair in July. Stay here at the **Grapevine Hotel** (0451–30344) in Sheep Street or at **Old Stocks Hotel** (0451–30666) on The Square. The lunches and the baking are recommended at **St Edward's Café**, also on The Square. TIC at Talbot Court (0451–31082).

Leave along B4068 west, and soon branch right to Lower Swell and then across countryside scattered with long barrows and tumuli, evidence of early Cotswold settlers. A right turn beyond Chalk Hill brings you to **Cotswold Farm Park** (*open Easter–Sept daily*), where rare breeds of farm animals and fowl lives in a natural environment. Traditional Cotswold sheep number large among the collection, and there is a children's corner and special exhibitions.

Continue downhill, across the Windrush, here no more than a stream, and turn right in Kineton. Bear left in Temple Guiting, cross B4077 in Ford, and head north towards Snowshill. For most of the year this is undisturbed countryside, ignored by the visitors who flock to the tourist honeypots, of which the Cotswolds has more than its fair share. The agriculture is largely arable, although scatterings of sheep remain.

The early 18th-century facade of **Snowshill Manor** (*NT, open May–Sept Wed–Sun, also April and Oct weekends*) conceals a Tudor house, now full of a remarkable collection of artefacts and antiques assembled by Charles Paget Wade, the former owner: musical instruments, toys, weaving and spinning tools, armour. There are fine terraced gardens with roses and shrubs. **SNOWSHILL** itself is an atrractive quiet hamlet with cottages, an inn and a pub looking on to the green.

Follow the minor road east from the village, and climb, bearing left, alongside Middle Hill and out on to the broad expanse of Broadway Hill, 1,024ft, on the scarp slope of the Cotswolds. The 65ft tower, a late 18th-century folly, is a landmark for miles around. From the top, you can see, it is claimed, no fewer than 12 counties. On a clear day, the high Welsh hills stand out in the distance, with the long ridge of the Malverns in the

*Woolstaplers Hall, Chipping Campden*

foreground. The tower is the focal point of **Broadway Tower Country Park** (*open April–early Oct daily*), where there are nature walks along the hillside, rare animals and birds, and craft displays in the 150-year-old, typically Cotswold Tower Barn. The 100-mile **Cotswold Way** runs through the Park; this is a fine walk along the scarp from Bath to Chipping Campden.

In the Vale below, **BROADWAY** is an enormously popular spot with visitors. Along the broad, chestnut-lined main street stands the luxurious **Lygon Arms**, a traditional coaching inn (0386–852255). TIC in Cotswold Court (0386–852937).

Beyond the Country Park, turn right on to A44, away from Broadway, and then immediately left along B4081. The great curving main street of **CHIPPING CAMPDEN** is lined with handsome stone houses that reflect the solid affluence the wool trade brought the town. The largely 15th-century church, St James, has a magnificent nave, its pillars soaring to the roof, and many brasses, including one of wool merchant William Grevel and his wife; Grevel's house, with its two-storey gabled bay window, stands in the main street. Look at the 17th-century market hall and at the lovely almshouses raised above street level. Among the town's oldest buildings is **Woolstaplers Hall** (*open April–Oct daily*), now a museum of local history. Among several hotels are the **Seymour House Hotel** (0386–840429) and the **Cotswold House Hotel** (0386–840317), where the restaurant is also recommended. TIC in the Woolstaplers Hall (0386–840289).

Leave town along B4035, soon turning right on to B4081 and, after crossing the railway, right again to **Hidcote Manor** (*NT, open April–Oct daily except Tues and Fri*), where the gardens, created by the horti-culturalist Major Lawrence Johnston, consist of a sequence of separate 'rooms', each with its own characteristic colours, scents and shapes. Roses, carefully tended borders planned to flower in different seasons, camellias, rare shrubs provide a perfect backdrop to a magnificent Cotswold stone manor house (*not open*). Each summer a Shakespeare play is performed on the Theatre Lawn (tel. 0684–850051 for details).

Drive south from Hidcote through Ebrington to the junction with B4035, where turn left. This road slowly descends from the Cotswolds to the Vale of Red Horse, as the countryside around the river Stour is known: red because this is ironstone country, in contrast with Cotswold limestone.

**SHIPSTON-ON-STOUR** is a pleasant small market town whose wealth, as in the neighbouring Cotswold communities, was founded on sheep; the annual sheep fair was a great occasion in the town's life. There are many attractive Georgian buildings, including the **Bell Inn** in Sheep Street (0608–61443) and the **White Bear** (0608–61558) in High Street.

Shipston, Chipping Campden and any of the nearby villages would make an excellent starting-point for a trip to Stratford-upon-Avon, with its theatres and Shakespearean exhibitions.

Continue over A34 and the river along B4035 through the Brailes, Upper and Lower, to **BROUGHTON**, where moated **Broughton Castle** (*open mid-May–mid-Sept Wed and Sun afternoons, also Thurs afternoons in July and Aug*) is set in lovely parkland. The castle, largely 14th- and 15th-century but with an Elizabethan facade, has been the home of the Fiennes family for over 500 years. The house is full of treasures — fine plasterwork and carvings, paintings — and traditional narrow passages and stairways. The nearby church contains the tomb of Sir Thomas Broughton, who built the castle.

Turn right in the village, then right on to A361. **BLOXHAM** is a pleasant hill-top village full of thatched ironstone cottages and with a 200ft church spire, visible for miles around. The west door has elaborate mouldings and carvings, the interior (mostly 13th-century) a painted screen. **Bloxham Village Museum** (*open April–Sept Suns and Bank Holiday Mons, also 2nd Sun in month Oct–March*) contains exhibits on local life.

On the final stretch now, we head south on minor roads through the two Barfords (St John and St Michael, divided by the river Swere). Bear left in Barford St Michael, cross B4031 at Hempton, and drive south to **DUNS TEW**, a charming village of thatched cottages.

A left turn in Duns Tew takes you across the main A423 into North

Aston. Turn right here through Steeple Aston to **Rousham House** (*house open April–Sept Wed, Sun and Bank Holiday Mon afternoons, gardens daily*), a handsome mansion built in the 1630s and much redesigned inside by William Kent a century later. There is fine furniture and plasterwork, plus a great collection of paintings. Kent also landscaped the gardens, which run down to the peaceful river Cherwell, creating lovely waterfalls, vistas and walks. The Oxford Canal runs alongside the river.

The minor road south from Rousham meets A423, where turn left and return to Oxford.

# 3 WALES AND THE BORDERS

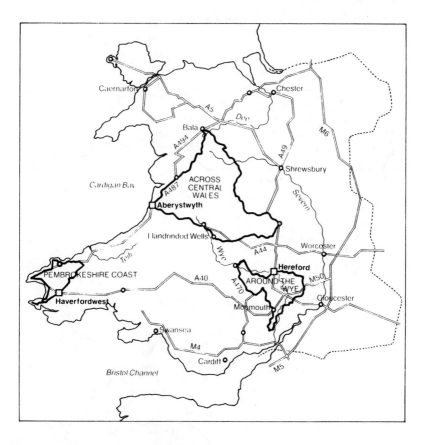

That Wales was once an independent nation which the English medieval monarchs could only subdue at the expense of considerable force is evident wherever you drive in the Principality or in the neighbouring English border lands. Great stone castles, strongly fortified and often spacious enough to accommodate garrisons of troops, rear up wherever there is a mountain pass or a river valley, an estuary or a settlement to be defended. These are the memorials of the conquerors. But the vanquished have their memorials too — not least in the sensation, in

Wales, of being in a land with its own distinct culture and way of life. The traveller has in addition scenery of unsurpassed beauty to enjoy: rugged mountain peaks, high moorland and fast-flowing rivers dropping sharply to a fine coastline in the west, in the east descending more gently to a fruitful, peaceful land scattered with handsome market towns and secluded villages.

## Around the Wye

*2–3 days/about 135 miles/from Hereford/OS maps 149, 162, 171, 161*

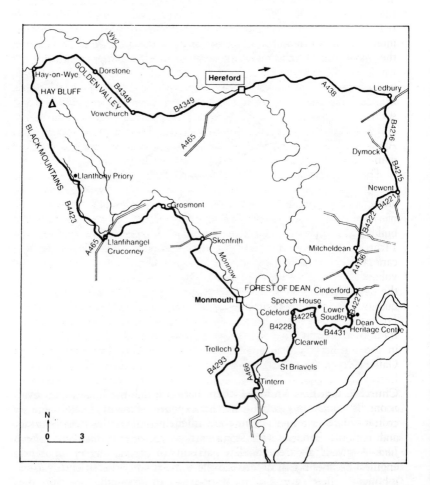

This circuit ranges wide through the varied landscapes of the English and Welsh borderlands, but always returns to the river Wye. From its source high up in the mountains of central Wales, this most delightful and unspoilt of all rivers traces a tortuous course towards the sea, through isolated hill country, across rich pasture land and at the foot of spectacular limestone cliffs. Nowadays, angling (especially for salmon), canoeing and walking are the chief activities along the Wye, but from the earliest times until well into the 19th century the lower part of the river was a major trading route, busy with boats carrying coal and iron, cider and corn. Besides the river, expect on this drive a variety of landscapes: the rich red pastures of Herefordshire, the centuries-old oaks of the secretive Forest of Dean, and remote sheep-covered Welsh hillsides.

We start at **HEREFORD** (pop. 47,600), the largest settlement alongside the Wye. The **cathedral**, originally Norman, has an early 14th-century red sandstone tower and much 19th- and 20th-century restoration. The interior is full of treasures. Look especially at the great Norman pillars in the nave, the lovely mid-13th century north transept with its tall windows, the elaborate tomb of St. Thomas Cantilupe in the north transept guarded by the effigies of 15 Knights Templar, and at the *Mappa Mundi.* This late 13th-century map of the world is one of the oldest surviving anywhere; the world is shown flat, with Jerusalem at the centre and England and Ireland on a remote edge. The **chained library** (*open April–Oct Mon–Sat, also winter Sats*) contains well over 1,500 books and manuscripts dating from the 8th to the 15th centuries.

The small city centre is enjoyable to walk around — there are some excellent shops (crafts, antiques, books, jewellery), a regular market and attractive old buildings. The **Old House** (*open Tues–Sat and Mon mornings, but closed winter Sat afternoons*), a 17th-century timbered building, is furnished in contemporary style. All Saints church (13th- and 14th-centuries) contains a 17th-century pulpit, beautifully carved and canopied choir stalls, and another chained library, this time with 300 volumes. (The chains were an early security measure to prevent theft in the days when books were hand-written or printed by hand in very low quantities.) The **Cider Museum** (*open April–Oct daily, Nov and Dec Mon–Fri mornings*) is devoted to the history of one of Herefordshire's traditional products; old equipment is displayed, and cider brandy is made in the distillery. Other museums include the **City Museum and Art Gallery** (*open Tues–Sat*), which has displays on local natural history, history and archaeology and a collection of 19th-century watercolours; **Churchill Gardens Museum** (*open Tues–Sat afternoons, also Sun afternoons in summer*), which concentrates on 18th- and 19th-century costume, furniture and paintings, and also contains a Victorian nursery and parlour; **Broomy Hill Engines** (*open afternoons; working exhibits June–Aug Suns, also Bank Holiday Suns and Mons*) are restored waterworks engines. **Bulmer Railway Museum** (*open Easter–Sept weekend afternoons*) is home to three restored steam locomotives, including the Great Western Railway *George IV*, and industrial locos and rolling stock.

**Marches** in Union Street offers a good selection of wholefood dishes. The **Green Dragon** (0432–272506), an old coaching inn, occupies a central position near the river and the cathedral. **Chesley House** (0432–274800) is a family-run guesthouse. TIC in the Town Hall Annexe (0432–268430).

Although the country on each immediate side of the border is the main focus of this route, we start by heading away from Wales. For **LEDBURY**, 14 miles east along A438, is not a town to be missed. Among its many black-and-white timber-framed buildings is the **Market House**, built as a corn market in the 17th century. Stroll along narrow cobbled Church Lane to the **Old Grammar School** (*open April–Sept daily, also winter weekends*), now a heritage centre devoted to the history of the town from Anglo-Saxon times. The spacious church is largely 14th-century, although the 200ft spire, a local landmark, is 18th-century; look for the monument of a priest in prayer, and also for the elaborate Skynner tomb. **Feathers Hotel** (0521–2600) and the **Talbot Hotel** (0531–2963) are both fine half-timbered buildings; the food at **Applejack Wine Bar** in The Homend is spoken of highly. TIC in St Katherine's (0531–2461).

Leave Ledbury along A449 towards Ross-on-Wye, but turn left soon on to B4216, turning left again in **DYMOCK** on to B4215. In the golden years of Edwardian England, before the carnage of the First World War, this handsome village was home to a group of young poets, among them Rupert Brooke, Edward Thomas and the American Robert Frost.

On the way into **NEWENT**, off B4215, at **Newent Butterfly Centre** (*open Easter–Oct daily*) free-flying tropical butterflies are on display, and the menagerie contains a large collection of creepy-crawlies: snails, scorpions, giant bird spiders, cockroaches, locusts and other such delightful creatures. To the south of the town, off B4216, the **Falconry Centre** (*open Feb–Nov daily except Tues*) is devoted to this ancient and noble pastime; the collection is the largest of birds of prey in Europe, and over 50 birds of varying species are bred each year. The breeding aviaries can be seen, and flying demonstrations are given daily, weather permitting. The small town centre has half-timbered and Georgian buildings. One of the pleasantest streets is Church Street, in which the **Shambles** (*open Easter–Oct daily except Mon*) is furnished as a late 19th-century tradesman's house. At the nearby **Cowdy Glass Workshop** (*open Mon–Fri*) you can watch exquisite glass pieces being crafted. TIC in the library, High Street (0531–822145).

Follow B4221 west, branching left on to B4222, and left again on to an unclassified road in Aston Crews. This leads through steep country to the junction with A40, where carry straight on to Mitcheldean. A right turn here on to A4136 leads you almost immediately into the **Forest of Dean**. Driving — or better still walking — through the Forest today, it is hard to believe that it was once the centre of a thriving mining industry, both for coal and iron ore. The Romans were the first to tap the forest's rich mineral resources, but large-scale production of iron began in the 17th century, of coal in the 18th century, and survived for a couple of hundred years. The last big coal pit closed as recently as 1965; before the Second World War a million tons of coal were dug most years. Nowadays, such activity would seem most incongruous in the peaceful forest glades, but on almost any walk you are quite likely to stumble across the traces of old ironwalks, or half-overgrown tram-roads or canals, or even one of the small private coal mines still in operation. The forest became a royal hunting forest early in the 11th century, and the remaining 27,000 acres are still Crown property, although administered by the Forestry Commission. The trees themselves are not especially old; whole plantations were felled to provide timber for the navy during the Napoleonic wars, and so most date from the early 19th century, although some massive 17th-century oaks remain. While roughly half the forest consists of conifers, there are also many oaks, beech, ash, elm and sweet chestnut.

Follow A4136 west from Mitcheldean, and turn left on to A4151 to **CINDERFORD** (TIC in the library, Belle Vue Road, 0594–23184). Take B4227 out of the town. A few miles south, on the edge of **LOWER SOUDLEY**, brings you to the **Dean Heritage Centre** (*open daily*), an excellent place to get an overview of Forest life. There are displays on archaeology, history and natural history, a reconstructed cottage and mine, a beam engine and a waterwheel, and lots of practical activities, including a smallholding and charcoal-burning demonstrations. The Centre occupies a handsome corn mill set by an attractive mill pond.

Retrace your route briefly along B4227, and turn left in Upper Soudley on to an unclassified road running south through the forest. Turn left on to B4331 and then right again on to another minor road that leads north to Speech House. Alongside these roads are many attractive parking spots with picnic tables.

Standing in the centre of the forest, **Speech House**, now a hotel (0594–22607), was built in 1680 as a meeting-place for the Verderers' or Speech Court, the body that administered the often severe laws that governed everyone who lived in the forest. Though their powers are now considerably reduced, the Verderers still meet here, and visitors may see the old court room.

Forest trails lead off through the woods around Speech House. If you are lucky, you might spot one of the two herds of fallow deer that still graze in the forest. In spring, the forest floor is carpeted with bluebells, wood anemone, primrose. Later in the year, when spring's fresh greens have turned a richer, deeper colour, there are butterflies in abundance, and the air is filled with bird song: nuthatch, tree-creeper, wood-warbler among many others. Autumn brings every shade of red and brown and gold, the crisp scrunch of leaves underfoot, and a wealth of fungi (make absolutely sure you know which varieties are edible before you start picking).

Follow B4226 west out of the densest parts of the forest to **COLEFORD**, a former mining centre (TIC in the Market Place — 0594–36307), where turn left on to B4228. Then a right turn on to a minor road in Milkwall will bring you to **CLEARWELL**, where

*Tintern Abbey*

**Clearwell Caves** (*open March–Oct daily*) are ancient iron mines worked for over 2,500 years until 1945. Eight of the caverns can be seen, and there are displays of mining equipment and vintage mine engines.

Return to B4228, and follow this road south-west to **ST BRIAVELS**, the forest's administrative capital in the Middle Ages, perched 900ft high above the Wye valley. There is a large church (originally Norman) and a 12th-century castle, partly ruined but partly used as a youth hostel.

A minor road descends through steep wooded country to the Wye, meeting A466 just before it crosses the river, which here forms the English–Welsh border, on Bigsweir Bridge. Turn left and follow the main road south down the gorge towards **TINTERN**. Shortly before the village, the restored **Old Station** (*open Easter–Christmas daily*) is a local heritage centre with a railway exhibition.

**Tintern Abbey** (*CADW, standard opening times*), built by Cistercian monks in the 12th century beneath towering limestone cliffs on a bend in the gorge, is a long-standing tourist attraction. Two centuries ago, Turner painted the abbey, Wordsworth wrote about it, and aesthetic theories of the picturesque were stimulated by the grandeur of the scenery. The impressive ruins, which include the chapter house, refectory and kitchen as well the Abbey itself, largely date from the 13th century; clearly this was a substantial community. It's a shame that the rest of the rather scrappy village looks so unprepossessing; something of the Abbey's unique atmosphere is lost. TIC by the Abbey (02918–431).

There are plenty of waymarked walks in the nearby woods, plus two longer-distance paths. The **Wye Valley Walk** (Chepstow to Hereford) runs along the Welsh side of the river, while **Offa's Dyke Path**, which we shall meet again later in this drive, follows the east bank.

Strike west from Tintern along the unclassified road from the centre of the village, which climbs through woodland and past old mine workings to Devauden, joining B4293 just before the village. Drive north, past **Beaufort Bird Gardens** (*open daily*), where the collection of tropical birds, rare pheasants, peacocks and ducks occupies attractive gardens, along this ridge road with fine views to **TRELLECH**. No more than a modest village nowadays, in the Middle Ages and before Trellech seems to have been an important township. Three huge standing stones — their purpose unknown — occupy a field close to the church, which contains a 17th-century sundial. There is also a preaching cross, perhaps dating back to the 5th century, and a natural spring, known locally as the Virtuous

Well. The local school has developed a short History Trail, which is well worth following. The **Lion** is a welcoming pub that serves delicious home-cooked food.

Continue along B4293 into **MONMOUTH**, a strategic stronghold astride the border since Roman times. Little remains of the town's early history, and the Norman castle, where Henry V was born in 1387, was largely destroyed during the Civil War. However, there is the lovely stone-gated Monnow bridge (the rivers Monnow and Wye meet just beyond the town walls), built in the late 13th century, and the town is a fine place to stroll around. There is a handsome market place and many 16th- and 18th-century buildings, including the timbered **King's Head Hotel** (0600–2177). A cheaper place to stay is the **Queen's Head Hotel** (0600–2767). **Monmouth Museum** (*open daily except Sun morning*) contains an unexpected Nelson collection with a wealth of memorabilia — unexpected because, apart from once passing through, he has no connections with the town — and displays on local history, including a section on the life of Charles Stewart Rolls, the Rolls of Rolls Royce, who was born in the town. TIC in Church Street (0600–3899).

So far the landscape has been relatively docile. That changes gradually as you head north-west out of Monmouth on B4233 into remote, sparsely populated country, with the prospect of high mountains ahead. Bear right on to B4347, and at the junction with B4521 turn right into **SKENFRITH**, a border village for centuries disputed between the English and Welsh. The **castle** (*CADW, free access*) was built in the early 13th century; a powerful central stone keep survives, together with some of the curtain walls. Skenfrith is one of the 'three castles' (the others are Grosmont (see below) and White Castle near Abergavenny) built to defend the Monnow valley against incursions from the Welsh, who were resisting the Norman takeover of their country.

B4347 continues north to **GROSMONT**, where the 13th-century **castle** (*CADW, free access*) stands on a hill above the village and river, defended by a deep moat. There are excellent views.

The next stretch of this exploration, as far as Hay-on-Wye, involves some difficult driving along narrow and at times mountainous roads. If you prefer not to tackle this, or if bad weather threatens, you can either return

*The 13th-century gated bridge over the river Monnow, Monmouth*

direct to Hereford along A465, or else make for Hay along B4347 from Pontrilas.

Our route continues along the minor road heading approximately west from Grosmont along Campston Hill to Llanfihangel Crucorney. Turn left here on to A465 and then almost immediately right on to B4423. The **Skirrid Inn** claims to be the oldest pub in Wales — possibly even in all Great Britain — and serves excellent food. The inn is a great favourite with walkers on **Offa's Dyke Path**, which passes through the village; it runs from Chepstow in the south of Wales to Prestatyn in the north. The Dyke was a defensive earthwork built by Offa, king of Mercia in the second half of the 8th century, as a barrier against the Welsh.

B4423 runs along the beautiful, secluded Ewyas valley to the ruins of **Llanthony Priory** (*CADW, free access*), founded in the late 12th century and now standing in a lovely setting of meadows and chestnut groves. The hills above are the Black Mountains, appealing in summer sun, but aptly named in lashing rain, or when threatening clouds gather low in the sky.

The road (which loses its B registration at the Priory) continues alongside the river through the tiny hamlet of Capel-y-ffin and climbs over Gospel Pass to descend alongside Hay Bluff (2,219ft) on the scarp slope towards Hay-on-Wye. From around the Bluff there are long views ahead, over the Wye valley and far beyond towards the peaks of central Wales.

**HAY-ON-WYE** is a busy hillside town, narrow streets clustering around the originally Norman castle, converted to a mansion in the 17th century. Its life nowadays largely consists of second-hand books, shop after shop of them, which gives it a rather odd atmosphere. There are some pleasant walks, however, through the winding streets and along the riverside Bailey Walk. Stay here at the **Old Black Lion** (0497–820841), and eat at the **Granary** on Broad Street: delicious pies, soups, casseroles, puds and cakes.

Almost immediately it leaves Hay, B4348 crosses into England, heading east for Dorstone at the head of the tranquil **Golden Valley** along the little river Dore. Delightful as it is, there's nothing specifically golden about the Golden Valley: it seems that the Normans misunderstood the Welsh *dwr* (water) for the French *d'or* (golden).

**DORSTONE** is a peaceful village — the sort of place where nothing ever seems to disturb the ordered calm. The church, originally 13th-century, was almost completely rebuilt in the late 19th. Arthur's Stone (*EH, open any reasonable time*) on the hill above the town is a prehistoric burial chamber. B4348 crosses to the east side of the river in Dorstone, but a better route is along the minor road on the west bank through Hinton and then across the river just below **PETERCHURCH**, which has a Norman church with a modern (plastic!) steeple.

Continue south on B4348 to **VOWCHURCH**, where the 14th-century church contains some magnifcent wood carving, and, now leaving Golden Valley, continue west on the same road, turning right on to B4349 at Gorsty Common. This road soon meets A465, where turn left for the short drive back to Hereford.

# The Pembrokeshire Coast

*1–2 days/about 110 miles/from Haverfordwest/OS maps 145, 157*

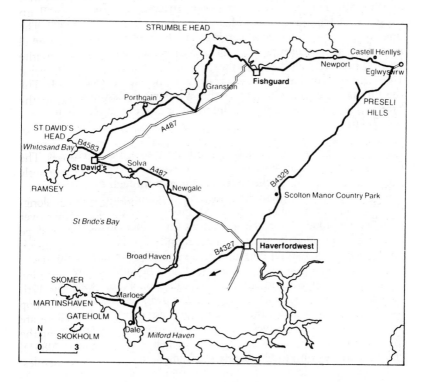

A rocky shore, home of seals and numberless sea birds, cliffs strewn with wild flowers, long stretches of unspoilt golden sand: these are the natural features of the Pembrokeshire coast that make it one of the loveliest in all Wales — if not in the whole of the British Isles. In the Preseli Hills inland from the coast ancient trackways and stone circles are a reminder of early settlers. St. David's, close to the shore but well hidden for security against attack from the sea, was the earliest Christian centre of Wales, whose founder — David, or Dewi — became the nation's patron saint. Almost the entire coastline, and some inland parts as well, form the Pembroke-shire Coast National Park.

**HAVERFORDWEST** is the main administrative and commercial centre for this southern part of Pembrokeshire: the Englishry, or 'little England beyond Wales' as it is often called. The Normans began their conquest of Pembrokeshire in the late 11th century. As they settled, they built new villages and imported people to live in them — at first from the west country, then groups of Flemish immigrants — and consolidate their hold

on the country. History has a way of making itself felt for many generations — and even nowadays English, not Welsh, is the language you will
hear in and around Haverfordwest. Today Haverfordwest is an agreeable
largely 18th-century town, whose main street climbs steeply from the
Western Cleddau River to St. Mary's Church (13th-century) which has a
fine oak roof and some good carving. The keep of the Norman castle is
now the **Castle Museum** (*open Tues–Sat*), which has displays on local
history, military collections and a regional art gallery. Stay here in the
16th-century **Hotel Mariners** (0437–3353), and eat alongside the river at
the **Granary** on Old Quay or at the **Wholemeal Restaurant** in Quay
Street. TIC and National Park Information Centre at 40 High Street
(0437–66141).

Leave town on B4327, heading south-west towards **DALE**, a little
yachting village on an inlet of Milford Haven. In August 1485, Henry
Tudor landed nearby, at the start of his march through his native Wales
and on into England, where he gained the throne from Richard III at the
Battle of Bosworth Field (see page 58). From the shore the stacks of the
oil refineries along Milford Haven are clearly visible; at night an intense
orange glow invades the sky for miles around. The Haven is one of the
finest deep-water natural harbours in the world. A trading centre since
time forgotten, it was also an important ship-building centre from the
16th century until the end of the 19th. Fishing on a large scale started in
the first years of the present century, but has dwindled drastically over the
last 40 years. Nowadays, the Haven's business is oil, tanker load after
tanker load of it; it arrives as crude and after refining is distributed
throughout the country — often via the pipeline that links the Milford
Haven refineries with the Midlands and Manchester.

Back to our exploration! Return along B4327, and soon turn left along
a minor road that runs through the fields to Marloes village. A left turn at
the entrance to the village brings you to the car park for **Marloes Beach**
(*NT*); the beach itself is about 10–15 minutes' walk — the path ends in a
short scramble.

Marloes is surely one of the best beaches in Britain. A wide expanse of
sand at low tide; safe bathing; rocks to scramble over, and rock pools to
play in; and, as clear as if laid out for a geology lesson, a fascinating
variety of rock formations and strata in the high cliffs behind the beach.

The **Pembrokeshire Coast Path** runs along the cliff tops. This is
perhaps the most satisfying of all the long-distance paths, at least for the
occasional walker. There's a good variety of scenery; the walking is not so
hard as to be off-putting, but hard enough to provide a real sense of
achievement; and wild flowers grow everywhere in abundance. This car
route can easily be combined with stretches of path-walking; call at any of
the National Park Information Offices to buy their very useful laminated
route cards, which include maps and notes about places of interest.

The road through Marloes village continues to **Martinshaven**, at the
tip of the peninsula. From here you can catch a boat to **Skomer**, the
nearest and largest of the three islands immediately off the coast. (*Boats*

*Marloes sands*

*daily except Mon; enquire at Information Offices for details or tel. Dale* (06465) 349.) Don't miss the trip, and bring binoculars and sandwiches. The island, uninhabited except by wardens and research scientists, is a nature reserve operated by the Dyfed Wildlife Trust. It takes no more than a couple of hours to walk round, but you will spend much longer than that absorbing the atmosphere. Together with neighbouring Skokholm — both names, incidentally, are of Scandinavian origin — Skomer has the world's largest colonies of Manx shearwater, estimated some years ago at 135,000 pairs. There are also puffins, guillemots, razorbills, kittiwakes and fulmars on the cliff edges, black-backed gulls, oystercatchers, lapwings, wheatears and many others in the interior. You are also bound to see rabbits — the strip of water that separates Skomer from the mainland spared the island's rabbit population from the scourge of myxomatosis — and you might just spot the Skomer vole. This is thought to be a unique subspecies, less shy and more confident than its mainland cousins from which it has evolved independently.

Return through Marloes to B4327, but where the main road branches right continue straight on to Talbenny and then on the steep descent to **LITTLE HAVEN**, a tiny fishing and yachting village. (The stretch of coastal path from Martinshaven to Little Haven is an excellent walk —

about 9 miles.) At **BROAD HAVEN** the National Park Information Centre (0437–781412) has a well-equipped children's activity room. The Park Authority organises a wide range of talks, walks and other activities throughout the season. Also in Broad Haven is a delightful 1½-mile woodland walk through Haroldston Wood.

Partly because of the Gulf Stream, this part of Pembrokeshire generally enjoys a benign climate, and in sheltered spots particularly, away from the sea winds, you will find wild flowers in bloom in almost every season. Snowdrops appear in February, and daffodils too — for daffodils must be worn on St. David's Day, 1 March — and in March primroses, black-thorn and wood anemone among many others. And so it is throughout the year: in late spring, bluebells in the woods and thrift on the cliff tops, heather and thyme in high summer.

North from Broad Haven, the road hugs the coast for a few miles, then turns inland to meet A487. Turn left on to this road, which returns to the coast at Newgale Sands. **SOLVA**, at the head of a small inlet, is a rather over-touristified village that cries out for the adjective 'picturesque'; at least it makes you realise how blessedly undeveloped most of the rest of the county is. The **Nectarium** (*open Easter–Sept daily except Sun morning*) includes a tropical butterfly house and insect galleries, as well as a shop selling crafts and designer clothes, and a café/restaurant called **The Hungry Caterpillar**.

The richly decorated **cathedral** at **ST. DAVID'S** dates largely from the

*St. David's Cathedral*

late 12th century, but was substantially restored in the 19th. Look especially at the nave with its oak roof and at the riotous misericords. The substantial ruins of the **Bishop's Palace** close by (*CADW, standard opening times*) seem more a fortress than a palace: battlements, gatehouse, curtain walls and an arcaded parapet decorated with sculptured stone heads. The palace was largely built in the first half of the 14th century and was destroyed in the 16th. Stay here at **St. Non's Hotel** (0437–720239), just south of the city, which is hardly more than a village in size. TIC and National Park Information Centre in the City Hall (0437–720392).

There's a marvellous stretch of coast all around the city. To the south is St. Non's Bay, named after St. David's mother, with a ruined chapel dedicated to her. Rocky outcrops overlook the sound between the mainland and Ramsey Island, there's a mile-long stretch of sand at **Whitesand Bay**, while amid the windswept rocks and heather on **St. David's Head** you will find prehistoric enclosures and a burial chamber. Near Whitesand Bay is **Lleithyr Farm Museum** (*open Easter–Oct daily except Mon*), which contains collections of old farm equipment and machinery, domestic bygones and farm animals.

Take A487 out of the city, turn on to B4583, and almost immediately, where this road bears left, continue straight on along the unclassified road which runs parallel to the coast. A left turn in Llanrian leads to Porthgain. Now no more than a hamlet by a derelict narrow harbour, for some 60 or 70 years from the mid-19th century **PORTHGAIN** was a thriving community producing slate, granite sets and blocks and bricks, which were sent out by ship to towns and cities around the country; many municipal buildings are built of Porthgain granite. The village and the nearby coastline are littered with industrial remains. **Harbour Lights** is a friendly restaurant near the harbour — they even provided, unasked, an impromptu birthday cake for a 12-year-old.

Return to Llanrian, where turn left, following the road through Trevine and the tiny beachside hamlet of Abercastle and then inland a little through Granston. Our goal is **Strumble Head**, a rocky headland with a lighthouse (now unmanned) at its tip, reached along a succession of steep, narrow lanes. This is a fine place, just right for a breezy walk and excellent for bird-watching. The Head is clear of the surrounding coastline, and is also near the Irish Sea, which is a major 'fly-way' for migrating birds — many unusual species have been observed.

Follow lanes west past **Carregwastad Point**, where a disorganised group of French troops staged an abortive invasion in 1797, and eventually downhill into Goodwick and Fishguard. **FISHGUARD** served briefly as a port of call for Atlantic liners before the First World War, and later became a major port for Ireland. The upper town has some pleasant old streets and buildings, while in the lower town, further east, cottages cluster around a charming small harbour; *Under Milk Wood* was filmed here in 1971. TIC in the Town Hall (0348–873484).

Follow A487 east to **NEWPORT**, flanked on one side by some attractive sandy beaches, on the other by the peaks of the Preseli Hills, 1,760ft at their highest point. This likeable small town would make a good base for exploring the hills and the northern half of Pembrokeshire — different in character, for we are now in the Welsh-speaking districts. **Cnapan** (0239–820575) in East Street is a pleasant guest house that also serves delicious food. National Park Information Office in Bank Cottages, Long Street (0239–820912).

The 90 massive stones used to build Stonehenge were carried from **Carn Ingli Common**, in the hills about 1 mile south of the town. Early remains in the form of hut circles are visible on the Common.

Continuing east along A487, you pass the Iron Age hill fort at **Castle Henleys** (*open Easter and late May–mid-Sept daily*). Here traditional archaeological excavation has been taken a stage further, and the huts and stables of this 2,000-year-old settlement have been reconstructed; contemporary vegetables and herbs are grown, and contemporary crafts practised. It's an ideal place for giving children a feel for the remote past: there's room to rush around and pretend to be an ancient warrior.

Just before Eglwyswrw, turn sharp right on to B4329, which climbs to the summit of the Preseli Hills. In about 4 miles, at Brynberian, a minor road to the right leads to the huge **Pentre Ifan** burial chamber, or *cromlech*: three tall pillars and a massive capstone, some 17ft by 10ft and weighing 14 tons. This is the most impressive of the many stone circles, forts and trackways that ancient man constructed in the Preseli Hills.

Return to B4329. At the summit, there's a fine walk east on the **Bronze Age Road** along the summit ridge of the hills. Paths to the south lead to old slate quarries. The National Park organises guided walks in the hills, as well as along the coast; enquire at an Information Office.

B4329 returns direct to Haverfordwest, passing *en route* **Scolton Country Park** (*country park open daily except Mon, museum June–Sept daily except Mon*). Here, in 40 acres of landscaped grounds and woodlands, there are a butterfly garden, countryside exhibits and regular special events; the museum contains displays of natural and human history.

## Across Central Wales

*2–3 days/about 240 miles/from Aberystwyth/OS maps 135, 147, 137, 136, 126, 125*

Starting at the wide sweep of Cardigan Bay, this grand circuit runs through some of the remotest parts of central Wales, traditionally the least visited and least developed region of the Principality. The landscape is largely mountainous, rugged peaks and rushing streams, wild moorland and hidden lakes gradually giving way as England approaches to a softer, more pastoral scene. We make a brief cross-border incursion, but then return to Wales. Most of the route lies within what was, for a century or so in the early Middle Ages before the final subjection of Wales, the independent kingdom of Powys. There are some narrow switchback roads on this route: drive slowly, and don't try to force the pace.

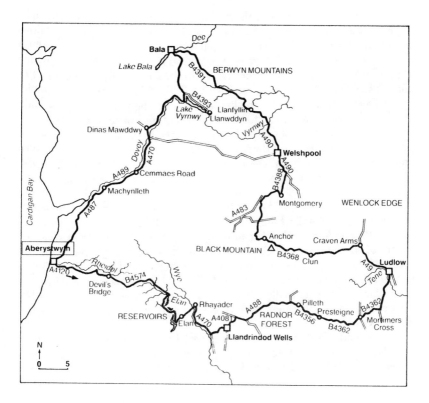

**ABERYSTWYTH** combines being a seaside resort, regional administrative and commercial centre, and university town. The National Library
of Wales and most of the university buildings, which include an Arts
Centre, stand on the hill overlooking the town. Down by the sea, the
town centre has some charming early 19th-century buildings. The ruins of
the 13th-century castle guard the harbour entrance and the seafront. At
the northern end of the promenade, you can ascend Constitution Hill by
means of the **Aberystwyth Electric Railway**, a funicular built at the very
end of the 19th century, or else walk up by the zig-zag path. The Railway
leads to the **Camera Obscura** (*both open Easter–Oct daily*), whose huge
lens gives wide views of the coastline and the mountains behind. See also
**Ceredigion Museum** (*open April–Oct daily*), which has displays on local
history and traditional life (Ceredigion = Cardiganshire). **Connexion** in
Bridge Street is a lively bistro. There are lots of hotels and guest houses in
Aber (as the town is generally called); try **Belle Vue Royal Hotel** (0970–
617558), overlooking the sea, or — in pleasant country 3 miles south of
the town — **Conrah Country Hotel** (0970–617941). TIC in Eastgate
(0970–612125/611955).

Leave town east on A4120, which reaches Devil's Bridge through hills directly above the Rheidol Valley, and parallel to the **Vale of Rheidol Light Railway**. At the time of writing, this line is operated by British Rail, although attempts are being made to sell it to a private operator. It is BR's only steam-operated and only narrow-gauge (1ft 11½in) line, and was originally built to carry ore from the lead mines of the Rheidol valley to the coast. (*Trains run Easter–Oct daily; tel. 0970–612378 for details.*)

At **Devil's Bridge**, where the line terminates, the river Mynach meets the Rheidol, tumbling some 300ft in a series of magnificent waterfalls set amid a beautiful wooded gorge. There are three bridges almost on top of each other — the devil's is the lowest, dating from the 12th century. It's a steep climb down to the falls — expect crowds, for this is a popular beauty spot. There are many other attractive waymarked walks and trails round and about.

Strike off east along B4574, at first past stretches of Forestry Commission forest. A 1½-mile Forest Trail starts at The Arch, 2 miles out of Devil's Bridge. Where the B road turns sharp right back on itself shortly before Cwmystwyth, keep to the minor road, straight on, which climbs through the village and then out into ever higher and remoter country towards the source of the river Ystwyth. Beyond the watershed, the infant river Elan, which eventually joins the Wye, accompanies the road. This is a vast and lonely wilderness, with scarcely a sign of human habitation for many miles.

In the early 20th century, four great lakes were carved out of the moorland to provide water for the people of Birmingham; a fifth was added after the Second World War, bringing total capacity to 22 million

*The sheep market at Rhayader*

gallons. Turning right at the head of the highest, Craig Goch, follow the road down the west side of this reservoir and of wooded Pen-y-garreg, and then down the east bank of Garreg Ddu. Water — sparkling blue in sunshine, a hostile grey in wind and rain — mountainside and the grey stone retaining walls (only Claerwen, finished in the 1950s, is built of concrete) make a spectacular combination. The reservoirs are renowned as a bird-watching centre — if you are lucky, you might see red kite, peregrine and merlin hovering over the hills — and the fishing is good.

At the foot of Garreg Ddu, follow the road east alongside the head of Caban Coch, the lowest of the reservoirs, and past Elan Village and the **Elan Valley visitor centre** (*open Easter–Oct daily*). Here are displays on the history and natural history of the area, audio-visual shows and a restaurant. Guided walks are also organised.

B4518 runs east into **RHAYADER** (Rhaeadr), a small market town tucked into a curve of the river Wye; the livestock markets (cattle, sheep and ponies) are famous throughout Wales. **Elan Valley Hotel** (0597–810448) is one of the many places to stay locally, **Workhouse Restaurant** in South Street one of the eating places. TIC in The Old Swan, West Street (0597–810591).

Follow the main A470 south out of the town, through lovely country alongside the Wye, and then bear left on to A4081. This road leads to **LLANDRINDOD WELLS**, an elegant, spacious Victorian health resort, full of well-kept parks and gardens. You can drink the waters of the chalybeate spring in the Pump Room, and for a week in late summer the town goes properly Victorian during the annual Victorian Festival; everyone dons appropriate costume, and much suitable entertainment is staged. The **museum** (*open Mon–Fri and Sat mornings*) illustrates local life from Roman times onwards, paying special attention to the growth of the spa; there are reconstructions of a Victorian kitchen, a chemist's shop and a pharmacy. The town would make an excellent exploring base for the surrounding countryside. **Hotel Metropole** (0597–2881) is an imposing Edwardian building in Temple Street in the centre of town, **Kincoed Hotel** (0597–2656) a smaller establishment in the same street. TIC in Rock Park Spa (0597–2600).

Leave along A483 north. Soon turn right on to A44, and then left on to A488, which runs north-west past Radnor Forest, a large stretch of hilly, often thickly wooded country. This is very much border country, scattered with the remains of castles and fortified places — both Welsh and English — strategically sited on spurs of rock commanding the river and stream valleys. A right turn on to B4356 brings you to **PILLETH**, a hamlet where in 1402 the supporters of Owain Glyndwr vanquished the English under the Earl of Mortimer; this was the first success in Glyndwr's long, ultimately unsuccessful, campaign to restore an independent Welsh state. Offa's Dyke, and the present-day **Offa's Dyke Path** (see page 80) cross the road east of Pilleth.

B4356 runs alongside the river Lugg into **PRESTEIGNE**, an attractive town with many black-and-white half-timbered buildings characteristic of the Marches. The **Radnorshire Arms** (0544–267406) in the High Street, established as an inn in the late 18th century, is a fine example. (The name Marches is given to the country on the English/Welsh border, where the feudal Norman marcher lords held sway.) The church (11th–15th century) contains a 16th-century Flemish tapestry. TIC in the Old Market Hall (0544–260193).

B4362 east from Presteigne enters England almost immediately and crosses A4110 at **MORTIMER'S CROSS**. Here, in 1461, the Yorkist forces under Edward Mortimer, Earl of March, won the crucial and bloody victory over the Lancastrian supporters of Henry VI that paved the way for his coronation, in London 19 months later, as Edward VI; some 4,000 men lost their lives. The **water mill** (*EH, open mid-March–mid-Oct Thur, Sun and Bank Holiday Mons*), built in the 18th century, was in use as recently as the 1940s.

Crossing the Lugg once more, stay on B4362, which passes the entrance to **Croft Castle** (*NT, open May–Sept Wed–Sun and Bank Holiday Mon afternoons, also weekend afternoons in April and Oct*). The Croft family has owned the castle since the time of the Norman Conquest, with the exception of a long gap from 1750 until the 1920s. They were great builders, for the walls and corner towers date from the 14th and 15th century, when this corner of Herefordshire was much trampled on by opposing armies, the battlemented facade from the 16th and 17th, while the interior was redesigned in the 18th, with some gorgeous plasterwork and a fine staircase. Footpaths through the park (*NT, open daily*), which contains an impressive avenue of 350-year-old Spanish chestnuts, climb up to Croft Ambrey, an Iron Age hill fort.

**LUDLOW** is our next destination, reached along B4362 and then left on to B4361 beneath steep and wooded hills. The town grew up round the Norman **castle** (*open daily except Jan and Dec*), strategically positioned on a bend in the river Tene; the chapel is Norman, the Great Hall dates from the early 14th century. The huge tower and that of St. Laurence church (the latter is taller) are both Ludlow landmarks. Inside the sandstone church, built in the 15th century, is a fine oak roof and vivacious carvings on the misericords, said to be among the best sets in the country. Castle and church are almost the only stone buildings in the town. The rest are brick (mostly Georgian) and timber-framed. Broad Street is astonishing: an almost complete street of 16th-and 17th-century houses, many with elaborate decorative details. The **museum** in Buttercross (*open April–Sept Mon–Sat, also June–Aug Suns*) covers the town's history from Norman times to the present day.

Take time to stroll around: Ludlow is one of Britain's finest country towns and well repays attention. Look especially at the Reader's House in the churchyard (part medieval, part 17th century), at the **Feathers Hotel** in Bull Ring (0584–5261) — as elaborate inside as it is outside — and at the **Angel** (0584–2581) in Broad Street. **Hardwick's** in Quality Square is well situated in a courtyard. TIC in Castle Street (0584–3857). The highlight of the annual Ludlow Festival, in late June and early July,is a Shakespeare play performed in the magical setting of the castle.

Ludlow castle was built to fend off the threat from the distant Welsh hills, towards which we now turn, for this drive penetrates no further into England. First there's a stretch of main road driving north on A49 to Craven Arms at the southern end of Wenlock Edge, a distinctive range of wooded hills. About 1 mile south of Craven Arms, directly off A49, **Stokesay Castle** (*open Mar–Oct daily except Tues, also Nov weekends*) is a fortified manor house built in the late 13th century. Its situation is delightful, with an early 17th-century half-timbered gatehouse and a church standing beside a small lake.

Turn left in Craven Arms and head west on B4368 along the Clun valley. The present-day tranquillity of the Cluns — immortalised as the 'four quietest places under the sun' in A.E. Housman's poem 'A Shropshire Lad' — belies their turbulent past, when this was frontier territory. Clunton succeeds Clunbury, and then comes **CLUN**, which the Welsh burnt down no fewer than four times between 1195 and 1400. The ruined Norman **castle** (*open daily*) stands high above a bend in the river. There's a **museum** (*open Easter–Nov Tues and Sat afternoons, also all day Bank Holiday weekends*) in the Georgian gaol, and a medieval saddle-back bridge across the river.

Increasingly lonely country lies ahead along B4368, which heads through Newcastle to the border just beyond Anchor, with its ancient inn of the same name. South of the road lies Black Mountain (1,469ft), north of the road Clun Forest, which is not a forest at all but a succession of rounded moorland hills dotted with earthworks and fortifications. The Clun and Kerry breeds of sheep come from hereabouts. B4368 crosses A489 just east of Kerry, but continue straight on, eventually descending to A483 at Abermule in the rich, green Severn valley.

A few miles away in **MONT-GOMERY**, east along B4386 from the main road, the **castle** (*CADW, standard opening times*) was built by Henry III in the 1220s and 1230s to guard the route into Wales along the Severn valley; only ruins now remain. In the town, which has maintained its medieval plan, are some attractive Georgian buildings, a 14th-century church and an appealing feeling of tranquillity.

Drive north on B4388, turning left on to A490 and then right on to A483 for Welshpool. One mile south of the town, the road passes **Powis Castle** (*NT, open April–Oct daily except Mon and Tues, also Tues in July and Aug and all Bank Holiday Mons*). This magnificent pile originated in

*Clun Castle*

the 13th century as a castle (when the square tower and stone hall were built), but has been much altered since then, both in the 16th century, when the Herbert family moved in, and again in the 19th. Inside there is a large collection of treasures, including weapons, paintings, tapestries, and a new museum devoted to the life of Clive of India. The lovely gardens and park were landscaped by Capability Brown. National Trust restaurant.

**WELSHPOOL** itself is the county town of Powys and a lively local centre with a good variety of shops and pleasant 18th-century buildings. One gruesome curiosity is the 18th-century hexagonal **Cockpit** (*open April–Sept Mon–Fri*), where cock-fighting took place at least until the 'sport' was outlawed in 1849, and probably illegally for some time after that. Among its local history collection, **Powysland Museum** (*open Mon–Fri and Sat afternoon, but closed Weds Oct–Easter*) has displays on cock-fighting. Just north of the town centre on A483 is the **Moors Collection** (*open mid-April–Oct Thurs–Mon*), a collection of poultry, waterfowl, pheasants, sheep and horses, including many rare breeds. There are good towpath walks along the **Montgomery Canal**, which runs through the town, and boat trips as well. A haven for wildlife, the canal was abandoned in 1944, but is now slowly being restored. Among the local restaurants is the **Granary** in the High Street. TIC in Vicarage Garden Car Park (0938–2043/4038).

Welshpool is also one terminus of the **Welshpool and Llanfair Light Railway** whose international collection of locomotives has been operating steam-hauled services since 1963. The line, which was built to a 2ft 6in gauge, originally opened in 1902 as part of the Great Western Railway, and finally closed in 1956. The main terminus of the line is 8 miles west at **LLANFAIR CAERINION**, where spare locos and rolling stock are on show. (*Trains run Easter–early Oct weekends, daily in Bank Holiday weeks and early July–early Sept, and on Tues–Thur in late June and early July; tel. 0938–810441 for details.*)

But we head north from Welshpool on A490, which, after crossing the river Vyrnwy, begins the long climb into the Berwyn Mountains. A490 ceases at **LLANFYLLIN**, a pleasing little market town alongside the wooded river Cain. B4391 heads north-west across the hills, descending to run alongside the river Tanat between Penybontfawr and Llangynog, and then climbing once more to cross the high moorland. Moel Sych (2,713ft) is the main peak on the right, Pont Cwm-byden (2,127ft) on the left.

This spectacular drive ends with the descent to the wooded Dee valley, across the head of Bala Lake to **BALA**, a mountain town that is a good base for exploring north into Snowdonia. There are interesting shops and lots of sporting activities. Stay at **Plas Coch Hotel** (0678–520309) in the High Street, or a little way outside the town at **Pen Isar Llan Farm Guest House** (0678–520507). Snowdonia National Park Information Centre in the High Street (0678–520367).

**Bala Lake** (Llyn Tegid) is Wales' largest natural lake. Along the south side runs the track of **Bala Lake Railway**, an enthusiast-operated narrow-gauge steam line from Llanuwchilyn to Bala. (*Trains run Easter–Sept daily* *except Mon and Fri, but also those days Bank Holiday weeks and in July and Aug; tel. 06784–666 for details.)*

Head south now, retracing our route on B4391 for about 1 mile, and then turning right to take an unclassified road that climbs through a thickly wooded valley to emerge on to the bare tops over Rhiw Hirnant Pass (1,641ft). This is a steep and difficult road, but an exhilarating one too.

The eventual descent brings us to the head of **Lake Vyrnwy**. The largest lake in Wales, 5 miles long and nearly a mile wide, it was created in the 1880s to supply water to Liverpool. The setting is marvellous, the water ringed by forests and mountains; there are excellent walks, fishing and bird-watching.

Follow the perimeter road, B4393, around the north side of the lake to **LLANWDDYN**. The original site of this small village is now underwater; it was dismantled and rebuilt as part of the reservoir project. **Vyrnwy Visitor Centre** (*open June–Sept daily, also weekends in April and May*), which occupies a former chapel, tells the story of the lake's creation and explains its effects on the local environment. Nearby, **Lake Vyrnwy Hotel** (069173–692) has magnificent views over the lake.

Continue on B4393 along the lake's south side. Shortly before the full circuit is complete, turn left on to the unclassified road that follows a tiny stream up into the mountains and then descends very steeply alongside Afon Dyfi (the river Dovey) to Dinas Mawddwy. From here, it is a matter of hugging the Dyfi, at first south along A470, then turning right at Cemmaes Road on to A489. These roads are liable to be crowded at holiday times, but unfortunately there is no avoiding them.

It was at **MACHYNLLETH** that in 1404 Owain Glyndwr was proclaimed king of an independent Wales, in the year when his revolt against English dominion was at its height. (Within six years, Welsh resistance had been crushed, and Glyndwr himself had vanished.) The majestic 19th-century Clock Tower marks the town centre. Nearby, Glyndwr's Parliament House has been incorporated into **Canolfan (Centre) Owain Glyndwr** (*generally open June–Aug daily, enquire at TIC in case of difficulty*), which contains displays on Glyndwr's campaigns and on the story of the earlier Welsh princes. The TIC (0654–2401) is part of a **Visitor Centre** (*open Easter–Oct daily, Mon–Fri in winter*) covering the history and natural history of the Dyfi Valley, including such topics as the slate and wool industries and the development of Nonconformist churches. The **Quarry Shop** in Maengwyn Street is a vegetarian restaurant run by the Centre for Alternative Technology (see below). Stay at **Wynnstay Arms Hotel** (0654–2941), also in Maengwyn Street.

The **Centre for Alternative Technology** (*open daily*) on A489 3 miles north of Machynlleth is well worth visiting for its stimulating and practical ideas about developing renewable technologies that reduce pollution and save resources. Among the displays are a conservation house, various forms of solar energy, water turbines, an organic vegetable garden and an ecological gardening display. There's a restaurant and a well-stocked bookshop.

From Machynlleth, return to Aberystwyth along A487.

# 4 THE WEST COUNTRY

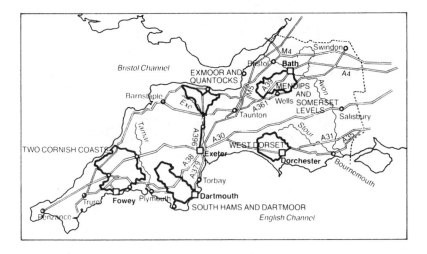

Stand alongside the M5 motorway or any west country main road on a Saturday in high summer, and nose-to-tail traffic will provide living proof that the west country is Britain's most popular holiday area. This is hardly surprising, given that its coastline supplies all the ingredients of the traditional holiday recipe: stretches of golden sand, generally safe bathing in water as warm as can be found anywhere off the British Isles, and a reasonable chance of fine weather. The two coasts have quite different characters, rugged in the north (where there are some fine surfing spots), gentler in the south, with many long, secluded estuaries. But the explorer who sticks only to the coastline misses much, for inland there is a striking diversity of scenery. Best known are the peninsula's three great stretches of heathery, peaty moorland, Exmoor, Dartmoor and Bodmin Moor. Below these wild tops lies a more pastoral landscape, of farmsteads and small villages nestling in wooded valleys, banks and meadows strewn with wild flowers, and crystal-clear rushing streams. There is much history in evidence too: the fortifications and places of worship of ancient societies, sites traditionally associated with the legendary King Arthur and, from much nearer our own time, the remains of the once flourishing tin- and lead-mining industries.

95

# The Mendips and the Somerset Levels

*2 days/about 85 miles/from Bath/OS maps 172, 182, 183*

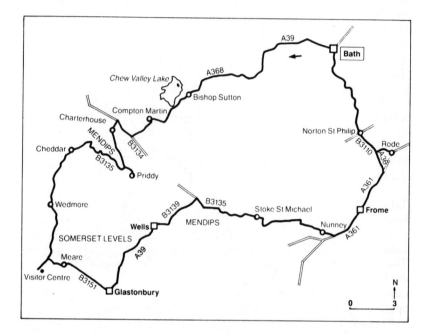

The limestone Mendip Hills, honeycombed with caverns and underground rivers and scored by great rugged gorges, and the flat expanse of the watery Somerset Levels are the main landscapes of this drive. Both have an intriguing air of mystery — perhaps because these ancient landscapes are traditionally associated with still potent myths and legends. A highlight of the tour is Wells, the smallest and perhaps the most perfect cathedral city in England.

We start with a contrast, for **BATH** (pop. 82,700) is hardly rural — indeed it represents a pinnacle of urban civilisation. Take time though to explore its elegant classical squares, crescents and terraces, laid out in the 18th century when the city became *the* fashionable centre for society. **Number 1 Royal Crescent** (*open March–Oct Tues–Sat*) is furnished as it would have been in the city's heyday two centuries ago, including a period kitchen. Look particularly at the superb sweep of Royal Crescent, 30 villas long, at Queen Square and The Circus, and at Landsdowne Terrace, with its commanding view over the city. Bath — better known then as *Aquae Sulis* — was also a popular resort in Roman days; the **Roman Baths Museum** (*open daily*), built around the remarkably well-preserved remains of pools, saunas and Turkish baths, tells their story in an interesting and unstuffy style. You can drink spa water, or take tea if you would rather, in the 18th-century **Pump Room** (*open daily*) above the Roman bath. Next door is the late 15th-century **Bath Abbey**. See also the **Assembly Rooms** (*open daily*), which house the **Museum of Costume** (*open daily*) with collections from the 16th century to the present day; and the **Botanical Gardens** (*open daily*). Shopping in Bath is excellent — clothes, paintings, pottery and other craft items, antiques, books — and a pleasure too in attractive streets and passageways. The city has a lively cultural life; try to take in a performance at the restored Georgian **Theatre Royal**, or come for the **Bath Festival**, which attracts top-class performers each June. Two of the city's many excellent eating places are the **Theatre Vaults** in Sawflies behind the theatre — pre-show dinner is served — and **Number Five** in Argyle Street, near Pulteney Bridge over the river Avon. Places to stay range from the luxury **Royal Crescent Hotel** (0225–319090) to more modest establishments such as the **Strathavon Private Hotel** (0225–23068). TIC in the Abbey Church Yard (0225–62831).

Take A39 west from Bath, turn right after 6 miles on to A368 shortly beyond Marksbury, and continue on this road for about another 6 miles, through Chelwood and Bishop Sutton and then alongside **Chew Valley Lake**, a reservoir used for sailing, trout-fishing and wildfowl-watching. There's a picnic area along this stretch of road. With the sharp cliffs of the hills coming ever closer, continue on A368 to Compton Martin, and turn left at the start of the village on to the unclassified road that climbs up, past a viewpoint, to the high plateau of the Mendips.

This seems flat, lonely and somewhat dull countryside at first sight — at least until a little geology and history puts it all in context. There are no surface streams flowing down from the Mendips. Instead, rainwater drains directly into the limestone or disappears through small fissures — swallets or slockers as they are known locally — to re-emerge many miles away at the foot of the hills. Inside the rock, the rushing, swirling, dripping of the water over many millions of years has carved out an enormous network about 30 miles long of chambers and passages, full of fantastical shapes and vivid colours. Often small depressions in the ground, especially noticeable after heavy rain, are the only indication of this below-surface world.

The Mendips are one of the most popular caving areas in Britain, attracting many enthusiasts each weekend — new discoveries are still being made. But don't go exploring on your own; contact a club if you want to try caving — if not, visit the spectacular show caves at Cheddar (see below) or Wookey Hole.

On the surface, the main activities have been mining and sheep-farming. The Romans mined lead and silver near Charterhouse, and in the Middle Ages lead-mining resumed around Priddy. The last lead mine closed in 1908, but the hills are still quarried for limestone.

To resume our drive, turn right off the unclassified road from Compton Martin on to B3134 and then left after about 2 miles on to another minor road, which brings you round, after another right turn, to

*Cheddar Gorge*

**Charterhouse**. There's an interesting walk from the car park around the old mine workings. Back on the road again, continue roughly south-west for about 2 miles, across B3371, to B3135. Continue straight on here to **PRIDDY**, where sheep hurdles are stacked on the village green in readiness for the annual Sheep Fair towards the end of August. There are many prehistoric remains in the fields around the village — long barrows and, to the north, the neolithic Priddy Circles. At over 1,000ft, Priddy is Mendip's highest village.

Return to B3135 and turn left to begin the long and dramatic descent of **Cheddar Gorge**, between great towering walls of bare rock. It is a shame that the bottom of the gorge is ruined by tawdry commercialisation — stop instead about a third of the way down, where a 1½-mile circular walk through Black Rock Nature Reserve leads off to the right.

Despite the surrounding mess, **Cheddar Caves** (*open daily*) at the foot of the gorge are a wonderful introduction to the underground world of stalagmites and stalactites, pools and grottos. The **Museum** (*open daily Easter–Sept*) contains displays on prehistory, with the 10,000-year-old Cheddar Man as the centrepiece, and there's also a fantasy grotto with a hologram exhibition. The TIC (0934–744071) is also in the Gorge. The nearby **Wishing Well Tea Rooms** are open all day for snacks, lunch and traditional cream teas.

B3151 runs south from Cheddar across the **Somerset Levels**. Originally an area of peaty marshland, crossed by rivers, frequently flooded and interrupted by small outcrops of harder rock (as at Glastonbury — see below), the Levels were drained and enclosed in the late 18th and early 19th centuries. Dead-straight ditches, called rhynes (pronounced 'reenes'), were built to draw off the water, and the present pattern of roads and fields was created. The rhynes feed rivers and artificial channels that eventually flow into the sea. Traditional farming methods — whereby cattle are grazed on the low-lying meadows in summer and then spend the winter on higher ground or near the farm — have lasted longer on the Levels than in many other parts of the country. Modern drainage techniques and more intensive farming methods, including greater use of weed-killers and fertilisers, could make this rich land even more productive — but at the expense of its unique character and extensive wildlife. Although the government is providing some financial assistance to farmers who stick to traditional methods, the threat to the Levels has by no means vanished.

The wildlife of the Levels is unusually rich, and many meadow flowers that have disappeared from more intensively farmed land still flourish. There are rare butterflies, such as the marsh fritillary, and otters; large

*Glastonbury Tor*

colonies of waders breed here, while wildfowl return from migration to winter on the Levels. Large numbers of willows grow on the banks of the rhynes, and basket-making remains an important local industry.

**WEDMORE**, astride a low ridge, is an attractive small town with 18th- and 19th-century stone houses and a large 15th-century parish church, whose features include a fine west front and south door (built about 1200) and, inside, a 17th-century pulpit. In 878, the Peace of Wedmore was agreed here between Alfred, King of Wessex, and the Danish leader Gudrum. Alfred led guerilla attacks against the Danish invaders from his stronghold at Athelney, further south on the Levels.

Continue south on B3151, which crosses North Drain, one of the main drainage channels, to Westhay, where take the unclassified road towards Shapwick. This soon reaches the **Peat Moors Visitor Centre** (*open daily*), which has displays on the history and natural history of the Levels, including reconstructions of the prehistoric timber tracks built across the marshes up to 9,000 years ago, and claimed to be the oldest man-made roads in the world.

Return now to Westhay, and turn right on to B3151. *En route* to Glastonbury — the Tor (520ft) is visible from miles off across this flat landscape — the road passes through **MEARE**, which until the 18th century lay beside a marshy lake, used in medieval times as a fish-pool for the Abbot of Glastonbury. The 14th-century **fish house** was built for the abbey official in charge of the fisheries, and was used for salting and storing the catch. (*EH, open any reasonable time — key from Manor House farm.*) Long before then, from about BC300 to 100AD, Meare was the site of a 'lake village', a small settlement of huts, built on wooden stilts to keep them clear of the marsh, whose inhabitants farmed the land immediately around. Finds from excavations here are displayed in Glastonbury Tribunal (see below).

Much myth surrounds **GLASTONBURY**, the Isle of Avalon of Arthurian legend, and the town is still a place of pilgrimage. At the beginning of the Christian era, a weary Joseph of Arimathea is said to have stuck his staff into the hillside where he sat down to rest. The staff took root and produced the winter-flowering thorn-tree, whereupon Joseph built a simple church and made the first conversions to Christianity in these islands. He is also said to have buried the chalice used at the Last Supper under the waters of a spring on the Tor. So far, however, no archaeological evidence has been produced to support any of these legends — the oldest find has been from the 7th century, while the abbey was founded by St. Dunstan in the mid-10th century. And whether the body of Arthur, a semi-mythical leader who led the West Country resistance to the Saxon invasions in the 5th and 6th centuries, really was brought to Avalon is also uncertain. After the abbey was burnt down at the end of the 12th century, a tomb inscribed as Arthur's was discovered in the ruins — but was it genuine or simply an attempt to boost the medieval tourist trade?

After climbing the Tor — good views all round, if it's wet it's easy to take yourself back to the time when the Tor was surrounded by miles of inaccessible peaty marsh — visit the **Abbey** ruins (*open daily*), and the **Somerset Rural Life Museum** (*open daily, but not Sat and Sun mornings*) in the 14th-century abbey barn, where the displays illustrate the traditional cycle of the farming year and local industries such as cider-making and peat-growing; the late 19th-century abbey farmhouse portrays the life of a local Victorian farm worker. **St John's Church** (15th-century) has a fine tower, and in the medieval courthouse, known as the **Tribunal** (*EH, standard opening times*), there is an exhibition of objects from the lake village. The mid-15th century **George and Pilgrims Hotel** (0458–31146) has a magnificent panelled facade, and retains the design of a traditional inn. **Rainbow's End Café** in the High Street serves vegetarian and wholefood dishes. TIC in Marchant's Buildings on Northload Street (0458–32954).

*The Chapter House steps, Wells Cathedral*

From Glastonbury, it's 5 miles along A39 to **WELLS**. The centre-piece of the town is the **cathedral**, built between about 1180 and the 1420s. Several hundred statues, each in its own niche, adorn the magnificent west front. Inside, there is a riot of stone carving, with abundant foliage and scenes from everyday life — including people suffering from tooth-ache and an old man being punished for stealing grapes. The great curved scissor arches were built in 1338 to support the massive tower, which was threatening to collapse. A graceful stone staircase leads up to the Chapter House, whose fan-vaulted ceiling is supported by a single central column, while the nearby astronomical clock marks each quarter hour with jousting knights — the same poor horseman is knocked off every time! The cloisters lead to the 15th-century library, which has a collection of medieval chained books and manuscripts.

In the cathedral precincts, see the 14th-century terraced houses of Vicars' Close, said to be Europe's oldest complete street. The originally 13th-century Bishop's Palace (*open Easter–Oct Thur and Sun, also Wed May–Sept*) is enclosed by a walled moat, where the swans used to ring the Gatehouse bell at meal times; whether through greed or exhibitionism, they rang so often that the bell had to be removed. Take time to explore the rest of the town, which has a lively market every Wed and Sat, and some interesting shops, including an excellent cheese merchant. The water from the natural springs in the Bishop's Palace grounds, that flows down open channels on each side of the High Street, was a gift from a medieval bishop to the people of the city. There are several old coaching inns such as the **Swan** (0749–78877) and the **White Hart** (0749–72056). The **Cloister Restaurant** provides bodily refreshment to supplement the cathedral's spiritual nourishment. TIC in the Town Hall, Market Place (0749–72552).

Leave the city on B3139 travelling north-east, and turn right on to B3135 after about 3 miles. This is a lonely road running along the eastern end of the Mendip range. At the junction with A37, turn right and immediately left on to a minor road. Cross A367 in Oakhill and follow the unclassified road through some pretty villages, Stoke St. Michael and Leigh upon Mendip; there is a good deal of roadstone quarrying in this area.

Bear right for **NUNNEY**, where the towers of the small moated 14th-century castle (*EH, open any reasonable time*) withstood attack during the Civil War. Attractive streets of stone 17th- and 18th-century cottages converge on a market square with a medieval cross.

Beyond the village, a left turn on to A361 takes you close to **Whatley Vineyard and Herb Garden** (*open Tues–Sun and Bank Holiday Mons*) into **FROME**. The town grew prosperous from the cloth industry, then declined in the early 19th century when the industrial revolution removed trade to the mills of the north. There are many well-preserved streets and alleyways to explore, including Cheap Street, lined with medieval buildings and with a water-course down the centre, Sheppard's Barton, a complete row of 18th-century weavers' cottages (Mr Sheppard, the clothier, lived in the manse at one end) and late 17th-century industrial housing in the Trinity quarter. The town is a bustling small commercial and market centre, without too much tourism, and so it's an excellent place for browsers too — whether for books or antiques. **Frome Museum** (*open Wed–Sat*) occupies part of the 1868 Frome Literary and Scientific Institute on North Parade and contains displays on local geology, archaeology and industry, plus a replica of a local pharmacy. **Jenner's** at the **Black Swan**, part of a craft centre on Bridge Street, serves tempting wholefood and vegetarian dishes. The **George** pub (0373–62584) occupies a central position on the market place. TIC in the Cattle Market Car Park (0373–67271).

For the last leg of this trip, back to Bath, take A361 north out of Frome, and bear left in Beckington on to A36. A right turn on to a minor road in Wolverton brings you to **RODE**, where many species of exotic birds can be seen in attractive landscaped gardens at the **Tropical Bird Gardens** (*open daily*).

Return to Wolverton, and follow B3110 through Norton St Philip. The **George Inn** at **NORTON ST PHILIP** started life as the wool store of the local priory; it was also used as a guest-house for merchants who came to buy at the village's two annual wool fairs. The oldest parts of the building date from the 14th century, and the half-timbered upper stories were added in the 15th. Following the dissolution of the monasteries in 1539 it became an inn.

Stay on B3110 to return to Bath.

## Exmoor and the Quantocks
*2–3 days/about 140 miles/from Exeter/OS maps 192, 180, 181*

Exmoor, home of red deer, shaggy, half-wild ponies and of countless sheep, is the principal focus of this route. There is marvellous scenery here: high, heather-carpeted moorland, hidden combes rich in wild flowers, sparkling rivers and a rugged coastline. Further east lie the rolling Quantock Hills, gentler and more wooded than Exmoor, but with equally fine walking and — an advantage in summer, when Exmoor's best-known beauty spots become clogged with crowds — far fewer people.

**EXETER** (pop. 86,500), all too often by-passed by visitors intent on destinations further west, has some attractive historic quarters, despite heavy bombing during the war and some remarkably insensitive rebuilding afterwards. The **cathedral**, built c. 1260–1394, is famous for its 300ft nave, whose columns dissolve in delicate fan-shaped patterns on the roof. Admire also the fine carving on the choir stalls, the bishop's throne, and the painted statues on the minstrel's gallery. Outside, statues of Saxon and Norman military leaders and monarchs stand in niches on the west front. The **cathedral close** has a pleasant mixture of domestic buildings of all ages, while nearby **Southernhay** is a Georgian terrace. In the centre are many interesting buildings reflecting the city's early prosperity as a centre of cloth manufacturing and trading: for instance, the 14th-century **Guildhall** (*open Mon–Sat*), where council meetings are still held, and the tiny 11th-century **St. Pancras Church**. Museums include the **Royal Albert Memorial Museum** (*open Tues–Sat*), with paintings by west country artists, a collection of Exeter silver and displays on local natural history and archaeology, and, near the remains of the Norman castle, the **Rougemont House Museum of Costume and Lace** (*open Mon–Sat*), where the exhibits include some exquisite examples of local lace, from Honiton in east Devon. The **Maritime Museum** (*open daily*), built around the 17th-century Custom House and other historic warehouses alongside the quay, boasts over 130 craft from every part of the world. It's a hands-on place — visitors are encouraged to explore many of the vessels for themselves. **Clare's Restaurant** in Princessay is spoken of highly as a cheap and cheerful place to eat, or else try **Coolings Wine Bar** in Gandy Street. The 200-year-old **Royal Clarence Hotel** (0392–58464) overlooking the cathedral claims to be the first establishment ever described as a 'hotel', while the **White Hart** (0392–79897) started life as an inn in the 15th century. TIC in the Civic Centre, Paris Street (0392–265297), and also in the service station at junction 30 of M5 motorway (0392–37581/79088), on the edge of the city.

While less spectacular than either the moors or the coast, the rolling farmland immediately around Exeter has an appealing pastoral quality. We set off north on A396, alongside the river Exe, which, although it reaches the sea below Exeter, has its source high on Exmoor, almost within sight and sound of the Atlantic coast. Set between wooded hills, **BICKLEIGH** is a charming riverside village of thatched cottages. **Bickleigh Mill Craft Centre and Farms** (*open April–Dec daily, also Sat and Sun Jan–March*) has studios for craft workers as well as a farm run on 19th-century lines, with shire horses and oxen, and a farming museum. On the opposite bank of the Exe, across a five-arched stone bridge, is **Bickleigh Castle**, which started life as a moated Norman manor house; the chapel and gatehouse survived the Civil War. There's a variety of historical exhibitions here, including one of 18th–20th century toys and another on Second World War spy and escape gadgets. (*Open June–Sept* *afternoons except Sat, also Easter–end May Wed, Sun and Bank Holiday afternoons.*)

**TIVERTON**, a market town with plenty of quiet character and handsome buildings, tends to get overlooked by tourists, and so is worth considering as an exploring base. Cloth was the mainstay of the town's economy for several centuries; the local speciality was kersey, a coarse cloth woven from long wool. The award-winning **museum** (*open Mon–Sat*) succeeds in bringing regional history and crafts alive in a way that other museums don't always manage. The **castle** (*open May–Sept Sun–Thur*) dates from the early 12th century but was largely destroyed during the Civil War; now a private house, it contains collections of clocks and furniture and a gallery devoted to Joan of Arc. **Angel Foods** in Angel Terrace is a reasonably priced wholefood restaurant. Hotels include **Tiverton** (0884–256120) and, at the cheaper end of the scale, **Bridge Guest House** (0884–252804). TIC in Phoenix Lane (0884–255827), and also at the service station (0884–821242) at junction 27 of M5, a few miles east.

**Knightshayes Court**, off A396 at Bolham, 2 miles north of Tiverton, is the work of the Victorian architect William Burges, who produced a sequence of richly decorated interiors. Attractive gardens contain many rare species. Light meals and snacks are available in the restaurant. (*NT, garden open April–Oct daily, house afternoons except Fri.*)

A396 winds through the steep-sided, wooded river valley, past a spur to Bampton, and across A361. About 2 miles after this junction, turn left on to B3222 for Exebridge and Dulverton, the road running alongside the little river Barle. Like many places on Exmoor, **EXEBRIDGE** appeared in R.D. Blackmore's novel *Lorna Doone*; the highwayman Tom Faggus was captured here, and his mare Winnie shot in the stable of the **Anchor Inn**, still going strong today.

**DULVERTON**, hidden in a wooded valley beneath the southern edge of the moor, is an important gateway town. The headquarters of the National Park are housed in a former workhouse, and include an information centre (0398–23665).

B3223 climbs up from the town for a first taste of high Exmoor country: miles of bleak, often boggy grassland, with stretches of heather and bracken. When the sun shines, it seems an exhilarating, top-of-the-world sort of place — but lonely and menacing in driving rain or swirling mist. The prehistoric remains — round barrows, hill-forts and enclosures — scattered across the moor bear mysterious witness to the presence of settlers thousands of years ago.

Exmoor is home to the largest wild herd of red deer outside Scotland; you'll be lucky to see these elusive creatures — they tend to keep out of the way of humans, although they sometimes feed in the open in the early mornings or evenings. During the autumn rut, or mating season, wild roars, known as 'belling', echo across the heather as the stags challenge one another for the hinds. Exmoor ponies, sturdy, dun- or brown-coloured beasts with a wiry coat designed to run off the rainwater, are the descendants of wild horses that survived the Ice Age. Four pure herds

*Exmoor pony*

have been established by the National Park Authority. Yellowhammer, winchat, linnet are among the birds that make their home in the sheltered valleys, skylarks soar and sing above the open moor, while high in the sky you may spot buzzards wheeling, or falcons or hawks.

There are two diversions off B3223 in quite short succession. The first is left down a steep lane to **Tarr Steps**, a medieval clapper bridge, 17 spans and 55yds long, over the river Barle. This is a well-known beauty spot and so likely to be very crowded in high season. There is a lovely walk alongside the river upstream. (You could even walk all the way to Withypool — see below; about 4 miles.) Alternatively, to avoid the aggravating traffic blockages on the lane leading down to the Steps, park on the main road (but make sure you don't block the traffic) and walk down all the way along often muddy footpaths.

B3223 breasts Winsford Hill. Now turn left again at the crossroads and descend to **WITHYPOOL**, a lovely little stone moorland village. Leave by the minor road running north out of the village, turn left on to B3223, and keep on this road as it sweeps west across the wild central part of the Moor to **SIMONSBATH**. The **Simonsbath House Hotel** (064383–259) dates from the 1650s. This part of the moor is known as Exmoor Forest — not that it has ever been forested; the word dates from the Middle Ages, when it signified a wilderness area used for hunting.

Now turn north, still on B3223, which passes Brendon Common on the right, and then starts to descend sharply. Turn right on to A39, and then shortly right again to **Watersmeet House**, which is an 1830s fishing lodge used as a National Trust information centre and restaurant (*open April–Oct daily*). The waters that meet here are East Lyn River and Hoar Oak Water; there's a spectacular waterfall and beautiful walks.

There are two alternative routes for the next section of this drive. If you want to visit picturesque but crowded **LYNMOUTH**, a little fishing village beneath high cliffs at the meeting of the East and West Lyn Rivers, or you don't fancy following some fairly narrow and twisting minor roads, continue on A39 — but be aware that this can be crowded at high season. Beyond Lynmouth there are fine views out to sea as the road crosses Countisbury Common. (National Park Information Centre at County Gate, Countisbury — 05987–321.)

The more peaceful alternative is to return to B3223, turn left almost immediately on to a minor road which climbs across a short stretch of

*East Lyn River*

open moorland and then descends again to the lush gorge of the East Lyn. Follow this road through Brendon and the hamlet of **MALMSMEAD**, where Badgworthy Water, the heart of what is known as Lorna Doone country, meets the main river. A memorial to R.D. Blackmore stands on the banks of the little stream. In the church at **OARE**, the next village, Lorna was shot on her wedding day by Carver Doone.

Beyond Oareford, turn left on to A39, and then almost immediately right again on to an unclassified road that, twisting and turning all the time, descends to the coast at **PORLOCK WEIR**. A small toll is payable. This stretch of coast is fine walking country, with the vivid colours of gorse and heather and magnificent views; in clear weather you can see across to the South Wales coast. You can follow the coastal path back towards Lynmouth or, on the far side of Porlock, explore the headland around Selworthy Beacon, which rises to over 1,000ft.

From Porlock Weir follow B3225 into Porlock, turn left on to A39, and right again just under a mile outside the village on to a minor road leading to West Luccombe and Luccombe. Turn right at the crossroads just before Luccombe, and climb steeply first through attractive woodland and then out on to open moorland again. On the right is **Dunkery Beacon**, at 1,705ft the highest point on Exmoor. You can park and walk up gentle paths to the summit, where fine views stretch out in all directions.

Beyond Dunkery Hill, follow B3224 east to Wheddon Cross, where turn left on to A396, which runs along the wooded river Avill to **DUNSTER**. Warm stone buildings along the main street, which ends in a sharp corner around the 15th-century Nunnery, the early 17th-century covered Yarn Market, built for the sale of locally produced cloth, and the fine early 15th-century church all make this a pleasant place to stay for a night or two. The castle, situated on a wooded hill overlooking the river, dominates the village. Founded in the 11th century, it came into the hands of the Luttrell family in 1376, who held it for no less than 600 years, when the National Trust took over. The interior includes much good 17th-century work, including a carved staircase and a plaster ceiling, and 19th-century restoration. The gardens include a terrace of rare shrubs. (*NT, castle open April–Sept Sun–Thurs, also Thur afternoon in Oct; garden and park, April, May, Sept Sun–Thurs, daily June–Aug, also Sun–Thur afternoon in Oct.*) At **Dunster Water Mill** (*open daily except Sat*) you can watch flour being produced and tour a collection of old agricultural machinery. Stay here at **Exmoor House Hotel** (0643–821268) or at **Yarn Market Hotel** (0643–821425). Don't be put off by the twee name of the **Tea Shoppe** on the High Street; the tea-time cakes are excellent, as are the pies, salads, cheeses and sweets served at lunch time. National Park Information Centre in Steep Car Park (0643–821835).

We leave Exmoor behind now and, just north of the town, turn right on to A39. Follow this fast road across the coastal strip to **WASH-FORD**. On the right of the road

*The Yarn Market and Castle, Dunster*

stand the ruins of 12th-century **Cleeve Abbey** (*EH, standard opening times*).
Hardly anything remains of the church, but the living quarters have
survived, including the 15th-century refectory, which has a fine timber roof.

Turn left by the radio masts at Washford Cross on to B3190, which
runs down to the sea at **WATCHET**. The town's unassuming character
largely derives from the fact that it is still a working port, as it has been
since Anglo-Saxon times. There's generally something of interest
happening in the harbour — a freighter or coaster negotiating the narrow
harbour entrance, fishing boats setting out to sea — and it's a pleasant
place for a stroll; there's good fishing, bird-watching and boating too.
**Market House Museum** (*open May–Sept daily*) records the history of the
port. TIC in the Council Chamber.

Watchet's station is on the steam-operated **West Somerset Railway**,
which runs between Minehead and Bishops Lydeard, just outside
Taunton. The entire 20-mile trip — the railway is Britain's longest
preserved line — takes 1½ hours in each direction. There are generally at
least two steam-hauled trains each day between Easter and late October,
and additional diesel railcar services as well. For details tel. 0643–4996.

Leave Watchet by the unclassified road that runs east along the shore
and then turns inland to West Quantoxhead, where the Quantocks drop
down to the sea. The hills — a narrow ridge roughly 12 miles long by 3
wide — are delightful country, well wooded, populated by herds of red
deer, and with peaceful villages nestling on the lower slopes. This is easy
walking country, with numerous footpaths, and a superb central ridge
route running the length of the hills, which you could follow south from
West Quantoxhead, meeting your driver again near Crowcombe (see
below).

Turn left in West Quantoxhead on to A39, and follow this road round
through Kilve to the eastern side of the range. Footpaths lead up on to
the hills from **HOLFORD**, hidden at the foot of a combe. William
Wordsworth and his sister Dorothy lived here for a year in 1796–7 — the
locals were most suspicious, and thought they were French spies — while
in next-door **NETHER STOWEY** their friend Samuel Taylor Coleridge
lived from 1796 to 1799, and wrote *The Rime of the Ancient Mariner*.
Visitors to **Coleridge Cottage** (*NT, open April–Sept Tues–Thur and Sun
afternoons*) are shown the parlour and reading room.

Take the minor road that climbs up from Nether Stowey to the top of
the hills. You meet the ridge path (see above) at Crowcombe Park Gate,
just before the road starts to descend again. Park here, and walk south,
alongside ancient cairns and woodland to Wills Neck, the highest point.
**CROWCOMBE** is a sleepy little community tucked in a fold of the hills;
there's a 13th-century market cross in the centre of the village.

Cross A358 and continue west on unclassified roads towards
Stogumber and Monksilver. The hills ahead are the **Brendon Hills**,
which in the mid-19th century were extensively mined for iron ore.
Stogumber is another lovely village with thatched, colour-washed
cottages and cobbled pavements and a red sandstone church. Turn left
in Monksilver on to B3188, which soon passes the entrance to **Combe**

**Sydenham Country Park** (*open Easter–Oct Mon–Fri*), created around an Elizabethan manor house which was the family home of Elizabeth Sydenham, Sir Francis Drake's second wife. Attractions here include the house and gardens, special interest walks, fly fishing and a trout farm; there's also a tea-room.

Continue south on B3188, and beyond Elworthy turn right on to the unclassified road that climbs up to the whale-back ridge of the Brendons. This road joins B3190, which follow south across the edge of Exmoor again back towards the gentler, lusher scenery of mid-Devon around Bampton. From here follow A396 south to Tiverton and Exeter.

## Two Cornish Coasts

*2–3 days/about 140 miles/from Fowey/OS maps 201, 200, 190*

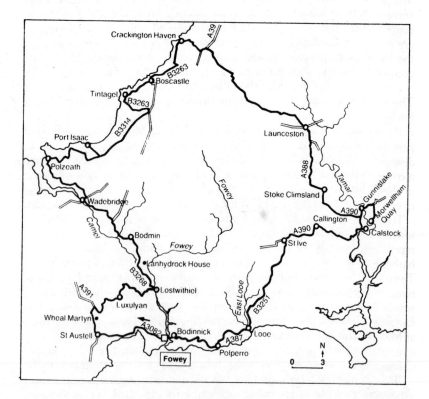

Cornwall's two coasts could hardly be more different. On the north, Atlantic rollers assault a wild and inhospitable shore, occasionally punctuated by narrow harbours half-hidden in mighty cliffs. In the more gentle and peaceful south, wooded estuaries gradually run down to a mellow coast broken by wide sandy coves and picturesque fishing villages. It is the south that experiences the beneficent effect of the Gulf Stream. Frosts and snow are unusual, and, because of the cooling effect of the sea, summers are rarely bakingly hot — a climate ideal for cultivating lush, colourful gardens densely planted with species hardly seen, at least in natural conditions, elsewhere in Britain.

The inland landscape is one of contrasts as well: granite moors, windswept and forbidding, give way to a land of deep-set lanes bordered by hedgerows filled with wild flowers — banks of primroses in spring, foxgloves, honeysuckle, red campion and many others — and of small farms, their fields divided by low stone walls and banks covered with ferns, gorse and flowers. The Cornish landscape is an industrial one as well, something that outsiders tend to forget. Tin has been mined since prehistoric times, although the earliest visible remains date from the Middle Ages, and most of the now deserted engine-houses were constructed in the late 18th and 19th centuries, the heyday of tin- and copper-mining in the county. Slate is still mined — most Cornish houses are roofed with local slate — and china clay forms an important part of the local economy: a visible one, too, with towering white heaps of spoil dominating the area around St. Austell.

This exploration of parts of eastern Cornwall begins on the south coast at Fowey, although any of the small coastal or inland towns visited would make an equally suitable starting-point. Fringed by buildings of every period, the tortuous narrow streets of **FOWEY** (pronounced Foy) descend sharply to the harbour, where yachts jostle with freighters moving upriver to collect their cargoes of china clay. Walk up to the top of the town for a panoramic view, or take the passenger ferry across the river to Polruan on the east bank. In the 14th and 15th centuries, bands of Fowey sailors — nicknamed the 'Fowey Gallants' — constantly harried towns along the French coast. After the French ransacked the town in a reprisal raid in 1457, forts, now ruined, were put up on each side of the harbour entrance; the 'Gallants' later turned to piracy. Fowey is the 'Troy Town' of Sir Arthur Quiller-Couch's stories; his home overlooked the river. Visit **Fowey Museum** (*open Easter and late May–Sept Mon–Fri*), which contains displays on local history, and the 14th-century church. Eat at **Food for Thought** on The Quay, and stay among many others, at **Marina Hotel** (072683–3315) on Esplanade or, somewhat less expensive, at **Polscoe Guest House** (072683–2407). TIC in the Post Office, Custom House Hill (072683–3616).

There's a fine walk along the coast through woodland and out on to windswept **Gribbin Head** (*NT*), where the red and white striped beacon tower was erected by Trinity House in 1832. The National Trust owns over 110 miles of the Cornish coastline, including several stretches east and west of Fowey. This walk follows the well-signposted **Cornwall Coast Path**, which runs the entire length of the county's two coasts. You could continue on foot to **POLKERRIS**, a small fishing village with a sandy cove and the remains of a pilchard house, where pilchards were pressed for oil, and meet your driver there.

A3082 runs west from Fowey, passing just north of Polkerris and above **Carlyon Bay**, notable for the Olympic swimming pool, international concert hall and other leisure facilities at **Cornwall Leisure World** and **Cornwall Coliseum** and through Charlestown to St. Austell. The **Visitor Centre** (*open April–Oct daily*) at **CHARLESTOWN** tells the story of the creation of this early 19th-century port to serve the expanding china clay trade; it remains a working port.

**ST AUSTELL** is deservedly described as the county's 'china-clay capital'. Pyramids of waste sand — actual clay forms only about one ninth of what is mined — punctuate the granite landscape to the north of the town, giving it an eerie, almost lunar effect. Discovered in 1755, china clay, or kaolin, is formed from decomposed granite and felspar, and is used to coat paper and for making house-paint, face cream and some medicines.

Set in a wooded valley 2 miles north of St Austell on A391 is **Wheal Martyn** (*open daily April–Oct*). The open-air museum, based on a restored 19th-century clay works, tells the history of this major Cornish industry and shows the extraction processes, with a working locomotive and waterwheels. There's also a nature trail.

Turn right off A391 at Stenalees and head along minor roads, turning left on to B3374 and then right off it again towards **LUXULYAN**, whose cottages and the 15th-century church with its battlemented tower are built of local granite. Beautiful **Luxulyan Valley** below the village is carpeted with daffodils and bluebells in spring. The massive viaduct, built by a local quarry- and mine-owner in 1842, once carried the railway and an aqueduct over the valley.

Now drive north-east through Lanlivery to join A390 south of **LOSTWITHIEL**, which in the 13th century served briefly as Cornwall's capital; the Old Duchy Palace dates from that period. It's a pleasant and compact place to stroll around, with 17th- and 18th-century houses, an 18th-century Guildhall and Grammar School, and pleasant riverside gardens; there are good shops too, especially crafts and antiques. **St. Bartholomew's Church** has a 13th-century lantern spire and, inside, a 14th-century carved font. TIC in the Community Centre, Liddicoat Road (0208–872207).

About 1 mile south of the town is the lovely little **St Winnow's Church**, delightfully situated on the east bank of the river Fowey. Cross the river by the 15th-century stone bridge, and then turn right, following tiny lanes until you reach the church.

**Restormel Castle** stands in a commanding position close to the river north of the town. Originally built by the Normans in about 1100 to subdue their traditionally independent-minded Cornish subjects — Cornwall had been an independent kingdom until as late as the 10th century — it was rebuilt in the late 13th century. The large oval shell keep, still in excellent condition, was surrounded by a moat. (*EH, standard opening times, plus summer Sun mornings; closed winter all day Tues and Wed mornings.*)

Leave Lostwithiel on B3268, and soon turn right on to B3269, from which signposts guide you to **Lanhydrock House**, one of the National Trusts's grandest Cornish properties (*open April–Oct daily, garden only daily during winter*). The house looks Tudor, but most of it was rebuilt in its original style after a fire in 1881; the Long Gallery's magnificent plaster ceiling of the Creation escaped destruction. The interior shows what late Victorian country-house life was like; much equipment and furniture is preserved, especially 'below stairs' in the kitchen, larder and servants' quarters. Beyond the formal garden, there are enjoyable walks in the park, which runs down to the river Fowey. National Trust restaurant, snack bar and shop.

A38 takes you into **BODMIN**, which became the county town of Cornwall in 1835; the Assize Courts still sit here, although the council offices are now in Truro. The most notable building is **St Petroc's Church** (15th-century), which includes a late Norman font and a 12th-century ivory and brass casket said once to have contained the remains of St. Petroc. **Bodmin Museum** (*open May–Sept, Tues, Thurs and Sat*) contains displays on local history, natural history and folklore, while the **Duke of Cornwall's Light Infantry Museum** (*open Mon–Fri, but closed in March*) in the former barracks records the regiment's history from 1702 onwards. TIC in Shire House, Mount Folly Square (0208–6616).

Head north-west on A389, past **Pencarrow House** (*open Easter–Sept Sun–Thurs*), a Georgian house with collections of paintings, furniture and china and with attractive grounds. Sir Arthur Sullivan composed *Iolanthe* here.

Lying a few miles inland, at the point where the river Camel begins to open out towards the sea, **WADEBRIDGE** is often more peaceful than nearby coastal centres. The 15th-century 14-arch (originally 17) 'Bridge on Wool' is said to have been paid for by wealthy sheep-farmers, who wanted to be able to cross easily. Or maybe its name came from the woolpacks said to have been used as foundations — as often happens, local traditions conflict. TIC in Town Hall (020881–3725).

There's sea in the air as B3314 heads towards the shore at the start of a long and exhilarating drive up the northern coast. Minor roads lead off to **POLZEATH**, where there is surfing, and rock pools and caves to explore, and to **TREBETHERICK**, a mile or so inland, where Sir John Betjeman, the poet, is buried in St Endoc's church; he spent childhood holidays in this area. The next hamlet north is **PORTQUIN**, hardly more than a tiny inlet, now owned by the National Trust. The stretch of coastline around Pentire Point is especially fine, with striking rock formations; it's well worth tackling along the coastal path.

**PORT ISAAC**, reached along B3267, is an ancient fishing village of narrow streets and passageways and slate houses descending to a minute harbour. **Slipway Hotel** (0208–880264) dates back to the 16th century;

the restaurant specialises in locally caught fish.

Return to B3314, which turns inland for a few miles, before turning left on to B3263 for **TINTAGEL**. The situation of the **castle** (*EH, standard times*) is spectacular, perched on its 'island' of rock high above the crashing waves. Small wonder that ancient legends, kept alive by more recent writers, have claimed Tintagel as Arthur's birthplace. Scanty historical evidence suggests that, as well as an Iron Age castle, there was some form of local stronghold, or perhaps a trading post, here between the 5th and 8th centuries — although the ruins now visible go back no further than the 12th century. Whatever the facts of the matter, Tintagel has become a place of pilgrimage, full of unappealing gift shops and cafés. An unusual building worth seeing is the **Old Post Office** (*NT, open April–Oct daily*), an originally 14th-century stone house used as a letter-receiving office in the 19th century and restored as such. Accommodation at the top end of the scale is provided by the **Atlantic View Hotel** (0840–770221), or more simply at **Castle Villa** (0840–770373).

The harbour at **BOSCASTLE** is a tiny fjord-like haven set between

*Tintagel Castle*

high slate cliffs, so difficult to approach by sea that rowing boats used to go out to guide incoming ships. The pier was built in 1547, originally for exporting slate and corn. The National Trust owns both sides of the harbour, and also stretches of the valley of river Valency, along which there are good walks to St Juliot, where the writer Thomas Hardy met his first wife; the district provides the setting for many of his poems. The small cottages of Boscastle village climb up the hillside behind the harbour. There are craft shops in the village, and also a **Museum of Witchcraft** (*open Easter–Oct daily*).

Our final port of call along the coast is **CRACKINGTON HAVEN**, reached by continuing on B3263 and then turning left on to a minor road. The sandy beach is approached via a long valley. This is Cornwall at its simplest and best: an unspoilt hamlet clustering around an attractive surf-beaten cove, with robust cliffs to each side and, behind, a landscape filled with gorse and wild flowers. Stay here at **Combe Bardon Hotel** (08403–345) or at **Crackington Manor Hotel** (08403–397).

Our route now strikes across the peninsula to the south coast, with Launceston the initial goal. Keeping to the minor road that runs on the north side of the stream, drive inland from Crackington Haven to A39, cross that road, and follow minor roads to Canworthy Water, Tremaine and Egloskerry. This is a quiet, empty part of Cornwall, with tiny hamlets, each with a few slate cottages grouped around the parish church, and occasional farmsteads. North of Egloskerry, in the village of **NORTH PETHERWIN**, you will find the **Tamar Otter Park and Wild Wood** (*open daily Easter–Oct*), a branch of the Otter Trust. The otters live in large natural enclosures, deer roam in the woods, and there is a waterfowl lake.

**LAUNCESTON**, the county capital until 1838, occupies an impressive hillside position, overlooked by an originally Norman castle (*EH, standard times but closed all day Tues and Wed mornings in winter*). It's enjoyable exploring the town on foot. As well as some good Georgian houses, worth seeing are the South Gate (the only survival of the three gates that controlled entrance into the medieval town) and the granite parish church, St. Mary Magdalene, whose exterior walls are covered with marvellously intricate carvings. **Lawrence House** on Castle Street is a local history museum (*open April–Sept Mon–Fri*), while in the attractive Kensey valley below the town the veteran locos of the narrow-gauge **Launceston Steam Railway** run for 1½ miles along the old North Cornwall Railway (*services operate daily May–Sept*). Eat at **Greenhouse Wholefood Restaurant** (Madford Lane) and stay at the **White Hart** (0566–2013) or, outside town, on **Hurdon Farm** (0566–2955). TIC in Market House Arcade, Market Street (0566–2321).

Head south now along A388, and turn left on to unclassified roads after about 7 miles for **STOKE CLIMSLAND**, where the Duchy of Cornwall has its home farm. Drive south through Downgate, and turn left on to B3257. Another left turn on to A390 will bring you across **Hingston Down**, scene of a great battle in 835 between the Anglo-Saxon and Cornish armies, to **GUNNISLAKE**, set on steep slopes high above the river Tamar, Cornwall's ancient frontier with the rest of England. Until Brunel built the Saltash railway bridge in 1859, the New Bridge here (built in 1520) was the lowest point at which travellers could cross the Tamar.

Until the beginning of the 20th century, this part of the Tamar valley was an important industrial area, with tin and copper mines, brickworks, and villages of miners' cottages. There are ruined mine-chimneys around Gunnislake, and at **Morwellham Quay** (*open daily*), reached by crossing into Devon on A390 and bearing right after 2 miles, the 1860s industrial community is brought to life. The port, the largest inland port in Devon and Cornwall, could accommodate up to six sea-going ships and had a storage capacity of 4,000 tons of copper ore. You can take a train ride underground into the copper mine, and explore the carefully restored cottages and quayside buildings.

Return to Gunnislake, turn left on to A390, and left again on to unclassified roads to **CALSTOCK,** a delightful riverside town whose streets climb steeply up to St Anthony's church, from where there are magnificent views up and down the wooded Tamar valley. Until the railway was built at the beginning of this century — the 12-arch viaduct strides across the town — Calstock was an important port.

Only a mile or so downstream by footpath or boat, but 6 miles on winding lanes, is **Cotehele House**, a grey granite manor house largely built towards the end of the 15th century. Inside, there is a wonderful collection of furniture, armour, hunting trophies and tapestries. Outside, attractive gardens run down to the Tamar and to Cotehele Quay, where the *Shamrock*, the last surviving Tamar barge, is moored. She was built in 1899 to carry limestone up river and granite, tiles, bricks and agricultural produce down. The mill has also been restored to working order. Meals are available in the barn and also on the quayside. (*NT, garden and mill open daily, house daily except Fri, April–Oct; garden only in winter.*) National Trust shop.

Head west on lanes through orchards towards A388, where turn right to **CALLINGTON. Kit Hill** (1,096ft) above the town was given to Cornwall by Prince Charles, Duke of Cornwall; there are magnificent views west to Bodmin Moor and east to Dartmoor from the summit, where stands an abandoned mine stack. The white-painted **Coachmakers Arms** (0579–82567) in Newport Square serves hearty pub food and provides pleasant accommodation.

Follow A390 west to St. Ive, where turn left on unclassified roads through the valley of the little river Tiddy to Menheniot. Cross the A38 main road beyond the village, and drive south on B3251 to the junction with A387. A right turn here will lead you alongside the East Looe river to the sea.

Both **EAST LOOE** and **WEST LOOE**, its neighbour on the opposite side of the little estuary, are primarily holiday towns nowadays, crowded with souvenir shops and cafes. But the little winding back streets bordered by fishermen's cottages are a reminder that the towns' prosperity was founded on fishing — pilchards in particular; stone and copper were also

*Polperro harbour*

exported during the 19th century. The **Old Guildhall Museum** (*open daily except Sat*) explains local history. Places to stay in the Looes (the name, incidentally, comes from the Cornish word 'logh', a lake or inlet) include **Commonwood Manor Hotel** (05036–2929) at the top end of the market and the family-run **Deganwy Hotel** (05036–2984). TIC in the Guildhall, East Looe (05036–2072).

A387 runs west to Polperro a little way inland. The coastal path offers good walking, past the beautifully coloured rocks of Talland Bay. It's a relief to escape the crowds, for in **POLPERRO** — perhaps the quaintest, neatest, most perfectly preserved of all Cornish fishing villages — you are likely to meet them with a vengeance. Underneath it all, this remains a lovely, simple village, with fishing boats in the harbour and rows of colour-washed cottages clinging to the hillside. Come out of season to appreciate it at its best. There is a **Museum of Smuggling** (*open Easter–Oct daily*), while **Land of Legend and Model Village** (*open Easter–Oct daily, but closed Sat except in high season*) presents a model replica of Polperro and an animated recreation of Cornish legends and history. At **Captain's Cabin** in Lansallos Street you can eat freshly-caught seafood.

The final leg of this drive is along minor roads to **BODINNICK** on the east bank of the river Fowey, where the car ferry crosses to Fowey.

# South Hams and Dartmoor

*1–3 days/about 115 miles/from Dartmouth/OS maps 191, 201, 202*

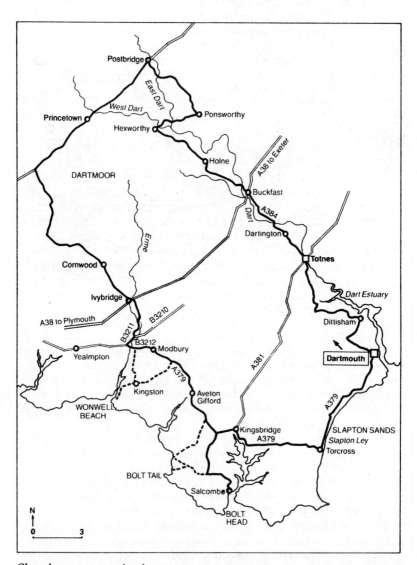

Sharply contrasting landscapes are encountered within a few miles of each other in this drive. Behind the rocky headlands, wide sandy beaches and wooded estuaries of the south Devon coast lies an idyllic landscape of tranquil villages and rich farmland. This in turn gives way to Dartmoor, still, despite the ever-increasing number of visitors, a wilderness of peat-covered windswept moorland, scattered with prehistoric sites and the remains of old mine workings and fringed by gentler, wooded valleys.

We begin at Dartmouth, but the route could be started from any number of equally attractive places — Kingsbridge, Salcombe, Totnes, or a larger town such as Exeter (see page 104) or Plymouth, which is only a few miles from the western edge of Dartmoor.

That **DARTMOUTH** was once a major port is hardly surprising, given its commanding position almost at the mouth of the river Dart and at the head of a magnificent natural harbour. Ships assembled here in the 12th century for the Second and Third Crusades, and in our own time before D-Day in 1944. Wool and cloth were the main exports, French wine a major import, and in the 16th and 17th centuries Dartmouth sailors crossed the Atlantic to fish Newfoundland waters for cod; the Pilgrim Fathers also set sail from here. When in summer the river is dotted with thousands of sails of every colour, you would think that yachts are the only boats on the estuaries. In fact, there's a large crab-fishing fleet, several warships visit the Naval College each year, and trawlers come in for repair, not to mention the freighters loaded with timber that dock upstream at Totnes.

Narrow streets and passages climb steeply from the water's edge, leading north to the **Royal Naval College**, which sits rather heavily over the town. There is a group of attractive 17th-century houses along cobbled **Bayards Cove** (where scenes from the TV series *The Onedin Line* were filmed). **The Butterwalk**, where dairy produce used to be sold, is also 17th-century, a row of overhanging timber-framed buildings decorated with carvings. Number 6 is **Dartmouth Museum** (*open April–Sept Mon–Sat*), which specialises in maritime paintings and ship models, and also has local history exhibits. See also the **Henley Museum** (*open Mon–Fri*), a remarkable collection of Victorian everyday possessions, and **St Saviour's Church**, with a 14th-century ironwork door, 15th-century screen and painted pulpit and 17th-century gallery. There's an enjoyable walk to the **castle** (*EH, standard opening times*) which guards the narrow estuary entrance; built in 1481, it was one of the earliest castles designed for artillery. Enjoy views back to the town from here, and also from the ferries that run across to Kingswear, on the opposite bank. Try the local crab and salmon at the **Spinning Wheel Café** in Hauley Road, while **Cherub Inn** in Higher Street serves a fisherman's lunch of hot smoked mackerel and salad. Stay at **Royal Castle Inn** (08043-4004) by the harbour, or more cheaply at **Townstal Farm House** (08043-2300) outside town. TIC in Royal Avenue Gardens (08043-4224).

Much the nicest route to Totnes is along the narrow lanes that link the little villages by the estuary shore. Cross wooded Old Mill Creek just north of Dartmouth and head through fields of fruit trees first for **DITTISHAM**, where a large brass bell is used to summon the ferry, and then for **CORNWORTHY** and **ASHPRINGTON**, a hill-top community. All these villages have attractive, well-maintained parish churches.

The handsome houses, largely 16th–18th-century, of **TOTNES** ascend from the quayside to the originally Norman **castle** (*EH, open daily except all day Tues and Wed morning*) with its 13th-century shell keep and curtain wall; the ruins aren't especially exciting, but the views are good. The principal street is Fore Street, which after passing through East Gate halfway up becomes High Street; there's quite a selection of craft, antique and book shops, and an Elizabethan costumed market is held every Tuesday in the new market place. One of the best-preserved Tudor houses on Fore Street, built for a local merchant in about 1575, is now the **Totnes Elizabethan Museum** (*open late March–late Oct Mon–Fri*). The construction of the house can be seen, including original plaster ceilings and 17th- and 18th-century panelling, and the displays recreate local life in Elizabethan and Victorian times, with dolls' house and furniture, childrens' games and clothes, and reconstructed Victorian grocer's shop. Another Tudor house in the arcaded Butterwalk at the top end of town houses the **Devonshire Collection of Period Costume** (*open May–Sept daily except Sat*), with costume and accessories from 1750 onwards. See also the 15th-century **St Mary's Church**, with an imposing red sandstone tower and, inside, a lovely stone screen, and the 16th-century **Guildhall** (*open Mon–Fri*), still used for council meetings. **Totnes Motor Museum** (*open April–Oct daily*) has a collection of some 30 historic cars. **Willow** and **Above Town Wholefood Eating House** (an explicit name if ever there was one) are both interesting and reasonably priced places to eat; Willow serves vegetarian food. **Royal Seven Stars** (0803–862125) is the town's oldest hotel. TIC on The Plains, near the quayside (0803–863168).

A little to the north along A384 is **DARTINGTON**. The **Cider Press Centre** (*open Mon–Sat and also Sun mid-July to mid-Sept*) is a collection of upmarket shops selling pottery, crafts, herbs, prints, toys, kitchen ware and so forth. Although many of the things on sale are of excellent quality — including Dartington Glass, which, however, is not made here but at a factory in north Devon — there's a slightly unsatisfactory atmosphere about the place; consumerism run riot. Much more genuine is **Dartington Hall**, restored in the 1920s as the centre of a hive of rural activities now run by a trust and including arts and education, agriculture and manufacturing (e.g. glass). In the **Great Hall** (*open daily when not in use*) hang tapestries depicting the work of the estate. In the lovely **gardens** (*open daily*), which run down to the banks of the Dart, sculptures, including a Henry Moore figure, stand amid lawns, specimen trees and banks of roses, camellias and azaleas.

A384 runs up the Dart to Buckfastleigh, although the best way to see this unspoilt stretch of the river is on the steam-hauled **Dart Valley Railway** (*services run at Easter and daily May–Sept; tel. 0364–42338 for details*). The **Leisure Park** (*open Easter and daily June–Sept*) at the **BUCKFASTLEIGH** terminus includes a museum and displays of rolling stock, and there is also a **butterfly farm** (*open Easter–Oct daily*).

On the far side of A38 (which use if you're joining this drive from Exeter) stands **Buckfast Abbey**. Founded in the 11th century, the abbey grew prosperous from sheep-farming on Dartmoor, fell into ruins after the Dissolution, and was rebuilt by a group of six Benedictine monks between 1906 and 1932. There is some marvellous stained glass, notably the figure of Christ in the east window of the abbey. Shops sell honey from the abbey bees and the monks' own tonic wine. (*Church open daily, exhibition daily Easter–Oct.*)

The abbey lies in a secluded riverside spot, but the view north to the brooding granite mass of Dartmoor gives a sense of wilder country ahead. From the abbey, follow narrow, steep lanes that wind to **HOLNE**, where the novelist Charles Kingsley, author of *The Water Babies*, was born, and then out to the moor proper. Parking spots near Venford Reservoir look down to Holne Moor, scattered with cairns, stone rows and hut circles erected, often for ceremonial purposes, by Dartmoor's Bronze Age settlers. Further off are old tin workings; between the 12th century and the 17th, almost every valley on the moor was streamed for tin; more recent centuries have seen open-cast mining shafts.

Dartmoor ponies are the main inhabitants of the high moorland plateau, together with black or dun-coloured Galloway cattle and Cheviot and Blackface sheep. All are hardy creatures able to withstand the snows of winter and to live off gorse and tussocky grass. The ponies, probably descendants of a domestic breed let loose on the moor over a thousand years ago, are rounded up in the autumn pony drift for branding

*Clapper bridge at Postbridge*

and as a culling measure, but otherwise are allowed to roam freely — though they generally stick to a relatively small home patch. Golden plover and dunlin breed on the moor; other birds you are likely to see include buzzards and ravens, skylarks, meadow pipits and perhaps a red grouse.

Beyond Hexworthy, the road descends to cross the West Dart. Turn right for **DARTMEET**, a honeypot for visitors, but attractive none the less; the two Dart rivers, East and West, meet here. The old clapper bridge (the word comes from the Saxon *cleaca*, meaning large stones) was used by packhorses before the present road was built. Continue east for about 1 mile, and turn left on to the minor road towards Ponsworthy. Just before the road descends to the village, turn left and follow this road to **BELLEVER**, where you can picnic beside the East Dart and follow forest trails.

One and a half miles later, the road meets B3212 just before **POSTBRIDGE**, where the National Park Information Centre (0822–88272) will suggest good local walks. The clapper bridge here is made of massive granite slabs.

Turn left on to B3212 (i.e. away from Postbridge), and drive through Two Bridges to **PRINCETOWN**, dominated by the grim buildings of the prison, originally built in the early 19th century to house French prisoners captured during the Napoleonic Wars. Top-security prisoners are no longer confined here, only those in so-called categories B and C, who are serving anything from 18 months to life. National Park Information Centre in the Town Hall (082289–414).

B3212 gradually descends towards Yelverton. Turn left about 1 mile before the village on to an unclassified road that runs along the edge of the moor through the little villages of Wotter and Cornwood to Ivybridge. (If you're joining this route from Plymouth, drive out to Ivybridge on the fast A38.)

Suddenly there's a complete change of scene, with a landscape of soft undulating hills and sleepy villages that embraces rather than challenges. Our route through South Hams will be along the coast — but expect slow progress, since the roads have to work their way round a succession of estuaries cutting far inland.

From Ivybridge, drive south on B3211 alongside the river Erme, turn right on to B3210 in Ermington, and then left on to A379 towards Modbury. (Three miles west along A379 — i.e. to the right — in **YEALMPTON** is the **National Shire Horse Centre** (*open daily*) and the spectacular rock formations of **Kitley Caves** (*open Easter and daily late May–September*).)

There's a delightful but quite time-consuming diversion alongside the out-of-the-way estuary of the Erme. Turn right off A379 on to an unclassified road shortly before Modbury, and follow this, through ups and downs, to **KINGSTON**, where the **Dolphin Inn** serves good food. An even tinier road leads off here to **Wonwell Beach** (pronounced 'Wonnel'), a lovely stretch of almost deserted sand. On the return trip, drive from Kingston to Seven Stones Cross, where take B3392 north to the junction with A379.

*Salcombe*

Beyond Aveton Gifford (pronounced 'Orton Jifford'), where A379 crosses the river Avon, you can use any of the minor roads running south to reach the coast. The most exciting stretch is the 4 miles or so of cliff top between two headlands known as **Bolt Tail** and **Bolt Head**, which you can walk on the well-signposted coastal path. To reach Bolt Tail, follow B3197 for a short distance, and then turn right through South Milton and Galmpton to **Outer** and **Inner Hope**, two neighbouring villages directly beneath the headland. Bolt Head is beyond Salcombe; the path leads past **Overbecks Museum and Garden** (*NT, museum open Easter–Oct daily, garden always*) at Sharpitor. The Edwardian house contains model boats, butterflies, ship-building tools and many other interesting things, while the gardens are full of exotica.

Even if a cliff-top walk doesn't appeal, you will not want to miss **SALCOMBE**, whose narrow streets tumble down to the estuary shore. It's a perfect place, with wooded walks and sandy beaches, and hosts of exotic plants and trees: fuchsias, palms, oranges. The **Maritime and Local History Museum** (*open late May–Sept daily*) contains displays on shipwrecks — once common on this rugged coastline — and other aspects of maritime and local history. Hotels include **Charborough House** (054884–2260) and **Woodgrange** (054884–2439). TIC at Russell Court, Fore Street (054884–2736).

A381 runs back up the estuary to **KINGSBRIDGE**, although an altogether pleasanter way to travel would be by river launch. The town was a major port from the Middle Ages until the last century, but now tourism provides most of its income. William Cookworthy, who discovered china clay, was born here in 1705. The **Cookworthy Museum** (*open Easter–Sept Mon–Sat, also Mon–Fri in Oct*) in the 17th-century grammar school is devoted to rural life in south Devon, with a Victorian pharmacy and school kitchen and displays of costume and agricultural machinery. TIC on the Quay (0548–3195).

Crossing an inlet off the estuary, A379 runs through Chillington to meet the sea at Torcross and **Slapton Sands**, a long shingle ridge used by US forces to rehearse the D-Day landings in Normandy; local people were evacuated for nine months. Behind the beach is **Slapton Ley**, a freshwater lake with reed beds and many interesting species of native and visiting wildfowl. A nature trail runs along the northern edge.

From Torcross it is 7 miles along A379 to Dartmouth.

## Hardy Country
*1 day/about 55 miles/from Dorchester/OS maps 193, 194*

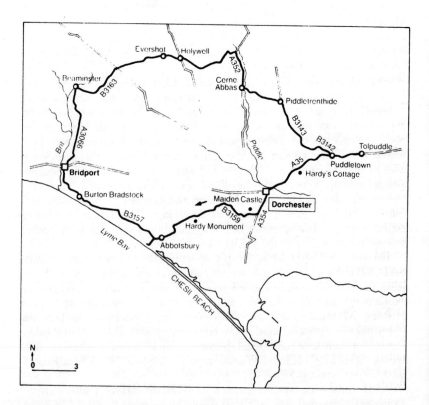

Rolling chalk downs, hidden river valleys and a fine, largely unspoilt coastline of cliffs and the unique Chesil Beach are the main components of this drive through remote and restful countryside. This is the heart of the Wessex portrayed by Thomas Hardy in his novels. It is also a landscape of great antiquity, with evidence of settlement dating back several thousand years, to the peoples of Stone Age Britain.

The **County Museum** (*open Mon–Sat*) in **DORCHESTER** (Hardy's 'Casterbridge') is a good place to start, for it gives an excellent overview of local history. There are finds from Maiden Castle (see below) and from the Roman town, and many Hardy relics, including a full-scale reconstruction of his study from Max Gate, the house (not open to the public) he had built on the western edge of the town; the Rural Craft Collection helps to bring the world of Hardy's characters to life. Dorchester — Roman *Durnovaria* — was built in about AD70, soon after the Romans settled in this country; near County Hall the foundations of a town house with heating systems and a veranda have been excavated, and you can follow the course of the Roman walls along The Walks. Dorchester is now a lively market town and local commercial centre with many 18th- and 19th-century buildings. Other, not locally rooted attractions are the **Dinosaur Museum** (*open daily*) and the **Tutankhamun Museum** (*open daily*), which contains replicas of the Pharaoh's treasures. The baking, salads and hot lunchtime dish are all recommended at **Potter In** (Durngate Street). The **Casterbridge Hotel** (0305–64043) occupies a Georgian building in the town centre, not far from the **Wessex Hotel** (0305–62660). TIC in Acland Road (0305–67992).

Take A354 south out of town, and after a couple of miles turn right near Winterborne Monkton on to an unclassified road, which runs round the south side of **Maiden Castle** (*EH, open access*), a massive fort occupying a hilltop site approximately 1,000yds long by 500 across. First occupied a little less than 4,000 years ago, it was extended successively by Stone Age and Iron Age peoples, and was finally stormed in a bloody battle by Roman invaders in about AD43 or 44; several centuries later a small pagan temple was built at one end. In its heyday, the castle, one of many scattered all around Wessex, served as a grain store for the surrounding area; pits and small granaries were built to store the grain, which represented the community's wealth. The inhabitants lived in circular houses scattered around the fort. The defences are impressive: three rows of ramparts, one beneath the other, with a heavily guarded and intricately designed entrance at each end.

Now follow the unclassified road, turn right on to B3159 to Martinstown, where turn left on to an unclassified road that climbs up to Black Down and then descends steeply to Abbotsbury. Confusingly, the rather ugly **Hardy Monument** on Black Down commemorates not the novelist, but Sir Thomas Masterman Hardy, Nelson's flag captain at the Battle of Trafalgar. 'Kiss me Hardy' were Nelson's dying words. In good weather, there is a stupendous view all along the coast, from the Purbeck

Hills in the east right across to Start Point in south Devon.

The descent to the coastal strip marks a distinct change of mood, for **ABBOTSBURY** is a gentle village full of honey-stone thatched cottages standing on pavements raised above the road. See here the **Sub-tropical Gardens** (*open daily mid-March–mid-Oct*), dating from the 1760s, with camellias, magnolias, lily ponds and many rare plants, all sheltered from the sea wind by a bank of trees; abbey ruins, including a massive 14th-century tithe barn (not open to the public); the 15th-century St Catherine's Chapel, built on an isolated hilltop; and the 15th- and 16th-century parish church. The **Swannery** (*open daily mid-May to mid-Sept*), south-east of the village, was founded by the local monks in the 14th century; several hundred mute swans breed here each year in the brackish waters of the Fleet, the lagoon trapped behind Chesil Beach. There is also a historic duck decoy, built in 1655.

It is worth driving down to the sea to inspect **Chesil Beach**, a 16-mile-long high bank of pebbles swept up by the sea that stretches all the way east to Portland Bill. In calm weather the sea looks benign, but swimming is dangerous at all times; in winter the waves thunder on to the shore, sucking up countless pebbles in a vicious undertow. Over the years, there have been many wrecks along the Lyme Bay shore.

The **Dorset Coast Path** runs along the shore, so if you want a walk, follow it along to Burton Bradstock, or even as far as West Bay, which is the resort for Bridport. For most of the time the road, B3157, runs half a mile or so inland, along the cliffs that drop sharply down to the beach. **BURTON BRADSTOCK** is a neat village with a pleasant green, yellow stone walls and thatched cottages.

**BRIDPORT** grew prosperous from rope- and net-manufacturing from the Middle Ages onwards, using locally grown hemp and flax; nowadays artificial materials are used. ('Bridport dagger' was 17th-century slang for a hangman's noose.) The town centre is largely Georgian, with wide streets once used for twisting and drying ropes and attractive little alley-ways. Noteworthy buildings include the late 18th-century town hall and the 13th-century parish church. The little **Museum and Art Gallery** (*open weekday mornings, and also June–Sept Mon–Wed and Fri afternoons*) includes displays on rope-making and local history and an international collection of dolls. Stay in simple but pleasant style at the **Bull Hotel** (0308–22878) in the centre of town and eat at nearby **Monique's**. TIC in South Street (0308–24901).

A3066 runs north from Bridport along the secluded valley of the river Brit. **Parnham House** (*open April–Oct Wed, Sun and Bank Holidays*) is a Tudor mansion with additions by the Regency architect John Nash; it is now owned by the furniture designer John Makepeace, who runs his school for wood craftsmen here. The 14 acres of grounds contain topiary, fountains, cascades and fine trees. **BEAMINSTER** (Hardy's 'Emminster') really does qualify for the cliché, 'untouched by time'. Streets built of local yellow-golden stone radiate from the market square, and the church has a 16th-century tower decorated with sculpture figures.

B3163 east is the start of a long stretch on minor roads across the steeply undulating downs which conceal deep, sheltered coombes in summer still rich in wild flowers. A couple of miles outside Beaminster bear right to visit the terraced hillside gardens with 18th-century fish ponds at **Mapperton Manor** (*open early March–early Oct Mon–Fri afternoons*); the Tudor house is not open to the public.

Follow B3163 to the junction with A356, and carry straight on here on an unclassified road that runs up and down through Evershot to the A37 at Holywell. Keep straight on again here, on another minor road, along Batcombe Hill, past a viewpoint with parking space at **Gore Hill** and alongside woodland to A352. Turn right here through **MINTERNE MAGNA**, where at **Minterne Gardens** (*open April–Oct daily*) Chinese and Himalayan rhododendrons, Japanese cherries and roses grow in abundance. **CERNE ABBAS** is a charming village with a duck pond, a lovely originally 15th-century church with a 17th-century pulpit, and an attractive variety of houses, including a row of overhanging timber-framed cottages.

Walk from the village past the remains of a Benedictine abbey, up to

*The church tower at Beaminster*

the great phallic and club-wielding **giant** cut 180ft tall and 167ft wide in the chalk hillside. His origins are unclear — possibly Roman, possibly earlier — but his association with fertility rites is quite unambiguous. Maypole dancing, another traditional fertility rite, used to take place nearby.

Turn right at the far end of the village, beyond the church. This road climbs steeply and then descends sharply again to Piddletrenthide. Turn right on to B3143 here alongside the little (I almost wrote piddling) Piddle, more of a stream than a river, and then left beyond Piddlehinton on to B3142 which leads to Puddletown. All these villages, and more around, take their evocative names from the river — those upstream of Puddletown (which, to confuse you still further, was called Piddletown until the 1950s) are all 'piddles', those downstream 'puddles'.

There's a fine largely 15th-century church in **PUDDLETOWN**. The

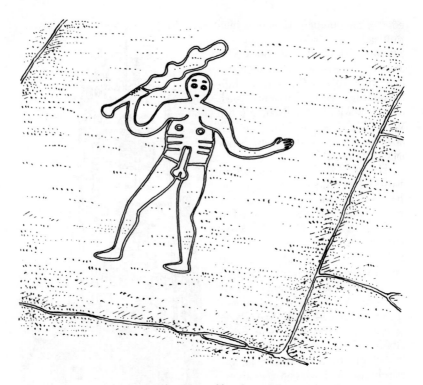

*The Cerne Abbas Giant*

interior is mostly 17th century, with box pews, a balcony and a canopied pulpit, and handsome effigies in the south aisle of a local knight and his lady. 'Weatherby', was the name Hardy gave the village in *Far from the Madding Crowd*.

Before returning to Dorchester, make a short diversion east along the A35 trunk road. After about 1 mile you pass **Athelhampton Hall** on the left (*open Easter–Sept Wed, Thur, Sun and Bank Holiday afternoons, also Tues and Fri in Aug*). The house dates from the 15th century and contains a fine timber-roofed Great Hall; outside are lovely walled and terraced gardens, with a 14th-century dovecote.

Another mile and a half further east is **TOLPUDDLE**, where at the end of 1833 local agricultural workers formed a friendly society to press for increased wages. The following year, six members — the Tolpuddle Martyrs — were arrested, convicted at Dorchester Crown Court of administering secret oaths, and sentenced to seven years' deportation to Australia. Following nationwide protests, the six were eventually granted a free pardon, returning to England several years later. The Martyrs' Tree, an old sycamore under which the martyrs met, stands on the village green, and there is also a small museum attached to the TUC memorial cottages, built in 1934. (*Key from warden*).

A35 descends from Puddletown to Dorchester across the westernmost edge of the great heath, Hardy's Egdon Heath in *The Return of the Native*, that stretches east almost as far as Bournemouth. Turn left off the main road to visit **Hardy's Cottage** in Higher Brockhampton (*NT, April–Oct daily except Tues mornings*). The interior of the cottage, which is at the end of a 10-minute walk through woodland from the car park, may only be seen by prior arrangement with the tenant (tel. 0305–62366). The furnishings are much as they were when Hardy was born here in 1840. With the exception of the five years he spent in London, he lived here until his marriage in 1874, writing *Under the Greenwood Tree* and *Far from the Madding Crowd*.

# 5 THE SOUTH-EAST

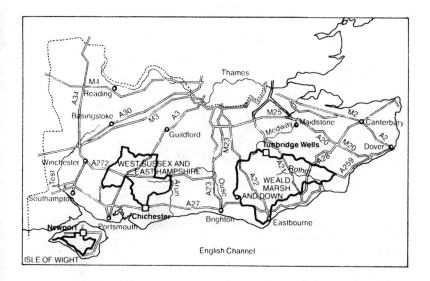

In this populous region are some of England's most crowded roads, and it sometimes seems impossible to escape the unceasing streams of traffic. You don't have to be a pessimist to believe that things are likely to get worse during the next few years. Increasing wealth will produce increasing pressure on land, with demands for the development of green-field sites and for new motorways, which will in turn generate more traffic. Furthermore, it is the south-east that will bear the brunt of the additional road traffic generated when the Channel Tunnel opens in the 1990s.

That said, for the moment large-scale suburbanisation is confined to specific areas (e.g. the Thames Valley, north Hampshire, the Solent conurbation, north Kent). In between there remains much delightful countryside, although, other than in occasional stretches, the coastline has been marred by ribbon development. Two ranges of chalk hills, the North and South Downs, enfold the fertile, well-wooded Weald, scattered with orchards and hop-fields, well-preserved villages and small towns and distinguished country houses. There are few dramas, few places where you catch your breath in astonishment, but in compensation many gentle, pleasing landscapes.

# The Isle of Wight
*1 day/about 56 miles/from Newport/OS map 196*

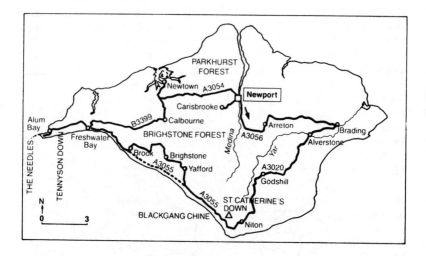

The strip of sea that separates the Isle of Wight from the mainland turns the journey into something of an occasion: an ocean voyage in miniature, with all the business of embarkation and casting off, a stretch of open water with a salt wind blowing, and then the boat slowly easing into dock again. Perhaps this is all the product of an over-vivid imagination — but on this small island, only 23 miles wide and 13 from north to south, you do somehow feel translated to a slightly more old-fashioned version of England. Especially along the south and west sides of the island, the pace of life is slower and not always quite so commercialised — there are no major highways, for instance, and many farmers have retained their traditional hedgerows, home of varied animal and plant life. And, although there are holiday crowds, it is easy to escape into beautiful and almost deserted countryside, even at the height of the season. A final word: come prepared to leave your car and walk, for many miles of easy, well-signposted routes criss-cross the island, leading you, in a surprisingly short time, through a remarkable variety of landscapes: high chalk downs, woodland, including a few remnants of ancient forests, chalk and sandstone cliffs, and marshy estuaries.

Transport across the Solent to the island is easy. Three separate ferry services carry cars: Lymington to Yarmouth and Portsmouth to Fishbourne (both operated by Sealink — 0705–827744) and Southampton to East Cowes (operated by Red Funnel — 0703–330333). Advance booking is advisable, essential at peak times.

It's most convenient to start at **NEWPORT**, the island's capital and probably also the most characterful of all its towns — if only by virtue of the fact that it is not a major seaside resort. One of the warehouses along the river bank — Newport stands at the head of the Medina estuary — has been converted into the **Quay Arts Centre** (*open daily except Mon and Sun morning*), with craft workshops and art galleries. Elsewhere there are handsome Georgian houses, a classical Guildhall in the High Street dating from 1813 — its architect was John Nash, the Prince Regent's crony, who also built Brighton Pavilion — the 17th-century Castle Inn and St Thomas's church (19th century, but with a 17th-century oak pulpit saved from the original church). **Newport Roman Villa** (*open Easter–Sept daily except Sat*) on the southern edge of the town, which was built in the late 2nd century AD, has a well-preserved bath range; reconstructed rooms, with acted-out scenes from Roman life, are intended to take you back to Roman times. Eat at **God's Providence House**, another fine old Newport building, dating back to 1701, and stay at **Newport Quay Hotel** (0983–528544) or more cheaply at **Orme House** (0983–522977). TIC in town centre (0983–525450).

About 1 mile south-west of the town, **Carisbrooke Castle** (*EH, standard opening times*) is well-preserved, with a 12th-century keep and artillery fortifications built in the 1590s against a Spanish invasion. Charles I was held prisoner here for 10 months in 1647–8. Until 1944, the Island Governor had his official residence here; now the **County Museum** occupies the Governor's Lodge. In **CARISBROOKE** village, St Mary's church is worth seeing for its Norman nave and massive 15th-century tower.

Leave Newport by A3056 towards Shanklin. **Arreton Manor** (*open April–Oct daily except Sat*), a 17th-century house built of mellow stone, contains collections of dolls and dolls' houses, old prams and toys and many other things, as well as the **National Wireless Museum**. At **Arreton Country Craft Village** (*open daily except Sat*), you can see artists and craftspeople at work, and buy their products.

Drive north from Arreton on a minor road over the downs and turn right in Downend along the hillside towards Brading. There are plenty of walks around here, with some fine views as well. **BRADING**, poised between the downs and the water meadows of the Yar estuary, used to be a small harbour until a century or so ago. The church, St Mary's, is one of the oldest on the island. The **Roman Villa** (*open April–Sept daily*) contains exquisite mosaic floors. Other, more touristy, attractions here include **Lilliput Museum of Antique Dolls and Toys** (*open mid-March–Dec daily*), with over 1,000 items, some dating back several thousand years, and **Osborn-smith's Wax Museum** (*open daily*), which recreates scenes from Island history. At the south end of the village is **Morton Manor** (*open April–Oct daily except Sat*). The house, which dates back to the 13th century but was largely rebuilt in the 1680s, is set in attractively landscaped parkland, with a rose garden, a sunken Elizabethan garden and a vineyard.

A3055 would take you south to Sandown and Shanklin, but instead branch right at the south end of Brading, following an unclassified road through Alverstone (good walks along the little river Yar) and Winford.

Carry straight on at the junction with A3056, and then turn right on to A3020. The thatched cottages and hilltop 15th-century church at **GODSHILL** inevitably define it as 'picturesque'. Underneath the all-too-twee holiday trappings — souvenir and antique shops, tea rooms, a **model village** (*open April–Sept daily*) — a traditional English village is struggling to escape. Visit out of season and you might just be able to appreciate it.

The **Worsley Trail**, one of the Island's eight long-distance paths, passes south of Godshill. Follow the Trail west for a fine walk (about 8 miles' easy going) along the belt of chalk downs that runs across the southern half of the island; you can meet your driver again in Brighstone Forest (see below).

Turn south on unclassified roads to Southford and **NITON**, a double village, the top half sheltered in the downs, the lower part set in that curious geological formation known as the undercliff. Repeated landslips over many centuries have created this sheltered strip of land squeezed between the sea and the steep downs; lush vegetation flourishes in its warm, humid climate. Below, **St Catherine's Point**, the southernmost tip of the island, is a good place for bird-watching, especially during the spring and autumn migrations.

Drive north-west along A3055, past **Blackgang Chine**, where there is an imaginative **fantasy theme park** (*open April–Oct daily*) with, in addition, a replica of a 19th-century sawmill and an exhibition of

*Freshwater Bay and Tennyson Down*

shipwrecks and smuggling. Chine is the local word for a ravine cut in the cliffs; the land hereabouts is still unstable — there was a landslip as recently as 1978.

Climb up to St Catherine's Hill and, behind it, St Catherine's Down (*both NT*), a spectacular viewpoint with panoramas across the island. A3055 continues along the cliff tops, soon bringing the best view in the island: the great sweep of unspoilt coast along to Freshwater Bay and Tennyson Down dropping sheer into the water, and beyond to the Needles, with — visible on a fine day — the Dorset coast in the far distance. Inland green meadows gently browse in the sunshine, and between high banks filled with wild flowers narrow lanes wander among peaceful villages.

You can either continue along the coast road, A3055, to Freshwater Bay, or else turn inland by the holiday camp at Shepherd's Chine to YAFFORD. (A third possibility is to walk along the coastal footpath.) All the machinery at Yafford Mill (*open April–Oct daily*) is in full working order, and you can wander through water gardens and along a nature walk, examine collections of old farm machinery, and look at rare breeds of cattle and sheep. Beyond the village, turn left on to B3399 for BRIGHSTONE, nestling in a fold in the downs.

A right turn in Brighstone on to an unclassified road leads you to the top of the downs, where there's a 2½-mile forest walk through Brighstone Forest, which is largely beech; red squirrels live here. The forest is also the end point of the Worsley Trail (see above), and from here you can also follow the Tennyson Trail, either on to Freshwater Bay (about 5 miles) and Alum Bay (another 2½ miles — see below) — a bracing hill- and cliff-top walk with lovely views — or back through the agricultural heart of the island to Carisbrooke (about 5 miles).

Descend to Mottistone, another peaceful village complete with Tudor manor house and church with lych gate, and rejoin the coast road at BROOK, where Hanover House serves afternoon teas. The golden sands of Compton beach are every child's delight, with excellent bathing.

Though not especially attractive itself, FRESHWATER BAY makes a good base for exploring the western end of the island. The Poet Laureate Alfred, Lord Tennyson, lived here for nearly 40 years; the early photographer Julia Margaret Cameron was a near neighbour. Tennyson's home, Farringford House, is now a luxury hotel (Farringford Hotel — 0983–752500); other nearby hotels are Blenheim House (0983–752858) and Saunders (0983–752322). Walk up from the beach on to the glorious downs — the air, Tennyson said, was 'worth sixpence a pint' — past the Tennyson Monument and on to the Needles. Rare species of orchid grow here, as well as many other tiny chalkland plants; this part of the downs is also a bird sanctuary.

By car, follow the minor road past Farringford Hotel and on past Alum Bay to the Needles. This trio of chalk sea-stacks — there was a fourth until it collapsed in 1764 — is all that remains of the chalk hills that once, before the Isle of Wight became an island, extended to the Purbeck Hills in Dorset. The Needles Old Battery (*NT, open April–Oct daily except Fri and Sat, but open those days in July and Aug*) is a fort built in 1862, in anticipation of a French invasion; a 200ft tunnel leads to the searchlight position (excellent views of the Needles and lighthouse), and the former Powder Magazine houses an exhibition.

The coloured sands of **Alum Bay** — there are more than 20 shades, most vivid after rain — are caused by the varying presence of minute quantities of minerals. Souvenirs filled with sand can be bought in the **Needles Pleasure Park** (*open April–Oct daily*) from where a chair lift descends to the sands. At **Alum Bay Glass** (*open Easter–Oct daily, but no glassmaking on Sat*) you can watch glassware and jewellery being made, and there is also a **Museum of Clocks** (*open July–Sept daily except Sat*) nearby.

For the final leg of the drive, return to Freshwater Bay and take B3399 along the central ridge of the island past **Calbourne Mill** (*open Easter–Oct daily*). The 17th-century mill is in full working order, and there is also an exhibition of rural life, with old machinery and woodland walks.

Turn left in Calbourne village, then left again on to A3054, and then almost immediately right towards deserted **Newtown**. The island's capital in the 12th and 13th century, the village was destroyed by a French raiding party in 1377 and never rebuilt, although the **Old Town Hall** (*NT, open April–Sept Mon, Wed and Sun afternoons, also Tues and Thurs in July and Aug*) was rebuilt in about 1700, and the church dates from 1835. Beyond this ghost village, its streets still just discernible, there is a fine 3-mile walk through the mudflats and former salt pans of Newtown Nature Reserve, with good opportunities for bird-watching.

A3054 runs east to Newport, past **Parkhurst Forest**, a remnant of the woods that in the Middle Ages stretched across much of the north of the Island. There are two trails here through pleasant mixed deciduous and conifer woodland.

# West Sussex and East Hampshire
*1–2 days/about 90 miles/from Chichester/OS maps 185, 186, 197*

The gentle chalk downs of West Sussex and the south-eastern part of Hampshire deserve to be better known. This is not for the most part a dramatic landscape — the exceptions are the steep northern slopes around Midhurst and the thickly wooded beech hangers near Selborne, both of which offer fine views — but a pastoral one with tranquil villages built of local stone and some grand country houses. It all provides welcome relief from the coastline, marred by rather ugly and scrappy development, and the huge and ever developing conurbation around Portsmouth and Southampton.

The 277ft **cathedral** spire marks **CHICHESTER** (pop. 24,900) from miles off. The church (largely early 12th-century, but with later additions) contains inspiring work from many different periods: for instance, two

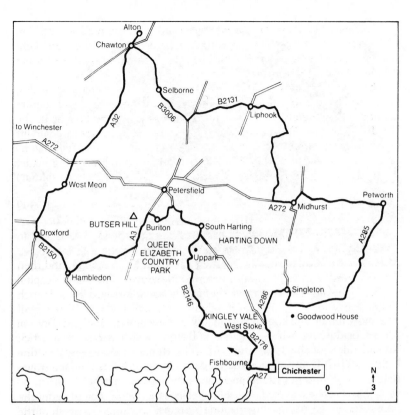

12th-century sculptures, a beautiful carved stone screen from 1475, intricately worked choir stalls, and, from our own time, John Piper's vivid altar tapestry, stained glass by Marc Chagall, and a painting by Graham Sutherland in the Chapel of St Mary Magdalene. The compact, elegant city follows the ground plan of the original Roman settlement, with four main streets meeting at the late 15th-century Market Cross. There are many attractive Georgian buildings — look especially at the lanes known as the **Pallants**; **Pallant House Gallery** (*open Tues–Sat*) in North Pallant (built 1713 and recently restored) houses a collection of modern art. **St Mary's Hospital** (*open Oct–March Tues–Sat*) was built in the 13th century as a hospital and chapel, and now serves as almshouses. See also the **Guildhall Museum** (*open June–Sept Tues–Sat*), which contains impressive local archaeological finds, and the **Mechanical Music and Doll Collection** (*open Easter–Sept daily, also winter weekends*), with barrel and fairground organs, Victorian dolls. The 1960s **Festival Theatre** stages an annual summer season, generally of not-too-demanding classics, and there are regular plays, concerts, etc throughout the rest of the year. Eat at **Chat's Brasserie** or at **St Martin's Tea Rooms**, and stay at **Nags** (0243–785823), a half-timbered pub in the town centre; **Dolphin and Anchor** (0243–785121) is a more upmarket hotel, with a good view of the cathedral. TIC in St Peter's Market, West Street (0243–775888).

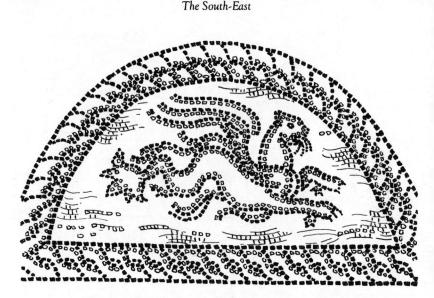

*Winged sea-panthers mosaic from Fishbourne Roman Palace*

The most important known personality in Chichester's early history was King Cogidubnus, who, although a Briton, was a friend of the new Roman rulers of the 1st century AD. His **Roman palace**, discovered at **FISHBOURNE** just outside the modern city in 1960, is the largest and richest ever found in Britain, and one of the largest anywhere. The north wing has been excavated, revealing elaborate, richly coloured mosaic floors, tesselated pavements, heating systems, corridors and courtyards, all now part of a modern building which also contains an informative museum. Outside, part of the garden has been replanted to its original plan with plants believed to have grown in Roman times. To reach the villa, take A259 west from the centre of Chichester, join the fast A27, and turn right almost immediately. (*Open March–Nov daily, also Dec–Feb Sun only.*)

Drive north from Fishbourne on a minor road, turn left on to B2178 and then right on to another unclassified road to West Stoke. Park beyond the village and walk up Stoke Down to **Kingley Vale National Nature Reserve**, where groves of ancient yew trees, some 500 years old, stand on a spur of the downs amid a line of Bronze Age remains. A 2-mile trail runs through the reserve, with lovely views across open downland.

Continue along the minor road to Funtington, where join B2146, which runs first west and then north through hilly wooded country, climbing gradually towards the high plateau of the Downs. On the right is the entrance to **Uppark** (*NT, open April–Sept, Wed, Thur, Sun and Bank Holiday Mon afternoons*), a fine late 17th-century red-brick mansion commanding superb views towards the coast. The interior has hardly been changed since the mid-18th century, with good furniture, carpets and paintings, and a Queen Anne dolls house, complete with its own period furnishings; the 'below stairs' rooms are Victorian. Humphrey

*Uppark*

Repton landscaped the gardens, which include a tea room, in the early 19th century.

Beyond Uppark, B2146 descends steeply towards South Harting. For some excellent views, and also equally excellent walking, turn sharp right on to B2141, which climbs to the top of **Harting Downs**, a popular spot with kite-fliers and hang-gliders. You can follow the long-distance **South Downs Way** west, rejoining your driver at Butser Hill (7 miles — see below) or — a shorter but more exhilarating walk, this — stride out east to Beacon Hill (1 mile, but a steep climb). This part of the Downs consists of mixed woodland and open grassland, the latter scattered with wild flowers, including many varieties of orchid. Sheep, the mainstay of local agriculture from the 15th century until well into the 20th, still graze, but, as everywhere along the South Downs nowadays, arable crops (notably barley and oilseed rape) are more profitable. Ahead, the view is of the small fields and scattered farmhouses of the clay Weald.

Descend to South Harting, recognisable by the green copper spire of its church, and follow B2146, turning left after about 2½ miles on an unclassified road through **BURITON** with its village pond to A3. A left turn on to this busy dual carriageway (take care — this is a dangerous stretch of road) leads you through a great cutting in the bare chalk to the **Queen Elizabeth Country Park** (*open daily*). There's an exhibition of forest life in the Visitor Centre, which is the starting-point for a variety of rambles, through beechwoods and up to the top of **Butser Hill**, at 889ft the highest point on the South Downs, and also the western end of the range, a massive full-stop in the chalk, visible from miles off. Butser is littered with ancient earthworks, and the Country Park is also the centre of an Ancient Farm Research Project, which investigates the way of life of

139

our Bronze and Iron Age ancestors. A replica roundhouse has been built alongside A3, and demonstrations of ancient crafts are given.

Continue south on A3 for just over 1 mile, then turn right through Clanfield (not a pretty village) and continue on unclassified roads alongside **Broadhalfpenny Down** to **HAMBLEDON**. This is hallowed ground for cricketers, for in the late 18th century the Hambledon Club was the first to lay down formal rules for the game. A monument near the club's pitch on the Down shows the curved bat and two stumps originally used. All this calls for a drink at the **Bat and Ball Inn**.

Follow B2150 north from Hambledon to Droxford, where turn right on to A32, which runs up the Meon valley. There are some delightful riverside villages here — elegant Georgian houses in **DROXFORD**, an originally Saxon church in **CORHAMPTON**, and in **EXTON** a massive Norman church tower. Turn off A32 to the right to **WEST MEON**, with plaster and timber cottages, many thatched. Buildings of many different styles contribute to the harmony of these unspoilt villages.

It's a welcome measure of the lack of organised tourism in this area that there are few places actually on this route to spend the night. **WINCHESTER**, 12 miles west along A272, is the obvious place for an overnight break, even though negotiating the by-pass to get into the town centre is a bit of a bind. Hotels here include, in descending order of cost, **Wessex** (0962–61611), **Wykeham Arms** (0962–53834) and **Southgate** (0962–51243); **Mr Pitkin's** is a nicer than average wine bar. Things to see include the cathedral, the buildings of Winchester School, the City Museum and the Great Hall, the only remnant of the medieval castle. TIC in the Guildhall (0962–840500).

Our route continues north on A32 to **CHAWTON**, a small and unpretentious village where the novelist Jane Austen lived from 1809 until her death in 1817. The red-brick house, which belonged to her brother, is now the **Jane Austen Museum** (*open April–Oct daily, Nov, Dec and March Wed–Sun, Jan and Feb weekends only*). It's moving to see the table at which she worked, concealing her manuscript whenever anyone else entered the room; *Mansfield Park*, *Emma* and *Persuasion* were all written here, for these were the years of her literary success. Letters and personal possessions are also displayed.

A mile or so beyond Chawton, **ALTON** is a pleasant small Georgian market and manufacturing town. The parish church still bears bullet marks from a Civil War battle. **Curtis Museum** (*open Tues–Sat*) has imaginative displays on local archaeology, history and natural history. The **Swan Hotel** (0420–83777) is an old coaching inn dating back to the 16th century. The town is at one end of the **Watercress Line**, a steam-operated railway running to Alresford. (*Services operate most days June–Aug and at weekends in April, May, Sept and Oct; tel. 096273–3810 for details.*)

B3006 runs south-west through thickly wooded country to **SELBORNE**, another literary shrine — to the pioneering naturalist Gilbert White, the local curate and author of *The Natural History of Selborne*, which he published in 1789. Truth to tell, **The Wakes** (*open*

March–Oct daily except Mon), the house in which he lived, is rather dis-appointing. The displays, which cover both White's life and work and the lives of several members of the Oates family, including Captain Lawrence Oates, who accompanied Scott's Antarctic Expedition, are rather amateur and old-fashioned. But first of all the five acres of gardens, left much as White knew them — you may also see descendants of Timmy, the naturalist's tortoise — and then the wonderful countryside around more than make up for this. Climb up the **Zig-Zag** (well signposted), the winding path White built in 1753 up the hanger, and then follow paths through woodland above the village and out across Selborne Common — all land little changed since Gilbert White made his observations here. You can walk for miles, descending the steep downland spurs to sleepy wooded valleys. In the village is also the **Romany Folklore Museum and Workshop** (*open daily*), which has displays of Romany history, crafts and costume and a large collection of living-waggons; the workshop restores and decorates waggons still in use.

Continue on B3006, turn left on to A325, and then almost immedi-ately right to **LIPHOOK**, where **Bohunt Manor Gardens** (*open daily*) has a large collection of waterfowl in attractive gardens. Also in the village is **Hollycombe Steam Collection and Gardens** (*open Easter–early Oct Sun and Bank Holiday Mons, also daily for 1 week in early July and another in mid-Aug*), where there is a working Quarry Railway, agri-cultural and fairground locomotives, and woodland walks.

From Liphook, strike south on unclassified roads to Woolbeding, and then left along A272 to Midhurst. Now the long, smooth ridge of the Downs forms the constant backdrop to the landscape.

**MIDHURST**, a smart little town with lots of pricey antique shops, has a pleasing jumble of buildings of different ages. Street names such as Wool Lane and Sheep Lane indicate the source of the town's prosperity. The 16th-century timbered Market Hall by the church was later used by the grammar school. Just to the north of the town centre, on the far bank of the river Rother, are the ruins of **Cowdray Castle**, built in the 1530s and burnt down in 1793. The town's two main hotels — the **Angel** (073081–2421) and the **Spread Eagle** (073081–2211) — are both old inns, the latter dating from the late 15th century.

Leave Midhurst by A286 north, and almost immediately bear right on to A272, which runs along the edge of **Cowdray Park**, famous for its polo club. Much land around Midhurst belongs to the Cowdray estate — its houses are distinguished by being painted a very bright yellow.

It is easy to overlook the attractive buildings, many half-timbered, and market square of **PETWORTH**, for the town seems to huddle under-neath the walls (which, encircling the park, extend to 13 miles) of **Petworth House**. This is a truly grand mansion, built in the late 17th century by the 6th Duke of Somerset and landscaped in the mid-18th by Capability Brown. The interior is stupendous: frescoes, carvings, paintings (by Rembrandt, Holbein, van Dyck, Turner among others), furniture. (*NT, House open April–Oct daily except Mon and Fri; gardens daily.*) National Trust restaurant, in the servants' quarters, and shop.

A285 south from Petworth crosses the Rother valley and then climbs to the top of **Duncton Down** — fine views as you look back. Turn right through woods towards **Goodwood House**. There are parking spots along this road, and signed forest walks. The house is another grand aristocratic mansion built by James Wyatt in the early 18th century, and contains more superb collections: paintings by Stubbs, Canaletto, van Dyck and Reynolds, fine French porcelain, furniture and tapestries, and an eclectic array of relics — e.g. Queen Victoria's walking stick and Napoleon's chair. Horse-racing started in 1802 — there is regular racing throughout the summer, plus a meeting at the start of August and the European Dressage Championships in July — and motor-racing after the Second World War. The **Goodwood Park Hotel** (0243–775537) occupies a former coaching inn. (*Open May–Sept Sun and Mon only, also Tues–Thur in Aug, but closed occasionally closed on those days* — *tel. 0243–774107 to check.*)

Beyond Goodwood, the road passes an ancient hillfort known as The Trundle and occupied since at least 2000BC — radio masts are the 20th century's bequest to future archaeologists — and **St Roche's Arboretum**, where there are fine specimens, including many conifers, before reaching A286 at Singleton. A left turn here brings you almost immediately to the **Weald and Downland Open Air Museum** (*open April–Oct daily, also Sun and Wed in winter*). This is a collection of historic buildings from Sussex, all carefully dismantled on their original site and re-erected here. Sussex builders have traditionally worked with local materials, and it is fascinating to see the variety of techniques and materials used over some 500 years. The buildings here include a 19th-century village school, a toll cottage, a market hall and a 15th-century farmhouse. Plenty of background information is provided to make the bricks and mortar come alive, and there are frequent demonstrations of rural crafts and skills.

Just off A286 on the right are **West Dean Gardens** (*open daily April–Sept, nursery all year*). There have been gardens here since the 17th century — some of the trees date back that long — and they are a pleasing mixture of styles, with Victorian arboreta and glasshouses, a gazebo, and a walled kitchen garden. A nursery sells shrubs and plants.

Return to Chichester along A286.

# Weald, Marsh and Down

*1–2 days/about 130 miles/from Tunbridge Wells/OS maps 188, 189, 199, 198, 187*

Three distinctive landscapes are encountered on this route. First, the Weald, a great band of rich wooded country that runs across south-east England, bordered by chalk downs to north and south. Nowadays fertile farming country, the Weald was formerly the source of timber for the forges of the iron industry that flourished here from Roman times until the 17th and 18th centuries. Then we cross on to the edge of Romney

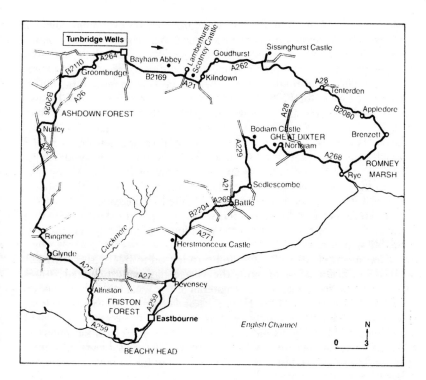

Marsh, lonely, sparsely populated and mysterious, especially when the winter mists roll in off the sea. Finally, we reach the South Downs where they run into the English Channel at the steep chalk cliffs of Beachy Head: 'the blunt, bow-headed, whale-backed Downs' as the poet Rudyard Kipling described them.

In the 18th and 19th centuries, **TUNBRIDGE WELLS** (pop. 55,900) was Bath's greatest rival in the attempt to gain the patronage, and thus the purses, of fashionable society. The town is formally known as 'Royal Tunbridge Wells', but that is a quite recent title, bestowed by Edward VII in 1909. Chalybeate springs were first discovered here in the early 17th century, and the town was firmly established as a spa resort by the early 18th. In 1735, Beau Nash, who had laid down the elaborate ground rules by which social life was conducted in Bath, came to do the same thing for Tunbridge Wells.

The town retains something of an 18th-century atmosphere, notably around **The Pantiles**, an elegant parade of shops (so called because of the clay, or pan, tiles with which the street was paved), and the lower end of the High Street. It's a pleasant place to stroll and to window-shop. Somewhat predictably, antiques are the speciality: will England never run out of antique knick-knacks and bric-à-brac, or are they all simply recycled every generation or so? The **Museum and Art Gallery** (*open*

*Mon–Sat, but closed Bank Holiday Mons and Tues*) in the Civic Centre on Mount Pleasant contains local history and archaeology displays, with a special feature on 'Tunbridge Ware' woodwork, and dolls and toys. **Pilgrim's** on Mount Ephraim (one of the distinguished-looking 19th-century quarters of the town) is a cheerful vegetarian restaurant. Stay in style at the **Spa Hotel** (0892–20331) or more modestly at the **Wellington** (0892–42911). TIC in the Town Hall (0892–26121).

Leave Tunbridge Wells on A267 south, soon turning left on to B2169, which runs east through undulating, thickly wooded countryside. A left turn after 5 miles or so brings you to the ruins of **Bayham Abbey** (*EH, standard opening times summer only*), delightfully situated on the banks of the little river Teise. The abbey was founded in the early 13th century, and, having been abolished by Henry VIII, was preserved in order to form the backdrop for the view from the mansion built in the 18th century on the hill opposite.

Continue east along B2169, and turn left on to B2100 to **LAMBER-HURST**. Set amid steep hills, the village has many timbered houses: timber is the traditional building material of the Weald. North-west of the village, the gardens of **Owl House** (*open daily*) contain rhododendrons, azaleas, woodlands and a sunken water garden; the cottage (*not open*), tile-hung and half-timbered, is said to have been used by wool smugglers. At 50 acres, **Lamberhurst Vineyards** (*open daily, guided tours July–Sept*), are said to be the largest in south-east England; take a bottle of 'Lamberhurst Priory' wine home with you.

Drive south on the main A21 for about 1½ miles, braving the almost incessant flow of traffic, and turn left to visit **Scotney Castle** (*NT, garden open April–mid-Nov, Wed–Fri and Sat, Sun and Bank Holiday Mon afternoons; house same days May–Aug*). Scotney is one of the many castles and fortified manor houses dotted across Kent (evidence of turbulent times in the post-Conquest centuries). The massive turreted tower was built in the late 14th century, while the manor house is Tudor, and not to be confused with the newer 19th-century Tudor-style castle. The romantic hillside gardens are a 19th-century creation too. National Trust shop.

Return to A21, turn left, and then left again on to the unclassifed road running north through **KILNDOWN**, where the village church is a fine example of the mid-19th century Gothic Revival style. The original vivid colours are now rather faded, but the red and yellow tiles, the stained glass and the stencilled wall patterns remain impressive.

This is quite steep countryside, and there's a top-of-the-world feeling about **GOUDHURST**, reached by turning right on to A262. The view from the top of the 17th-century tower of St Mary's church is glorious: a peaceful Kentish scene, with woodland, hop fields and orchards — the garden of England indeed. The rest of the church dates from the 15th century; see especially the monuments, including those of the Culpepper and Bedgebury families, both major landowners hereabouts and active in the Wealden iron industry. There are some handsome tiled and weatherboarded houses in the town, product of its prosperity gained from the cloth trade.

A262 runs east to Sissinghurst, where the garden at **Sissinghurst Castle** (*NT, open April–mid-Oct Tues–Fri afternoons and all day Sat and Sun*) is among the most celebrated and therefore most visited in the country; it is often crowded, especially at weekends. The fine gatehouse and entrance buildings, all nearly in ruins, were all that remained of the 16th-century house when Harold Nicholson, diplomat turned writer, and his wife, the novelist Vita Sackville-West, bought it in the 1930s. Restoration of both house and garden was an immense task, which took much of the rest of their lives to complete. The garden was designed, in Vita Sackville-West's words, as a 'combination of long axial walks . . . usually with terminal points such as a statue or an archway or a pair of sentinel poplars, and the more intimate surprise of small geometrical designs opening off them, rather as the rooms of an enormous house would open off the arterial corridors. There should be the strictest formality of design, with the maximum informality in planting.' Her plan was achieved triumphantly. Each small 'room' — the rose garden, the herb garden, the white garden, Delos (inspired by the Greek Island) — has its own character and also its own distinctive colours, and is planned to flower at a different season. National Trust shop and restaurant.

Return along A262 to **SISSINGHURST** village (white weatherboarded cottages), where turn left on to the minor road leading south to Golford hamlet. Turn left here on to another unclassified road which runs south-east through woodland to the outskirts of **TENTERDEN**. Turn left on to A28 to reach the town centre.

This is a beautiful small market town, still relatively unspoilt and uncrowded. The church dominates; from the top of the 100ft tower, on a clear day, you can see the Channel, and on a very clear one, the French coast. The houses and shops are Tudor to Georgian, with the latter

*Sissinghurst Castle*

predominant. The **museum** (*open Easter–Oct daily, usually afternoons only, also winter weekend afternoons*) in Station Road recalls the town's history. In the 15th century it was a cloth-exporting port on the river Rother (since then, the river has silted), and belonged to the Confederation of the Cinque Ports (see below). The **Kent and East Sussex Railway**, a steam-hauled private line, runs alongside the Rother from the town. Rolling stock can be seen at the restored Edwardian station at Tenterden and also at Rolvenden station. (*Static displays open Easter–Christmas daily; trains run Easter–New Year weekends and Bank Holidays, daily in Bank Holiday weeks and mid July–early Sept, also Tues–Thurs in June and July; tel. 05806–2943 for details.*) Tenterden would make an excellent base from which to tour west Kent and East Sussex; there are several old coaching inns along the main street, including the **White Lion** (05806–5777). TIC in the attractive late 18th-century Town Hall in the High Street (05806–3572).

Leave along B2080, which runs east to **APPLEDORE**, which stands on the border between the wooded Weald and the flat land of Romney Marsh, barely higher than sea level and criss-crossed by drainage channels and embankments. It all seems peaceful now, but in 1380 the village was sacked and the church burnt by a French raiding party. When Napoleon threatened invasion just over 400 years later, the **Royal Military Canal** was built across the back of the Marsh from Rye to Hythe, so forming a kind of defensive moat. B2080 crosses the now disused canal (walks along the bank) and then runs across the Marsh to Brenzett. Sheep were once the mainstay of Marsh agriculture, but now there is extensive arable farming as well.

Turn right in Brenzett, and head along A259 towards **RYE**, which rises sentinel-like out of the surrounding marshes. In the Middle Ages, it was one of the Cinque Ports, an association of five (*cinque* = five in French) Channel ports originally formed to defend the coast and after the Conquest granted extensive privileges in return for supplying the monarch with men and ships; the other four towns are Sandwich, Dover, New Romney and Hastings. The sea has long since receded.

Rye is very much a town for strolling, enjoying the shops and well-preserved old buildings, notably along cobbled Mermaid Street. The church (12th-19th centuries) has a magnificent mahogany altar and a turret clock, where the quarter hours (but not the hours) are struck by the figures of two boys. **Lamb House** (*NT, April–Oct Wed and Sat afternoons*) was the home of the American novelist Henry James from 1898 to 1916, and later of the writer E.F. Benson. The **museum** (*open April–mid Oct daily*), housed in a 13th-century defensive tower known as the Ypres Tower, contains displays on local and Cinque Port history. The **Swiss Patisserie** in Cinque Ports Street is recommended not only for cakes and pastries of all kinds, but also for savoury dishes. **Jeakes House** (0797–222828) is a pleasant bed-and-breakfast establishment in Mermaid Street, while there are fine views over Romney Marsh from the **Old Vicarage** (0797–225131) in East Street. TIC at 48 Cinque Ports Street (0797–222293).

Leave town on A268 north, which soon turns north-west. Beyond Peasmarsh, at Four Oaks, turn left on to B2088 towards Northiam, which joins A28 at the entrance to the village. **Great Dixter** (*open April–mid-Oct afternoons except Mon*) is a lovely 15th-century timber-framed manor house; the great hall was restored in 1911 by the Edwardian architect Sir Edwin Lutyens. He also designed the gardens, which are full of topiary, yew hedges and flower borders.

The woods behind Great Dixter overlook the Rother valley, where, not distant as the crow flies, Bodiam Castle stands guard. To get there by road, return to the centre of the village, and then follow minor roads through Ewhurst Green and over the little river bridge to Bodiam.

**Bodiam Castle** (*NT, open daily except Suns Nov–March*) comes straight from the pages of a picture book of traditional England, great stone walls and battlemented towers rising from a shimmering moat scattered with water-lilies. Bodiam was one of the last military castles built in England — in 1385, against a French invasion that failed to materialise — and was slighted after being besieged during the Civil War. Inside, the layout of the rooms is quite easy to understand, and some of the towers can be climbed. A Second World War gun emplacement on the sward in front of the castle is a reminder of preparations for a more recent invasion; the Rother would have made as good a defensive position in 1940 as in 1385. National Trust shop and café.

Drive through Bodiam village to A229, where turn left and drive south to Sedlescombe. Turn right here on to an unclassified road which crosses A21 and runs through Whatlington to **BATTLE**, a bustling small town which takes its name from that most famous event in all English history: the Battle of Hastings in 1066, when England fell to the invading

*Bodiam Castle*

Norman armies. At the far end of the High Street stand the excavated foundations of the **abbey** (*EH, standard opening times*) erected by William I in gratitude for his victory. The high altar was erected over the spot where King Harold was killed, and information boards at strategic points enable you to work out the ebb and flow of the fighting. The impressive abbey gateway dates from the 14th century. The **museum** (*open April–Sept daily except Sun morning*) tells the story of the battle and also has displays on local history, especially the local iron industry. There are old buildings in the rest of the town. **La Vieille Auberge** (04246–2255) is a 15th-century inn standing on the High Street. TIC at 88 High Street (04246–3721).

Leave Battle on A269 west, and where the road bends sharp left continue straight on along B2204 to the junction with A271. Turn right here and continue along the ridge, which has fine views south towards the shore, turning left on to a minor road signposted **Herstmonceux Castle** (*open April–Sept daily*). The castle is the home of the Royal Greenwich Observatory, which moved here from London in 1957. Two rooms of the castle are open, with displays on modern astronomy, together with telescopes, and the attractive grounds.

The road descends and crosses Pevensey Levels. Turn right on to the main road, and continue straight on at the junction on A27, which runs directly underneath the walls of **Pevensey Castle** (*EH, standard opening times*). This Norman castle was built within a Roman fort constructed in the 4th century; much of its walls are still standing. Soldiers have been regularly stationed here: during the Spanish Armada, the Napoleonic Wars and most recently, during the Second World War. TIC (summer only) in castle car park (0323–761444).

Our next destination is Beachy Head on the far side of Eastbourne, a town which it's virtually impossible to avoid. Turn left on to B2191 in Pevensey, then left again on to B2104, then right on to A259. Approaching the town centre, make sure you are on the seafront road (B2103), and stick to that, driving the entire length of the front and then climbing up steeply on to the Downs at the far end of town; turn left, following signs for Beachy Head.

**EASTBOURNE** (pop. 83,600) has attractive parks and gardens, a Victorian pier, sandy beaches and all the usual resort amenities, but provided in a fairly tasteful style. TIC at 3 Cornfield Terrace (0323–411400) and also (summer only) at the Pier.

It is at the steep chalk cliffs of **Beachy Head**, 532ft above the waters of the Channel that the South Downs meet the sea. Splendid views, wheeling seabirds, soft turf and salt breezes all invite you to leave the car and stride out along the downs. This is also the eastern end of the **South Downs Way** long-distance path (the western end is described on page 139), which you could follow across the undulating Seven Sisters (there are in fact eight cliffs, but seven is traditionally a magical number) and then inland along Cuckmere River, meeting your driver at Seven Sisters Country Park (6 miles).

The unclassified road follows the coast from Beachy Head to Birling

Gap, and then turns inland to East Dean. Turn left here on to A259, which descends steeply to the Cuckmere valley. The car park for **Seven Sisters Country Park** is on the left. There are walks towards the sea and in Friston Forest on the other side of the main road, and a well-laid out **Visitor Centre** (*open Easter–Sept daily, also winter weekends*). **Living World** (*open April–Oct daily, also winter weekends*) is an indoor exhibition of insects, butterflies, and marine life, all displayed in their natural surroundings; watch out for spiders and scorpions!

Turn right just before A259 crosses the river on to a minor road running alongside the forest and through Litlington, turn left and left again to reach Alfriston. All around are the swirling chalk domes of the downs, cut through with narrow steep-sided valleys and patches of dense woodland. **ALFRISTON** is a charming village (almost too charming for its own good) with half-timbered houses, including the **Star** (0323–870495) and the **George Inn** (0323–870319); the **Singing Kettle** is a pleasant small teashop. **Alfriston Clergy House** (*NT, open April–Oct daily*) is a half-timbered and thatched 14th-century priests' house opposite the lofty 14th-century church.

Head north out of the village and turn left on to A27 near Berwick. **Drusillas Zoo Park** (*open April–Oct daily, also winter weekends*) boasts monkeys, penguins, llamas, tropical butterflies and other attractions such as a miniature railway.

Drive west along A27, where signposts point the way to **Charleston Farmhouse** (*open April–Oct Wed, Thur, Sat, Sun and Bank Holiday Mon afternoons — timed ticket system*), a 17th- and 18th-century farmhouse that belonged to Vanessa and Clive Bell and Duncan Grant, luminaries of the inter-war Bloomsbury Group.

Now turn right off A27 on to the unclassified road leading to **GLYNDE**. **Glynde Place** (*open June–Sept Wed, Thur and Bank Holiday Mon afternoons*) is a handsome 16th-century manor house (remodelled in the 18th century) with a panelled long gallery and some fine portraits. Travelling north, we pass **Glyndebourne**, the celebrated little opera house tucked in a quiet fold of the Downs.

The final, and quite lengthy, leg of the journey is through the wooded Sussex Weald: not as dramatic perhaps as the bare-backed Downs, but lush, peaceful countryside, and surprisingly isolated (so long as you stay away from the main roads). Turn right on to B2192, then almost immediately left through Ringmer village to the junction with A26. Turn right here and then left after about 1½ miles on to an unclassified road running north through Isfield, straight over A272 and on to Nutley. Turn left here on to A22, and almost immediately right on to a minor road. Turn left on to B2026, which heads through **Ashdown Forest**, a marvellous high-level stretch of mixed woodland and heath, sadly ravaged by the great storm in October 1987. It was in Ashdown Forest that Christopher Robin, Pooh, Piglet and their friends lived — and, who knows, perhaps they do so still, for those with sufficient innocence to find them. In Hartfield, turn right on to B2110, and then, beyond Groombridge, right again on to A264, which returns to Tunbridge Wells.

# 6 EAST ANGLIA

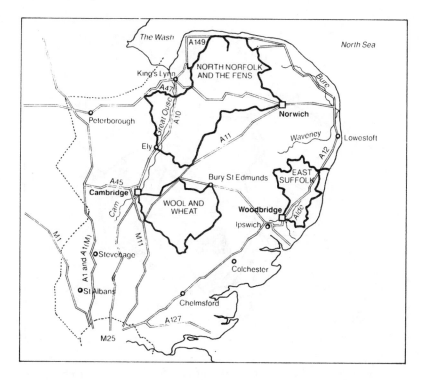

Wide skies filled with clouds scudding in ever-changing patterns; richly decorated churches, testimony to the wealth and faith of their builders 500 years and more ago; vast, intensively cultivated wheat fields; and a coastline broken by long estuaries and marshy creeks, where land and water merge gradually and imperceptibly. These are some of the traveller's impressions of East Anglia, an area whose subtler pleasures though long appreciated by *aficionados*, are only now beginning to be more widely known. It is a grand area to tour, for the side roads are relatively empty, the driving is easy, and, as well as the varied rural landscapes, there are many handsome country towns and villages to explore.

151

# East Suffolk

*1–2 days/about 100 miles/from Woodbridge/OS maps 169, 156*

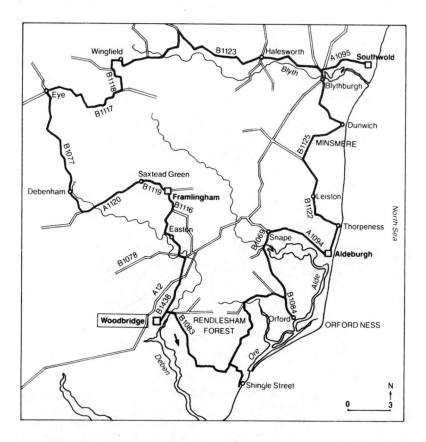

As they approach the sea, the rivers of east Suffolk — the Deben, the Alde, the Blyth — mere streams inland, widen into long tidal estuaries, whose lonely salt marshes and reed beds are the home of many seabirds. Immediately behind the shore lies a belt of woodland and sandy heath known as the Sandlings, where Scots and Corsican pine alternate with patches of vivid gorse and broom. A series of small fishing communities punctuates this inaccessible coastline, each with its own definite character. Inland from the Sandlings, on the far side of the A12, lies an attractive area of arable countryside dotted with relatively unvisited villages and small towns.

We start at Woodbridge, but for convenience only, as several other places on the route — Orford, Aldeburgh, Southwold, Framlingham — would make an equally pleasant base. **WOODBRIDGE**, at the head of the Deben estuary, is largely 18th-century, with some 16th-century buildings, notably the Shire Hall, the ground floor of which was originally used as a covered market. The church contains a monument to Thomas Seckford, a senior Court official in Elizabeth I's time, who was responsible for building much of the town. There are local history displays in the **museum** (*open April–Oct Thurs–Sat, also Sun and Bank Holiday afternoons*). The town's once busy ship-building and timber-exporting industries along the quay declined as ships grew too large to sail up the estuary; now the harbour is full of yachts, and there are thriving yacht-building concerns. The restored 18th-century **Tide Mill** (*open June–Oct weekends, also Bank Holiday weekends, Wed–Fri in July and Sept and daily in Aug*) contains working machinery, historic photographs and drawings. **Seckford Hall**, just outside town, was built by Thomas Seckford's father in about 1530 and is now an elegant country house hotel (03943–85678). Another place to stay is the **Bull Hotel** (03943–2089), a former coaching inn in Market Hill. The town also operates an unusual bed and breakfast scheme, in which one third of the (very reasonable) charge is donated to Oxfam; tel. 03943–2740 for details.

Leave Woodbridge on A1152 across the estuary, and immediately turn right on to B1083, which soon passes **Sutton Hoo**, where in 1938 was discovered, deep in the sand, a 7th-century ship filled with burial treasure — gold jewellery, gold coins in a gold purse, a magnificent sword with its scabbard, a battle standard, buckles and mounts. The treasure, which belonged to an Anglo-Saxon king, most likely Aethelhere, who was killed fighting the Northumbrians in 654, is now in the British Museum. Excavations — interrupted by the outbreak of the Second World War — have now resumed. (*Guided tours May–Sept weekends 2–4 pm.*)

Follow B1083 south through Sutton to Shottisham, where branch left on minor roads to Hollesley (pronounced Hozeley). A right turn in the village will take you out to **SHINGLE STREET**, a lonely village facing the North Sea, an ideal place if your fancy runs to sea, sky (often filled with scudding clouds), marshland and not much else. Back in Hollesley, head for Butley along a minor road that runs along the edge of **Rendlesham Forest**. The Sandlings are good walking country, and there are numerous paths through woodland and across the open heath. In Butley, a right turn on to B1084 brings you to Orford.

Now little more than a holiday village, **ORFORD** has seen more important days. In the 16th and 17th centuries, ships slowly made their way up the river (which is called the Ore downstream of Orford, the Alde upstream) between mudflats and marshes to the quay to collect cargoes of Suffolk wool for export to the continent. Even in the present century, the town had its own schooners and ketches, and craftsmen to build and repair them. Henry II built the **castle** (*EH, standard opening times but closed Thurs and Fri morning in winter*) for coastal defence in 1165–72. All that remains is the imposing 90ft keep (polygonal outside, cylindrical inside), which contains a chapel, great hall and cellar. From the top there are grand views over the river and Orford Ness, the long sand spit that stretches along the coast from Aldeburgh. The first performances of

Benjamin Britten's *Noye's Fludde* and *Curlew River* were given in the church (14th-century with a ruined Norman chancel), and at least one of his works is performed here during the annual Aldeburgh Festival. The Craft Shop in Front Street contains the **Dunwich Underwater Exploration Exhibition** (*open daily*), which tells the story of the exploration of Dunwich by marine archaeologists. There's a fine walk along the river bank to Chantry Point and beyond, with views over **Havergate Island**, which is a RSPB reserve with breeding avocets and terns. (*Permits in advance from the warden, 30 Mundays Lane, Orford; open April–Aug Sat, Sun, Mon and Thurs.*) The **Jolly Sailor** and **King's Head Inn** are two waterside pubs (the latter with accommodation — 0394–450271), while the **Crown and Castle** (0394–450205) is a more upmarket establishment.

*Orford castle*

Leave by the way you came, along B1084, but where the B road veers left after about 1 mile continue straight on through Sudbourne and alongside Tunstall Forest to join B1069 at **Snape Maltings**, in a wonderful situation on the edge of the marshy estuary. Used for storing grain for brewing until 1965, the Maltings were converted to a concert hall in 1967, and are now world famous as the focal point of the annual Aldeburgh Festival each June.

The Festival was founded by Benjamin Britten in 1948, and through his inspiration and guidance grew from most modest beginnings to become one of the liveliest and most exciting events of the musical calendar. Britten himself found the inspiration for much of his work from this windswept corner of Suffolk; *Peter Grimes*, with its vivid portrayal of the dour fishing community, is based on a poem by George Crabbe, who was born in Aldeburgh. A Mozart festival is held at the Maltings in late August/early September each year, and there are regular concerts throughout the year. (For details of the Festival programme and other concerts tel. 072885–2935). The complex of buildings also contains a craft shop, garden shop, art gallery and tea shop.

You can walk along the north bank of the Alde most of the way into Aldeburgh. By road, continue north on B1069 and then turn right on to A1094 at Snape church.

Nowadays, **ALDEBURGH**'s early 16th-century timber-framed **Moot Hall** (*open June–Sept daily, also Sun and Bank Holidays in May and June*)

*Snape Maltings*

stands on the sea front. When it was built, it was in the town centre — the rest of the old town has vanished into the sea. The hall contains local history displays. There is a fine shingle beach, with a Martello Tower a little way to the south, from which fishermen sail — herring and sprat are local delicacies. Stay here at **Uplands Hotel** (072885–2420), in the childhood home of the pioneer woman doctor Elizabeth Garrett-Anderson, or at **Brudenell Hotel** (072885–2071), and eat in the **Regatta Restaurant**. TIC in the Cinema in the High Street (072885–3637).

Take the coast road north to **THORPENESS**, a purpose-built resort created at the beginning of this century, where the 19th-century post mill (*open July and Aug Tues–Sun afternoons, also Easter and weekends and Bank Holiday Mons May, June and Sept*) is still in working order; it is now an information centre for the Suffolk Heritage Coast. North along the coast is Sizewell Nuclear Power Station, and the site of Sizewell B, now being built — expect delays because of construction traffic.

Turn inland on B1353 and then right on to B1122 to **LEISTON**. The **Long Shop**, now a museum (*open April–Sept daily*) was built in 1853 to house a pioneering production line for the manufacture and assembly of steam engines; also on show are examples of agricultural machinery manufactured here. North of the town on B1122 are the ruins of **Leiston Abbey** (*EH, open any reasonable time*), built in the 1360s; the Lady Chapel is still in use as a church, and the farmhouse built on to the side of the abbey is now a music-making centre.

Follow B1122 through Theberton, and then turn right on to B1125. In Westleton, turn right on to the unclassified road that runs to the shore at Dunwich. In Norman times **DUNWICH** was already an important port and monastic centre, and it grew in size during the Middle Ages, with numerous churches and chapels. Hardly anything now remains: an inn, a 19th-century church, the ruins of a 13th-century priory and a small museum (*open March–Oct weekends, also Tue and Thur in June and July, daily in Aug*). The rest has vanished under the sea, as the cliffs have yielded over the centuries to the beating waves. There are good cliff-top walks in both directions here, north towards Walberswick, south to Dunwich Heath (*NT*) and the RSPB's **Minsmere Reserve**, which consists of mixed heath, woodland, marsh and lagoon. (*Observation hides accessible from Dunwich Heath at any time; reserve open daily except Tues, but RSPB members only Sun and Bank Holiday weekends.*) This is a wonderfully remote spot, with hardly a sound except the regular swoosh of waves on shingle and the calling of seabirds.

Drive north-east from Dunwich through woodland to B1125, where a right turn brings you to **BLYTHBURGH**. Here the glorious 15th-century church is a landmark from miles distant, a great ark of faith riding up from the surrounding marshes. In the Middle Ages, Blythburgh was a town of some importance; the river was crowded with vessels, there were two annual fairs, and the town had its own gaol and mint. The church was built to match, 127ft long, 54ft wide, with fine carvings on the roof and pews and a marvellous sense of light and space.

A1095 runs east to **SOUTHWOLD**, an elegant little seaside resort with a mixed sand and shingle beach, a pier and a small harbour. In the town behind, narrow streets link a series of spacious greens, mostly surrounded by attractive houses, in which Dutch and Flemish influences are apparent; the greens were created after a fire swept through the town in 1659. The fine church (15th century) contains a beautiful painted screen and a carved and painted pulpit. The **museum** (*open late May–Sept daily*) has displays on local life, including the Battle of Sole Bay in 1672 between the Dutch and English fleets off Southwold. See also the **Lifeboat Museum** (*open late May–Sept afternoons*) and especially the **Sailors' Reading Room** (*open daily*), which contains books, models, paintings and photographs of boats and the sea. Stay at the **Crown** (0502–722275) in the High Street, and eat there too (not surprisingly, fish is a speciality); sample a pint of Adnam's beer as well — it is brewed in the town and delivered to local pubs by horse-drawn dray. TIC in the Town Hall (0502–722366).

Leaving the coast behind, we head now for the hinterland. Return along A1095, turn right on to A145 and immediately left on to B1123 through Halesworth and Chediston to Metfield. This is a gentle pastoral landscape, each village with its impressive church built from the profits of wool, which was the county's staple industry until the 17th century. In Metfield turn left on to the minor road leading to **FRESSINGFIELD**, where the church has a fine hammer-beam roof and delicately carved bench ends. The old timbered guildhall is now the **Fox and Goose Inn**, with a far-flung reputation for good food; advance booking is advisable (037986–247). Look too at the church in **WINGFIELD**, 2 miles west, which has elaborate effigies of the Dukes of Suffolk. A 16th-century house has been built into the moated castle (*not open*) with its gatehouse, drawbridge and towers, while **Wingfield College** (*open April–Sept weekends and Bank Holiday Mons*) is a timber-framed building hidden by an 18th-century facade; it has recently been restored, and regular concerts and art and craft exhibitions are held.

Beyond the village, turn left on to B1118, then right on to B1117 in Stradbroke, heading for **EYE**. The name means 'island', and indeed the Norman keep (now replaced by a 19th-century folly) did stand out above the surrounding country. The 15th-century church boasts a magnificent 101ft tower, there is a lovely early 16th-century guildhall and a flamboyant Victorian town hall. Take time to explore the network of narrow streets, and look out for brickwork built in wavy undulations, a Suffolk style known as 'crinkle crankle'.

Head south on B1077 through **DEBENHAM**, an unspoilt village with some good buildings, including a timber-framed guildhall and a largely 15th-century church, and then drive north-east along A1120 to **SAXTEAD GREEN**. The 18th-century **post mill** (*EH, open April–Sept Mon–Sat*) is preserved in perfect working order, a rare survivor of the many windmills that marked the Suffolk landscape until well into the present century.

Two miles east along B1119 you come to **FRAMLINGHAM**, where from the distance the massive 12th-century **castle** (*EH, standard opening times*) looks just as a castle should, all massive stone walls and battlemented towers, although Tudor chimneys somewhat spoil the effect! Inside, you can walk along part of the walls (good views over the town), but otherwise virtually nothing remains of the original structure. During the 18th century the great hall was converted to a poorhouse, part of which is now a museum. In 1553, Mary was proclaimed Queen of England here, and rode off to London to claim her throne. The compact little town has many attractive buildings, especially on Market Hill and Castle Street, while the church has a remarkable collection of tombs. At **Tiffins** in Fore Street you can enjoy morning coffee or tea; the cafe occupies part of an antique shop. Stay at the **Crown** (0728–723521) on Market Hill.

Follow B1116 south for about 1½ miles and then turn right on to an unclassified road leading to **EASTON**, where **Easton Farm Park** (*open Easter–Oct daily*) offers such attractions as two dairies (one Victorian, one filled with the latest milking equipment), nature trail, blacksmith's shop, old farm machinery and lots of farm animals. From Easton drive south alongside the river Deben, turn left on to B1078 and then almost immediately right on to B1438, which leads back to Woodbridge.

# Wool and Wheat

*1–2 days/about 90 miles/from Cambridge/OS maps 154, 155, 167*

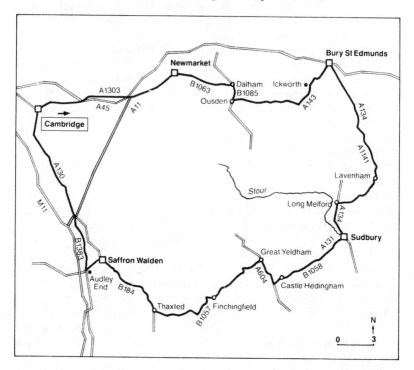

Landscape is as much the creation of man as of ancient geological forces. In much of Suffolk and northern Essex today, vast hedgeless fields of wheat and barley, broken only by occasional wooded valleys and small streams, stretch out to the horizon. Only a few hundred years ago the scene was quite different. In the 15th and 16th centuries, sheep and timber were the two foundations of East Anglia's prosperity. Numerous small towns grew rich on the production of fine-quality cloth, exported both to London and to the continent. Merchants and weavers built themselves grand timbered houses ornamented with elaborate plaster decoration and endowed magnificent churches, memorials now as much to themselves as to their faith.

Start in **CAMBRIDGE** (pop. 85,200) England's second oldest university city (only Oxford is older), and nowadays also an important commercial and industrial centre. The best way of absorbing the atmosphere of the 20-plus colleges is simply to wander round as your fancy takes you, exploring narrow alleys and elegant courts and enjoying the view from the 'Backs', the stretch of the river Cam that runs behind some of the colleges. Buildings range from 13th-century (at **Peterhouse**, the oldest

158

college) to ultra-modern, with something from every period in between. Most college dining-halls and chapels are open to the public, but since students and fellows (teachers) live and work in the colleges, access is often restricted, especially at exam time in May and early June. Highlights not to be missed include: **King's College Chapel**, a glorious Gothic building with exquisite fan-vaulting, elaborately carved choir stalls and Rubens' *Adoration of the Magi* hanging behind the altar; **Trinity College**, with its 17th-century Great Court and library designed by Christopher Wren; **Queen's College**, mostly 16th-century, and the 18th-century Mathematical Bridge, originally held together without any nails; and the cool classical buildings of **Downing College**.

The **Fitzwilliam Museum** (*open daily except Mon*) has a massive collection of almost everything, including Egyptian antiquities, glass, coins, paintings (the miniatures are especially fine), sculpture, clocks, furniture and a pleasant coffee shop where you can recover from such a concentration of treasures. Rather less daunting are the 20th-century paintings and sculpture at **Kettle's Yard** (*generally open Tues–Sat afternoons*), which was originally the private home of Jim Ede, who built up the collection; a gallery houses temporary exhibitions. Almost next door is the **Cambridge and County Folk Museum** (*open daily except Sun mornings*).

Cambridge has plenty of interesting eating places, though they all tend to be crowded during the tourist season. **Henry's** in Pembroke Street is a good coffee shop, while the menu at nearby **Brown's**, opposite the Fitzwilliam, starts with sandwiches and moves up to full-scale meals. Stay at the **Garden House Hotel** (0223–63421), which backs on to the river, or more cheaply at the **Royal Cambridge Hotel**(0223–351631). TIC in Wheeler Street (0223–322640).

A1303 is the Newmarket road from central Cambridge. If you're coming from London stay on A11 and follow signs for Newmarket; from the west or north take A45 around Cambridge, and look out for Newmarket signposts.

**NEWMARKET** means horses, hundreds of them, for the town is the centre of English racing, with the headquarters of the Jockey Club and the **National Stud**, where visitors are shown behind the scenes to see how it's done, visiting stallions, the foaling unit, mares and foals and the nursery yards. (*Tours April–Sept Mon–Fri at 11.15am and 2.30pm and also at 11.15am on race Sats; advance booking advisable* — tel. 0638–663464.) There is also the **National Horseracing Museum** (*open April–Nov Tues–Sat and Sun afternoon, also Bank Holiday Mons and all August Mons*) — but perhaps the best way to catch something of Newmarket's spirit is to watch the racehorses being exercised each morning on the Heath west of the town.

Take B1063 east out of town, past private stud farms, to Ashley. Continue straight on along an unclassified road to **DALHAM**, a pretty, almost winsome village with little footbridges across the river Kennet. Turn right here on to B1085, and then left after about 1½ miles through

*The rotunda at Ickworth*

a succession of small villages, Ousden, Hargrave Green, Chevington, to the junction with A143. A left turn here, and then another in Horringer, will bring you to **Ickworth** (*NT, open every May–Sept afternoons except Mon and Thurs, also April and Oct weekend afternoons*).

The centre of this astonishing house — one might almost call it a folly, but it is a folly on a monumental scale — is a domed rotunda, 104ft high, from which curved corridors extend to two wings, originally intended to house collections of paintings and sculpture; the length of the house, from one wing to the other, is some 600ft. The house was started in 1794 by Frederick Hervey, 4th Earl of Bristol and more or less completed by his son in 1830. Inside there is a dazzling collection of paintings — including works by Hogarth, Gainsborough, Titian and Reynolds — furniture and silver. The formal gardens and park were the work of Capability Brown, who concealed the house behind a screen of oaks and cedars, thus heightening its impact when it finally comes into view. National Trust shop and restaurant.

A143 runs north into **BURY ST EDMUNDS** (pop. 30,000). This elegant town, largely 17th and 18th century in appearance but with a much longer history, would make an excellent touring base, far less busy than Cambridge. Apart from the imposing **Norman Gate**, only ruins (now a botanical garden) remain of the great Norman abbey built here on the burial place of Edmund, the last king of East Anglia; he was beheaded in 869 by invading Danes, and was later canonised. There are two fine churches in the town, St James and St Mary, the latter especially beautiful with an angel roof in the nave and a blue and gold wagon roof in the chancel. Admire a succession of handsome buildings as you walk up Angel Hill, notably **Angel Hotel**, which appeared in Dickens' *The Pickwick Papers* and is renowned for good food and accommodation (0284–753926), **Angel Corner**, an early 18th-century house which is now a museum of clocks (*NT, open daily*), and the Athenaeum, used in the 18th century for balls and assemblies. See also the **Theatre Royal**, a perfect late-18th-century playhouse still in regular use; if you haven't time to take in a performance, at least visit the interior (*NT, generally open Mon–Sat, but closed Aug and early Sept*). You'll find numerous pubs as you explore the town — the minute **Nutshell** in The Traverse is one of the smallest in England. For good-value wholefood meals, try **Beaumonts** in Brentgovel Street. TIC in Angel Hill (0284–63233/64667 evenings and weekends).

Take A134 south, turning left on to A1141 just beyond Bradfield

Combust. **LAVENHAM** is perhaps the best known and most visited of all the Suffolk wool villages. The 140ft church tower is visible from miles distant. Inside the church, built largely in about 1500 when the wool trade was at its most successful, there is fine carving in both stone and wood, notably in the porch and in the Spring and Branch chapels; both families were prosperous local weavers who financed the building of the church. The town is full of Tudor timber-framed buildings. The black of the oak beams and the white of the plaster contrast strongly. But this contrast may not always have been present four centuries ago — it seems that on at least some houses the beams were originally covered. Notable buildings include the **Guildhall** (*NT, open April–Oct daily*), where there is an exhibition on the history of the wool trade, the **Priory** (*open April–Oct daily*), which also has a herb garden, and **Little Hall** (*open April–mid-Oct weekends and Bank Holiday Mons*) — but simply strolling around is the best way to see the town. Both lunch and tea are available in the refectory of the Priory, and you can stay at the **Swan**, a handsome timber-framed building with a modern extension entirely in keeping (0787–247477). TIC in the Guildhall (0787–248207).

*Lavenham Guildhall*

Water — or rather the lack of it in any substantial quantity — is the reason why these wool towns and villages have survived virtually unscathed into the present century. When water began to be used for fulling cloth, the weaving industry moved first to the west country and then to the north, where there was also sufficient coal to power the machines developed during the Industrial Revolution. From being among the most industrialised counties of England, Suffolk became one of the least.

Drive west across country to Long Melford. Alternatively, walk along the track of the disused railway (an easy 3 miles), which has been turned into a footpath. **LONG MELFORD** is less intensely 16th-century than Lavenham and has a number of handsome 18th-century buildings, reflecting the town's later prosperity as a river port. But appearances are deceptive — some of the Georgian facades conceal earlier timber framing. The long main street, full of antique shops, leads to the Green and the massive church. Inside all is light — there are 97 windows in all — and delicate lofty stonework. **Melford Hall** (*NT, open May–Sept afternoons Wed, Thur, weekends and Bank Holiday Mons, also April weekends*) is a handsome three-sided Tudor brick mansion with some 18th- and 19th-century interiors and full for furniture and porcelain. Nearby **Kentwell Hall** (*generally open July–Sept Wed–Sun afternoons, April–June Thur and Sun afternoons*) is another Tudor mansion which is gradually being restored. Regular re-creations of Tudor life, plays and craft fairs are staged.

A134 runs south alongside the river Stour to **SUDBURY**, a busier and less exclusively tourist-oriented weaving town; silk is still manufactured here. **Gainsborough's House** (*open daily except Mon and Sun mornings*), the birthplace of the painter Thomas Gainsborough in 1727, is now a museum with a number of his paintings, and rooms arranged in period style. There's a statue of the painter, palette and brush in hand, on Market Hill, near St Peter's church (late 15th-century). Sudbury is another pleasant place to spend a night or two, especially if you want to explore south to 'Constable country' further down the Stour. The **Bull and Trivets** (0787–74120) is an attractive hotel dating back to the 16th century. TIC in the Library, Market Hill (0787–72092).

Now we cross into Essex on A131, branching right after about 3 miles on to B1058. This is a lovely drive through peaceful, gently undulating countryside dotted with attractive villages, each with its church, colour-washed cottages and timber-framed buildings, many with elaborate plaster decoration (pargeting). (Whoever first claimed that East Anglia is flat got it almost completely wrong. Admittedly, the Fens are flat, but almost everywhere else gentle hills and valleys add subtlety to the landscape.)

The **castle** (*open Easter and daily May–Oct*) at **CASTLE HEDINGHAM** is an imposing Norman keep almost 100ft high. Inside there is rich stone carving and a magnificent banqueting hall, complete with minstrels' gallery. A 16th-century bridge crosses the moat. The village has 16th-century and 18th-century houses, and lots of crafts and antiques shops.

A right turn on to A604 brings you to the **Colne Valley Railway**, whose restored steam locos operate from a little Victorian station. The railway's restaurant is highly recommended— no limp British Rail sandwiches! (*Station and exhibits open March–Dec daily; steam locos operate most Suns and some weekdays June–Oct — tel. 0787–61174 for details.*)

Just before Great Yeldham, turn left on to the unclassified road leading to **TOPPESFIELD**, where the **Museum of the Working Horse** (*open Easter–Oct daily*) contains wheelwright's and blacksmith's shops, a forge, and lots of waggons, ploughs and other equipment.

Continue south-west along minor roads to **FINCHINGFIELD**. The village well merits its reputation as a beauty spot — but as a result it's often crowded with visitors, especially at weekends. It's all so traditionally English: cottages cluster around the village green with its pond and climb up the hill towards the largely Norman church and the 15th-century **Guildhall** (*open April–Sept weekend and Bank Holiday afternoons*). There are lots of tea and craft shops.

B1057 leads south to **GREAT BARDFIELD**, another delightful village with pargeting on the cottages and a lovely guildhall. The **Cottage Museum** (*open April–Sept weekends and Bank Holiday Mon afternoons*), which occupies a 16th-century charity cottage, displays farm and domestic items.

Minor roads run west to **THAXTED**, whose former prosperity as both a wool town and a cutlery-making centre is indicated by the majestic church tower, 183ft high, and, inside, by carving and stained glass. The town's other notable landmark is the **windmill** (*open May–Sept weekends and Bank Holiday Mon afternoons*), built in 1804 and reconstructed in the 1970s (far views from the top). This is another town well worth strolling around: look especially at the 15th-century Guildhall, with three over-hanging storeys and, among others, at the houses in Stoney Lane. There's a music festival here in late June; the town is also a morris-dancing centre, with dancing most Bank Holiday Mondays.

Drive north on B184 to **SAFFRON WALDEN**, where many houses have elaborate pargeting, notably the old Sun Inn. The church (mostly built 1450–1550, when the town was thriving on cloth and saffron production) is impressive, with brasses and carvings. The **museum** (*open daily except Sun mornings*) has local historical and archaeological collections, plus furniture, ceramics, glass and costume. **Bridge End Gardens** (*open daily*) are attractive Victorian gardens, with pavilions, statues, a formal Dutch Garden and even a Garden Mystery Trail. **Eight Bells** in Bridge Street is a 500-year-old inn serving good food; there is limited accommodation (0799–22790). TIC in the Corn Exchange, Market Square (0799–24282).

Just west of the town is **Audley End** (*EH, open Easter–early Oct afternoons except Mon*), one of the great houses of England. Built in the early 17th century by Thomas Howard, James I's Lord Treasurer and the 1st Earl of Suffolk, and extensively remodelled by Robert Adam in the 18th, it is superbly decorated and full of treasures: furniture, pictures, books, even a collection of stuffed birds. Capability Brown landscaped the grounds, for which Adam designed temples, bridges and pavilions. There is a pleasant tea shop.

To return to Cambridge, drive north along B1383 to Stump Cross, where follow A130 into the city.

## North Norfolk and the Fens

*2–3 days/about 200 miles/from Norwich/OS maps 134, 133, 132, 131, 143, 144*

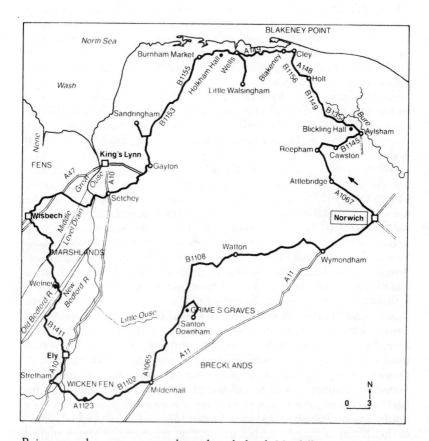

Being on the way to nowhere has helped Norfolk to preserve its traditional independence and self-sufficiency as a distinct region. Despite gradually improving communications with the rest of the country. it retains a noticeable sense of separateness, and Norwich remains a major economic and cultural centre, far more important to its region than other places of a comparable size. This route first of all wanders through the northern half of the county, where a belt of low sandy hills scattered with impressive churches and country houses built from the profits of Norfolk's now vanished wool industry gives way to a lonely coastline of salt marshes and small fishing villages. Then it moves west into the distinctive Fen country, criss-crossed by a network of drainage channels. The continuing efforts of drainage engineers from the 17th century onwards have transformed this once desolate, virtually uninhabited tract of bog into rich black earth, some of the most fertile land in England.

**NORWICH** (pop. 167,000), England's second city for much of the Middle Ages, is a most successful blend of the old and the modern. Although there is history everywhere you walk, it isn't roped off and labelled 'heritage', as so often happens elsewhere. Centuries-old streets and buildings are as much an integral part of this lively and prosperous working city as the shops and offices, factories and amenities built in recent years.

The castle keep and the cathedral spire dominate the townscape — the **cathedral** lies in a slight depression, and so the rest of this marvellous example of Norman architecture, indisputably one of the country's finest cathedrals, is only visible quite close-to. It is grand in large things and in small: the massive sweep of the nave with its three-tiered arches, the exquisite carvings on the misericords, the countless roof bosses. Look also at the cloisters (13th–15th-century) and then stroll around the precincts, where there are many attractive buildings, and down to the 15th-century watergate by the river. The **castle** keep is also Norman, a great square white block used as a prison until the end of the last century and now the renowned **Castle Museum** (*open daily except Sun mornings*). There are excellent displays of arms and armour, archaeology, history and natural history. But the paintings are the highlight of the collection, notably those by John Crome and John Sell Cotman, the leaders of the Norwich School, whose landscapes seem to capture the essence of the Norfolk counryside.

Between and around castle and cathedral runs a network of narrow streets and passages, well worth exploring, with a pleasing jumble of houses and churches (at one time Norwich was said to have a church for every Sunday in the year and a pub for every day — there are still lots of both). Two small museums worth seeing are **Strangers' Hall Museum of Domestic Life**, in which period costumes and furniture are displayed in a 14th–15th-century mansion, and **Bridewell Museum** (*both open Mon–Sat*), which covers the history of Norwich trades and industries. The nearby **Mustard Shop and Museum** (*open Mon, Wed, Fri, Sat*) is devoted to the history of Colman's Mustard, still manufactured in Norwich. The stately church in the Market Place, often mistaken for the cathedral, is **St Peter Mancroft** (mid-15th century).

Stay in Norwich at the **Castle Hotel** (0603–611511) or more cheaply at the **Georgian House Hotel** (0603–615655/617082). The city has numerous eating places: **Britons Arms Coffee House** in Elm Hill serves delicious light meals and snacks, as does the restaurant in the refurbished 18th-century **Assembly Rooms** above the market square. TIC in the Guildhall, Gaol Hill (0603–666071).

*Letheringsett watermill*

We make first of all for Aylsham, but by a rather circuitous route, so if time presses take the direct road north along A140. Otherwise, head north-west on the Fakenham road, A1067, as far as Attlebridge, where turn right on to the unclassified road leading north to **REEPHAM**, an attractive little 18th-century town; the church has some good carving. Now follow B1145 east, and soon turn left for **SALLE** (pronounced 'Saul'), where, in virtually deserted countryside, stands a spectacular 15th-century church built by three local families, including the Boleyns. (Anne Boleyn, second of Henry VIII's six wives, is traditionally but inaccurately said to have been buried here.) Tall piers lead up to the lofty roof; there are fine brasses, wood carving, and a beautiful font on which the seven sacraments are depicted in stone.

Return to B1145, which runs east to Cawston and Aylsham. At **CAWSTON** there is another magnificent church, with a hammerbeam roof decorated with carved angels and an unusual Plough Gallery, paid for by the local Ploughman's Guild.

Nowadays, this is largely arable countryside, but in the Middle Ages it was populated by large flocks of sheep. Weaving was the business of the local villages, and the profits were put towards church-building.

**AYLSHAM** is a likeable riverside town (on the Bure) with 17th- and

18th-century buildings (note the Dutch influences — very common in Norfolk) and a 15th-century church, where Humphrey Repton, the landscape gardener, is buried. B1354 runs north-west to **Blickling Hall** (*NT, house and gardens open April–Oct afternoons except Mon and Thurs, but gardens daily in July and Aug*). This great redbrick mansion was built for Sir Henry Hobart, James I's Lord Chief Justice, between 1616 and 1627. Gables and turrets decorate the facade; inside there is marvellous plasterwork — above all in the Long Gallery — and fine furniture, pictures and tapestries. The gardens, laid out in the 18th century (probably by Repton), contain rides, a lake, a temple and a mausoleum. National Trust shop and restaurant. The Trust's conservation workshop is based at Blickling (*open Tues and Wed afternoons*).

Follow B1354 to Saxthorpe, where turn right on to B1149 towards Holt. In a couple of miles on the right, at **Mannington Hall Gardens** (*open April–Dec Sun afternoons, also June–Aug Wed–Fri*), there are extensive rose displays, and also a scented garden and lovely herbaceous borders; you can follow nature trails and some 20 miles of footpaths through the countryside (*walks open April–Oct Wed–Sun*).

**HOLT** is a little Georgian town set in the attractive range of low wooded hills that runs behind the coast; much of the town centre was burnt down in 1708 and was rebuilt in a pleasing uniformity of architectural style. There are some excellent shops (toys and dolls' houses, clothes, books), and the **Owl** serves simple, well-cooked meals and snacks. Sir Thomas Gresham, a local man who went to London and became Lord Mayor, founded Gresham's School here in 1555. The **North Norfolk Railway**, an enthusiast-operated steam line, runs from Holt, east to Sheringham, where there is a museum. (*Trains run April–Aug Sundays and some weekdays; for times tel. 0263–825449.*)

**LETHERINGSETT** is a delightful village on the river Glaven about 1 mile west of Holt along A148. Domesday Book records a **watermill** here; the present one, built in 1802, has recently been superbly restored to full working order. (*Open Tues–Fri and Sat morning, also Sun afternoons June–Sept; flour-making Tues, Thur and Sun afternoons.*) The village church has a Saxon round tower. Opposite the mill **Glavenside Guest House** (0263–713181) occupies a rambling old house with gardens running down to the river.

Now at long last we reach the coast along B1156 from Letheringsett. At **CLEY-NEXT-THE-SEA** (Cley is pronounced Cly), you could almost be in Holland, with the large windmill (*open June–Sept daily*) and lonely marshes stretching out to the shingle embankment; there's a real edge-of-the-world feeling. The Norfolk Naturalists' Trust operates a **Visitor Centre** (*open April–Oct Tues–Sun*) overlooking the marshes, which are a nature reserve and bird sanctuary. There are fine walks along the shore: glorious when the sun streams down, eerie in the sea mists that suddenly descend. Cley was once an important port; there's a handsome custom house and a noble 14th-century church.

The **Norfolk Coast Path** runs along the whole of this stretch of coastline.

While Cley has an air of having seen better days, **BLAKENEY**, west along the coast road, A149, is quite clearly enjoying a prosperous present, with yachts crowding the magnificent sheltered harbour and beautifully maintained fishermen's cottages (far too expensive for any fisherman nowadays). Boats from the harbour take visitors out to **Blakeney Point** (*NT*), a 4-mile long stretch of sand dunes and shingle enclosing extensive saltmarshes where many species of seabird can be seen, and seals as well. (The seals suffered badly in late summer of 1988.) **Blakeney Hotel** (0263–740797) overlooks the harbour.

**WELLS-NEXT-THE-SEA** gains character from being a working port — coasters still call with cargoes of fertilizer or chemicals, and there are local fishing boats — and from its 18th- and 19th-century alleyways, but loses it by being maintained in a scruffy, down-at-heel way. The beach is a mile from the town across sand dunes. TIC in Wells Centre, Staithe Street (0328–710885).

For those so inclined, there's an interesting diversion inland from Wells along B1105 to **LITTLE WALSINGHAM**. In pre-Reformation days, pilgrims flocked to the shrine of the Virgin Mary built here in the 11th century. The cult was revived at the end of the 19th century, and nowadays many thousands join the annual pilgrimage (at least 100,000 in recent years). A National Anglican Shrine was built in the 1930s; the National Roman Catholic Shrine is 1 mile south at Houghton St Giles. The atmosphere is rather self-consciously devotional (at least for my taste), but the village does have some impressive buildings. These include the 15th-century **shirehall** (*open Easter–Sept daily*), where the main exhibit is a Georgian courthouse, and the remains of the medieval abbey (*open May–Sept Wed, Sat and Sun afternoons, also Mon and Fri in Aug and Wed in April*), whose grounds contain the original Shrine of Our Lady of Walsingham. As its name suggests, the **Old Bakehouse Restaurant** occupies a large, high-ceilinged bakery in the High Street. TIC in the Museum (032872–510).

A149 runs west from Wells past **Holkham Hall** (*open late May–Sept Sun, Mon and Thur afternoons, also Wed afternoons in July and Aug*), an elaborate mid-18th century classical mansion — severe outside, richly decorated and furnished within — designed by William Kent for Thomas Coke, 1st Earl of Leicester, who had returned home from the Grand Tour an enthusiast for Italian architecture. There are paintings by Titian, Gainsborough, van Dyck, Kneller and many others, as well as tapestries, statues and books. Capability Brown laid out the park, in which stands a statue to Thomas Coke — 'Coke of Norfolk' — the agricultural reformer who lived here for many years; he was a great-nephew of the original Thomas Coke. Other attractions at Holkham include a collection of Victorian and other bygones, a pottery, garden centre and tea rooms.

Opposite the main gates of the Hall, a road leads to a pleasant beach and to trails through **Holkham National Nature Reserve**, which is run by the Nature Conservancy Council.

Beyond Holkham, turn left on to B1155, which runs through **BURNHAM OVERY**, a pretty little village with a watermill (*NT, not* *open*). Once upon a time, Burnham Overy was a port, but over the centuries the sea has retreated as shingle and sand are swept down from the Yorkshire coast. Nelson was born in Burnham Thorpe, just to the south.

B1155 passes through **BURNHAM MARKET**, a good-looking little market town with a wide main street, and then brings a change of mood, turning away from the marshy coastline with its creeks and salt breezes to run south across a more pastoral landscape broken by gentle hills. A left turn on to B1153 at Great Bircham brings you to A148.

Much of the land hereabouts belongs to the Queen's **Sandringham** estate, which was bought by her great-grandfather Edward, Prince of Wales (later Edward VII) in 1861; the house, where the royal family spends its winter holiday, was built in 1870. The **house**, **gardens**, and a **motor museum** can be visited (*open April–Sept Mon–Thur and Sun, but closed 18 July–6 Aug approx.*).

To reach Sandringham, turn right on to A148 and then soon right again, following signposts. Otherwise continue on B1153 across A148 (right and then left) and south as far as Gayton. Turn right here on to B1145, then left immediately on to the minor road leading to East Winch, where turn right on to A47 and then left on to an unclassified road running through Blackborough End to Setchley. Turn left here on to A10 and then almost immediately right on to another minor road leading alongside the river Nar to a group of small villages known as the Wiggenhalls, strung out along the river Great Ouse.

The point of this rather complicated route, apart from avoiding busy main roads around King's Lynn, is to enter the Fens via the Norfolk Marshlands. The Fens, apart from isolated spots, have been inhabited only since the great drainage works of the 17th century. But the Marshland settlements, occupying higher ground above sea level and therefore less prone to flooding, have been in existence for many centuries. There is magnificent wood carving in the church at **WIGGENHALL ST GERMANS**, and more at **WIGGENHALL ST MARY THE VIRGIN**, on the far side of the river. Between the two villages a huge pumping station lifts water from the Middle Level Main Drain to the river. Footpaths run along many of the waterway banks.

Drive south alongside the river to **WIGGENHALL ST MARY MAGDALEN**, where there is fine 15th-century stained glass in the church, turning right just before the village. This unclassified road runs to A47, where turn left and head for Wisbech.

Before reaching the town, commonly called 'the capital of the Fens', a word about this strange, set-apart corner of East Anglia. The first major drainage schemes were organised by Sir Cornelius Vermuyden, a Dutch engineer who later took British nationality, in the 1630s–50s. Until then, the Fens were almost entirely marshland, regularly flooded during the winter. Vermuyden built two channels, the Old and New Bedford Rivers (the latter also known as the Hundred Foot Drain, for that is its width), straight across the Fens. These channels were designed to do three basic jobs: drain water from the land, receive water draining down from higher ground beyond the Fens, and cope with tidal waters flowing down the Ouse from the Wash. Supplemented by additional drains, sluices and channels, they still do those jobs today. First windpumps, then steam pumps and later still diesel and electric pumps were employed to prevent flooding. The result of all this labour was 300,000 acres of rich black earth — pure peat, in fact, and ideal agricultural land. Cereals and root crops — celery, potatoes, carrots, onions — are chiefly grown, with some fruit around Wisbech and bulbs in the north near Spalding.

Some people find the Fens harsh and unforgiving country — and when a winter east wind straight out of Siberia cuts across the land it is not hard to sympathise. But there is also a compelling beauty here, never more than in the evening, when the setting sun leaves vivid streaks of orange across the wide, wide sky.

**WISBECH** (pop. 22,600), is an elegant town. Two streets, North Brink and South Brink, divided by the river Nene, are full of Georgian buildings, notably **Peckover House** (*NT, open May–Sept afternoons except Thurs and Fri, also weekends and Bank Holiday Mons April and first 2 weeks in Oct*), built in 1722 and full of fine wood and plaster decoration; there is a 2-acre Victorian garden. See also the market place and Old Market, the Crescent and the **Wisbech and Fenland Museum** (*open Tues–Sat*), purpose-built as a museum in 1847, which contains a wide range of collections on local and natural history, folklore, and the fine and decorative arts. Wisbech remains an active port, even though it is now 10 miles from the sea, in contrast with three or four when the town was built as a port. Stay here at the **Rose and Crown** (0945–583187) in Market Place. TIC in the District Library, Ely Place (0945–583263/64009).

A1101 runs south across the Fens through Outwell and Upwell alongside the Wisbech Canal, once but no longer used by Fen lighters. Middle Level Main Drain is crossed at Three Holes, and at **WELNEY** the Old and New Bedford Rivers, their banks high above the surrounding land. The stretch of land between these two water courses is known as the washlands (not to be confused with the Wash on the coast), and is flooded during winter as part of the drainage control system. The Wildfowl Trust runs a **nature reserve** (*open daily*) at Welney. Thousands of wildfowl over-winter here, Bewick's swans, widgeon, teal among them, while many others nest in spring and summer.

Follow A1101 alongside New Bedford River for a short distance, and then carry straight on along B1411, which eventually turns south-east towards Little Downham and **ELY**.

The great Ely **cathedral**, the 'ship of the Fens', dominating the skyline was begun in the late 11th century: the sweep of the long Norman nave cannot fail to impress. In 1322 the central tower collapsed, and in its place was constructed an octagonal lantern with exquisite fan vaulting and tracery, one of the marvels of English medieval architecture. Look also at the Lady Chapel, which has more fine carvings (many mutilated during the Reformation), and at the magnificent west tower. The cathedral also contains a **stained glass museum** (*open March–Oct Mon–Sat and also Sun lunchtimes*). Attractive buildings, many used by King's

*The Prior's doorway, Ely Cathedral*

School, surround the cathedral. The **Old Fire Engine House** in St Mary's serves local specialities (eel pie among them). TIC in the public library, Palace Green (0353–2062).

Follow the main A10 south for 4 miles, and branch left to **STRETHAM**. At the end of a country road on the far side of A1123 you will reach **Stretham Beam Engine** (*open daily*), a parallel steam engine built in 1830 to pump water from the Fens.

East of Stretham, A1123 passes **Wicken Fen** (*NT, open daily*). This 600-acre nature reserve is the only remaining stretch of original, undrained Fenland, with fascinating plant and bird life. There's a 2-mile nature trail, and you can also wander freely along paths and droves, and use the Tower Hide for bird observation. Bring Wellington boots if the weather's at all wet.

Turn right from A1123 on to A142, and then soon left on to B1102 to **MILDENHALL**, a small town on the river Lark with a magnificent church, the roof of which is filled with beautifully carved angels, saints birds and beasts.

Leave town on A1101 south-east and then turn left on to A1065 towards Brandon, past the hideous screech of Lakenheath air base, the largest American air base in East Anglia. Now the Fens are giving way to the **Brecklands**. This stretch of sandy heathland was originally a most fertile spot, home of some of the earliest inhabitants of East Anglia. During the Middle Ages the villages were depopulated, and the land was enclosed for sheep, countless generations of which stripped it of all vegetation and left it desolate, suitable only for the cultivation of pheasants. All that has changed during the last 60 years or so, and now the area is thickly covered with Forestry Commission pines.

Turn right off A1065 beyond Brandon to visit **Grime's Graves** (*EH*, *open standard times*), a honeycomb of Neolithic flint mines, shafts and galleries. You can descend one of the shafts, and see the pick marks made thousands of years ago.

There are forest walks all around here — except, of course, on the extensive army battle area to the north, from which keep well away. The best are perhaps around the forest village of **SANTON DOWNHAM** alongside the river Little Ouse. To get there, continue east from Grime's Graves to A134, turn right, and then left on to a minor road through the forest and over the Norwich–Ely railway line.

To resume our route, return from Grime's Graves to A1065, where turn right and continue north, turning right on B1108 to **WATTON**. This is a quiet Norfolk country town on the edge of the Brecklands with a wide main street.

Continue east along B1108 through Hingham to Kimberley, where turn right on to B1135, which leads to **WYMONDHAM** (pronounced Windam). The abbey church here has two towers; inside there is a striking Norman nave and a 15th-century hammerbeam roof. The town has some handsome Georgian buildings.

Return to Norwich along A11 trunk road.

# USEFUL ADDRESSES

English Tourist Board
Thames Tower
Black's Road
Hammersmith
London
W6 9EL
(01–730 3400)

Wales Tourist Board
Brunel House
2 Fitzalan Road
Cardiff
CF2 1UY
(0222–499909)

## Regional Tourist Boards

Cumbria Tourist Board
Ashleigh
Holly Road
Windermere
LA23 2AS
(09662–4444)

East Anglia Tourist Board
Toppesfield Hall
Hadleigh
Suffolk
IP7 7DN
(0473–822922)

East Midlands Tourist Board
Exchequergate
Lincoln
LN2 1PS
(0552–531521)

Heart of England Tourist Board
2/4 Trinity Street
Worcester
WR1 2PW
(0905–613132)

London Tourist Board
26 Grosvenor Gardens
London
SW1W 0DU
(01–730 3450)

Northumbria Tourist Board
Aylzley Heads
Durham
DH1 5UT
(091–384–6905)

North West Tourist Board
The Last Drop Village
Bromley Cross
Bolton
Lancashire
BL7 9PZ
(0204–591511)

South East England Tourist Board
1 Warwick Park
Tunbridge Wells
Kent
TN2 5TA
(0892–40766)

Southern Tourist Board
The Old Town Hall
Leigh Road
Eastleigh
Hampshire
SO5 4DE
(0703–616027)

Thames and Chilterns Tourist
   Board
The Mount House
Church Green
Witney
Oxfordshire
OX8 6DZ
(0993–778800)

West Country Tourist Board
37 Southernhay East
Exeter
Devon
EX1 1QS
(0392–76351)

Yorkshire and Humberside Tourist
   Board
312 Tadcaster Road
York
YO2 2HE
(0904–707961)

## Offices of the British Tourist Authority

British Tourist Authority
Thames Tower
Black's Road
Hammerside
London
W6 9EL
(01–846 9000)

*New York*
40 West 57th Street
New York
NY 10019–4001
(212) 581–4700

**USA**
*Chicago*
875 North Michigan Avenue
Chicago
Illinois 60611
(312) 787–0490

**Canada**
94 Cumberland Street
Suite 600
Toronto
Ontario M5R 3N3
(416) 925–6326

*Dallas*
Suite 210
Cedar Maple Plaza
2305 Cedar Springs Road
Dallas
Texas 75201
(214) 720–4040

**Australia**
4th Floor
171 Clarence Street
Sydney
NSW 2000
(02) 298627

*Los Angeles*
Room 450
350 South Figueroa Street
Los Angeles
CA 90071
(213) 628–3525

**New Zealand**
3rd Floor
Dilworth Building
Corner of Queen and Custom
   Streets
Auckland 1
(09) 3031–466

# National Parks

Council for National Parks
45 Shelton Street
London
WC2H 9HJ
(01–240 3603/4)

Brecon Beacons National Park
7 Glamorgan Street
Brecon
Powys
LD3 7DP
(0874–4437)

Dartmoor National Park
'Parke'
Haytor Road
Bovey Tracey
Devon
TQ13 9JQ
(0626–832093)

Exmoor National Park
Exmoor House
Dulverton
Somerset
TA22 9HL
(0398–23665)

Lake District National Park
National Park Visitor Centre
Brockhole
Windermere
Cumbria
LA23 1LJ
(09662–6601)

Northumberland National Park
Eastburn
South Park
Hexham
Northumberland
NE46 1BS
(0434–605555)

North York Moors National Park
The Old Vicarage
Bondgate
Helmsley
York
YO6 5BP
(0439–70657)

Peak National Park
Aldern House
Baslow Road
Bakewell
Derbyshire
DE4 1AE
(062981–4321)

Pembrokeshire Coast National
  Park
County Offices
Haverfordwest
Dyfed
SA61 1QZ
(0437–4591)

Snowdonia National Park
Penrhyndeudraeth
Gwynedd
LL48 6LS
(0766–770274)

Yorkshire Dales National Park
Colvend
Hebden Road
Grassington
Skipton
North Yorkshire
BD23 5LB
(0756–752748)

## Other Useful Organisations

English Heritage
Fortress House
23 Savile Row
London
W1X 2HE
(01–734 6010)

CADW: Welsh Historic
   Monuments
Brunel House
2 Fitzalan Road
Cardiff
CF2 1UY
(0222–465511)

The National Trust
36 Queen Anne's Gate
London
SW1H 9AS
(01–222 9257)

Ramblers' Association
1/5 Wandsworth Road
London
SW8 2LJ
(01–582 6878)

The Royal Society for the
   Protection of Birds
The Lodge
Sandy
Bedfordshire
SG19 2DL
(0767–80551)

Automobile Association
Fanum House
Basingstoke
Hampshire
RG21 2EA
(0256–20123)

Royal Automobile Club
PO Box 700
Spectrum
Bond Street
Bristol
BS99 1RB
(0272–232340)

# A SHORT BIBLIOGRAPHY

**Guides**
The Companion Guides, published by Collins, provide reflective and well-informed comment on local history, architecture and customs. The series includes:
**East Anglia,** *John Seymour,* 2nd edition revised by *John Burke*
**Kent and Sussex,** *Keith Spence*
**Northumbria,** *Edward Grierson*
**Shakespeare Country,** *Jonathan Keates*
The **Shell Guides,** published by Faber and Faber, are also useful, and include:
**Buckinghamshire,** *Bruce Watkin*
**Cambridgeshire,** *Norman Scarfe*
**Devon,** *Ann Jellicoe* and *Roger Mayne*
**Hertfordshire,** *R.N. Healey*
**Nottinghamshire,** *Henry Thorold*
**South West Wales,** *Vyvyan Rees*

**Travel and Countryside**
Here is a small selection of the countless books inspired in one way or another by rural Britain:
**Coasting,** *Jonathan Raban.* An account of a sea voyage around the coastline of Britain
**David Gentleman's Britain** and **David Gentleman's Coastline,** *Weidenfeld and Nicholson.* An artist's view
**Dickens's England,** *Tony Lynch,* Batsford
**The English Country House,** *Olive Cook and A.F. Kersting.* Thames & Hudson
**The Illustrated Journeys of Celia Fiennes,** *edited by Christopher Morris,* Webb & Bower/Michael Joseph. Accounts by the 17th-century traveller
**Journeys into Britain,** *Robin Page,* Oxford University Press
**The Kingdom by the Sea,** *Paul Theroux,* Penguin. Another coastal journey
**Landscape with Machines,** *L.T.C. Rolt,* Alan Sutton. Recollections by the pioneering industrial archaeologist
**The Making of the English Landscape,** *W.G. Hoskins,* Penguin. A classic, pioneering account of the evolution of the countryside
**Millstone Grit,** *Glyn Hughes,* Pan. The Pennine landscape
**Travellers History of Britain and Ireland,** *Richard Muir,* Mermaid.
**Uppark and Its People,** *Margaret Meade-Fetherstonhaugh and Oliver Warner,* Century/National Trust Classics. A history of the house described in 'West Sussex and East Hampshire'.
**Vanishing Cornwall,** *Daphne Du Maurier,* Penguin

**Literature**
The work of many writers has been notably influenced by one part of Britain or another. The following are a few selected examples:

H.E. *Bates*, Bedfordshire/Northamptonshire and Kent
R.D. *Blackmore*, Exmoor
*Melvyn Bragg*, Cumbria
*The Brontë sisters*, Yorkshire
*Daphne Du Maurier*, Cornwall
*Thomas Hardy*, Wessex (an area now contained by parts of Dorset, Hampshire and Wiltshire)
*James Herriot*, Yorkshire Dales
*Thomas Hughes*, Vale of White Horse, Oxfordshire
D.H. *Lawrence*, Nottinghamshire
*Beatrix Potter*, Lake District
*Gilbert White*, Selborne, East Hampshire
*William Wordsworth*, Lake District

# INDEX

The names of individual routes are given in **bold** type.

travol